BE QUIET AND Listen

God Bless

Sheldon Larmore
+
Sara Belle

BE
QUIET
AND *Listen*

SHELDON LARMORE

TATE PUBLISHING
AND ENTERPRISES, LLC

Published by Tate Publishing & Enterprises, LLC
127 E. Trade Center Terrace | Mustang, Oklahoma 73064 USA
1.888.361.9473 | www.tatepublishing.com

Tate Publishing is committed to excellence in the publishing industry. The company reflects the philosophy established by the founders, based on Psalm 68:11,
"The Lord gave the word and great was the company of those who published it."

Book design copyright © 2012 by Tate Publishing, LLC. All rights reserved.
Cover design by Karla Durangparang
Interior design by Blake Brasor

Published in the United States of America

ISBN: 978-1-62147-559-0
1. Biography & Autobiography / General
2. Biography & Autobiography / Religious
12.10.25

DEDICATION

*T*his book is dedicated to the one I laugh with and love with all my heart and soul, Sara Belle, my wife and David's mother. Together we have learned the best and most beautiful things in this world are not things. They cannot be seen or touched. They must be felt with the heart. She has stood by me in life through thick and thin, tears and laughter. She has put meaning to the word *magical* throughout our lives together and is always near with a candle of hope in my darkest times. She is the reason for so many of yesterday's sweet memories and for the promises to come in the dawn of tomorrow.

Without her constant persistence and her loving encouragement I would not have been able to complete this manuscript because of the mental, physical, and tremendous emotional drain it had on both of us. She did not and she would not allow me to put aside this work. To us, our memories are just too priceless. Because of her our special times with David and the milestones in our life these memories will live on through the pages of this book.

Sara Belle is my wife, my best friend in good times, and my rock in times of sorrow.

I will love her with all of my heart and soul through eternity!

ACKNOWLEDGMENTS

*F*irst and foremost I must acknowledge and give praise to God for His relentless prompting of me to put into words the story of our son's spiritual walk with Him throughout his time on Earth. I am confident David and his Lord had a meaningful and personal relationship that gave him his inner strength and energy that served to guide him through life. He has guided our family through life into paths of peace, joy, and contentment. Even though we still find ourselves falling short in fully acknowledging the magnificence of God, we honor Him, praise Him, and put our total trust in Him each day. We are constantly working toward becoming better Christians.

Early in my life I invited God into my heart and prayed for Him to direct my steps, and He did. He answered my call for direction abundantly. By nurturing our faith in God we can accept and deal with whatever comes along, confident that in the end, things will work out according to His plan. We've learned, contrary to popular belief, God can take care of things much better than we can.

Secondly, I must acknowledge the patience, love, and support Sara Belle so generously gave me in the many months it took me to bring this task of love to completion. Without her guidance, encouragement, and memories of the past it would have been a difficult endeavor to bring any sense of continuity to the pages of this book. As we worked together compiling information she kept us grounded and focused by stating ever so often, "God is not finished with us yet. We are still a work in progress with much improvement to be done. We can't stop now in the middle of life."

The list of friends who have been such a significant part of our family and so generous with their love, support, and prayers over time is thankfully endless. Each time I included a name in the book to highlight an event or make a situation or point come alive I shuddered knowing full well I was leaving out other names of people who played an important, unforgettable part in making our lives more meaningful and joyous. I pray that since this is my first attempt at writing, my mistakes and my omissions of people and events will be forgiven. The important thing to know and to treasure is we know who you are and love you for caring so much. David knows who you are and is looking down on you and us with great joy and admiration.

We love each of you!

As is stated: "It is more blessed to give than to receive" (Acts 20:35)…and each of you gave to us abundantly and with a generous heart.

TABLE OF CONTENTS

PREFACE

fter our first date on December 2, 1966, Sara Belle and I knew our feelings for each other were more magical than we had felt following dates with others. If it's possible, ours was true love at first sight, but I know both of us were afraid to admit it. From December 2, 1966, until January 15, 1967, we did not miss a day without a date. In those forty-five days we fell hopelessly in love. We became engaged on January 15, 1967, and were married on April 7, 1967. Looking back over our many years of happiness we have come to the realization that people are brought together for a reason, and everything happens in God's time. We completed one another by filling in each other's missing spots with love.

Since both of us were teachers with a genuine love for the students we taught, our dream was to have a house filled with the excitement, joy, and love of several children. We looked forward to the time when we could watch, direct, and help in the raising of productive, caring, and giving young adults. We wanted to have the opportunity to provide a secure home, give sound advice, and put each of them on the right track to success as human beings. Jokingly, we used to tell our parents we wanted to have our children as soon as possible while they were still able to take care of them. I used to say, "After all, Mom, what is a home without having kids running around?" She would always respond with, "Quiet."

After two years of marriage, Sara Belle and I planned for the birth of the first of what we hoped would be four or five children. David was conceived the first of September 1969 and born May 6, 1970. This would give Sara Belle three and a half to four months with David before we returned to school in the fall. Two days before David's arrival, Sara Belle wrote the following letter to him without any thought of it being published someday. This letter had to be inspired by God. After reading the story of David and how he was touched and guided by his Father, I encourage you to reread this letter.

May 4, 1970

Dear_____,

This is your mother writing you a letter even before you are born. We don't know which you will be yet, but this we do know—whether you will be Jodie Lynn or David Jefferson, you will come into this world where your home will be filled with love.

A lot has happened since you were conceived. The world in just these nine short months has grown smaller. There are many more people. Wherever there are a lot of people, you will find that not everyone can be pleased all of the time. In due time you will learn to do what you think is best even if it creates hard feelings. You will be guided by God.

You have lost, even before you are born, two very dear and great uncles. They loved you even though they never got to know you. Uncle Norman, your father's uncle, was like a father to your dad. He was always around to give us a helping hand. He was a very caring and generous man. We never heard him say anything bad about anyone. Then there was Uncle Dudley Walker, on my side of the family. He, too, was always willing to give whatever he could to help make our life easier. Though you will never know them, I hope you will be like them in many ways.

Let me acquaint you with your father. He is a very dear person, and I hope you love and respect him as your father. He is the most considerate, sincere husband any woman could have. He fills the house with love, security, and laughter. You will soon learn without a doubt that he is "The Best Father in the Whole World."

We don't really know you yet, but so far you have been a good baby. You have let me work until May 6, and you're due on May 18. That's being very good. I have felt extra fine and have only gained about fifteen pounds. You didn't kick very much which didn't cause your mother to wear out so fast.

As I mentioned earlier, you will come into a home filled with much love. Love not from just your father and me but also our relatives and friends. They all have the same prayer for you—that you will take life as it comes and in stride and do something to help mankind—not destroy it. Your father and I have many wonderful plans, but whether we can carry them out depends a lot on you. Whatever happens to you in life and whatever happens to your dad and me, we want you to remember: Everything happens for a reason. God is your source of strength. Put your faith in God and never let go. Things are bound to get rough in your lifetime from time to time. But as long as you have faith things will smooth out and never be as bad as they really seem. Forget your faith and it will be like walking in darkness without any hope of ever seeing sunshine again.

That's all for now, but before you are born I want to acquaint you with your great-grandmother Green. She is your father's grandmother. She is an angel and a saint.

Love you,

Mother

Sara Belle and I have great faith and believed in our life together and our goals for the future. Each night we prayed for God's will in our marriage and to provide us with children to love and nurture. As you read David's story you will realize God's plan was for us to have one child. This we accepted, knowing some of God's greatest gifts are unanswered prayers.

BEGINNING THE JOURNEY OF PARENTHOOD

A baby is born with a need to be loved and never outgrows it.

—Frank Howard Clark

The morning sun was shining brightly in our bedroom as I woke up at six o'clock. Rubbing my eyes, I turned over in bed to see Sara Belle already awake and sitting up. Giving her a kiss on the cheek, I reminded her that it was her last teaching day of the school year.

"We'd better get up and get moving since you want to be in school early today," I said. I knew she had several last minute chores to complete in her classroom before she left on maternity. I jumped out of bed expecting Sara Belle to follow.

"I don't think I'm going to school today," she said.

"What? Why?"

"I'm having pains, labor pains I think," she shared with a smile followed by a low, slow groan. I very calmly (even though my insides were beginning to shake, rattle, and roll) sat on the side of the bed, held her hand and asked, "When did the pains start?"

"In the middle of the night about midnight, I guess."

"What? We'd better get ready to go to the hospital!"

"Not yet," she said.

"What do you mean *not yet*? You've had these pains for six or seven hours. Why didn't you wake me up? I'm calling the doctor. We need help!"

"It is only six thirty. The doctor's office won't be open until eight thirty."

"How far apart are the pains?" I asked.

"They are about three minutes apart."

"Oh my God! Don't you think we should go to the hospital now and be safe rather than be sorry? Remember, we're new at this. Neither one of us knows what to expect." At this point it was obvious to me we were having a baby *right then*; not two weeks from then on May 18 as projected.

The phone rang. I answered it to find out it was one of my teachers, Mrs. Smith calling to report she was sick and would need a substitute for the day. I wished her the best and told her not to worry and take care. I immediately hung up the phone and ran back to the bedroom to find out how Sara Belle was doing. She was still sitting up in bed very calmly looking through her latest *Family Circle* magazine. I told her about the phone call and that I was going to call my assistant principal at the intermediate school so he could get a substitute for Mrs. Smith. As I went down the hall to the kitchen to make the call, I couldn't help but wonder how she could be so relaxed and calm while I was inwardly falling apart at the seams anticipating the arrival of our baby at any time.

When I contacted my assistant principal, Emerson Holloway, I told him I thought our baby was coming. I asked him to get a substitute for Mrs. Smith and I would be in touch with him later in the morning. With that task done I ran back to check on Sara Belle. Finding her as happy as she was the last time I checked on her I decided to get dressed. I needed to be prepared for whatever emergency was about to happen. After I shaved and dressed, I looked at the clock. It was only 7:18 a.m. I panicked again! How could we wait one hour and ten minutes before calling the doctor's office? For the next thirty minutes or so I walked from one room to another constantly checking on Sara Belle. She got up, took a shower and got dressed with little or no difficulty. However, she stopped occasionally and gave out little groans as the pains came more frequently. I was saying prayers, wearing a path in the carpets, and constantly checking on her pain level. I'm sure I was becoming a greater pain to Sara Belle than the contractions. Only forty more minutes before I could call the doctor's office.

The phone rang again. Answering the call I found out it was my assistant principal at the intermediate school saying that Mrs. Smith had just arrived at school. She told the assistant principal she had not called me earlier for a substitute. He also told me that he had called Mrs. Jackson to substitute for Mrs. Smith, and she had just arrived in the office to begin work. He wanted to know what to do with Mrs. Jackson, the substitute. I told him since she was already there, he could share her with the sixth grade teachers. She could work with students in need of individual help. I stated that I would straighten out the matter when I returned to school. I was trying desperately to act as if I had everything under control.

It was my day to shine! I wanted to be known as the superman of expectant fathers even though my legs were weak and my knees were knocking. I wanted my assistant principal to be able to tell everyone that he had talked with me and I had assured him things were on target and I had everything under control. I told him I would be in touch with him as soon as I knew what was happening.

What I really wanted to say was, "You take care of the problems! Don't bother me with little silly concerns today! I'm having a baby!" I'm glad I could still reason to some degree while I was enjoying the emotions of expectant first-time dad syndrome of being overwrought, hysterical, and raging inwardly. Remember, it was my wife who was in labor and she was being so mature about it. She would not even consider going to the emergency room or doing anything else *so normal* until she has spoken to the doctor.

The phone rang. "Hello?" I said in my most pleasant but disguised voice.

"Hello, Sheldon," said the party on the other end of the phone. It was my assistant principal, Joyce Townsend, at the primary school.

"I know you may not be in school today. Tell Sara Belle we will be anxious to hear as soon as the baby is born. Give her our love. Sheldon, I hate to bother you. I'm concerned; Mrs. Barkley has not arrived at school yet. We were wondering if you had heard from her."

A light bulb went on. I thought, *Dummy! That must have been Mrs. Barkley who called you for a substitute and not Mrs. Smith.*

"Yes, I've made a big mistake, but the mystery of the lost substitute has been solved," I said. "Call the intermediate school and have them explain to Mrs. Jackson, the substitute, that your boss is having a baby and just got things screwed up this morning. Tell them to send her to the primary school so she can fill in for Mrs. Barkley."

After solving this problem, I hung up the phone and looked at the clock. I thought, *The clock is messing with my mind. By now it should be at least nine thirty.* The wall clock read 8:16 a.m. It seemed to have a grin on its face as if it were saying, "Cool it, Jack! You still have fourteen minutes before the doctor is in." Running back to check on Sara Belle, I found her very content watching the morning news and sipping on a cup of coffee. She was still groaning every three or four minutes. She looked at me and said, "Relax. I'm okay. You can call the doctor's office at eight thirty, and I will talk to him."

I stood beside her with the doctor's phone number scribbled on a half a sheet of paper crumbled from clenched fists and smeared with sweat from my palm.

The time arrived! It was eight thirty! I picked up the phone and dialed the doctor's number. I got a busy signal! I reminded my inner soul, *Stay calm, try again, don't overreact, it's only a mechanical device. Now take a deep breath and dial again.* This time the phone rang on the other end. I nervously handed the phone to Sara Belle and waited.

"Hello," she said, "this is Sara Belle Larmore. Is Dr. Hanson in?" As the telephone conversation continued, Sara Belle did tell the nurse that she thought she might be having labor pains. I heard her tell the person the pains were about three minutes apart. After further discussion, Sara Belle said, "Thanks. We'll be in the office at eleven thirty."

My first response was, "What! What? What! Eleven thirty! Where! Wow! Why!

"You mean to tell me that the doctor *does not* want to see you until eleven thirty?" It was now 8:48 a.m. When you subtract 8:48 a.m. from 11:30 a.m. you get 2 hours and 42 minutes or 162 minutes. That was the longest 162 minutes of my life.

What do you do with a pregnant wife who has increasing labor pains while waiting for 162 minutes to see the doctor? Well, what seemed like three nights and four days eleven o'clock finally arrived. I decided this was the magic hour for us to begin our ten-minute trip to see the doctor. Until this trip, I never realized how many bumps and ruts there were in any one stretch of road or how terrible other drivers can be. It seemed I constantly had to put on brakes to avoid collisions at stoplights. People ought to be taught how to drive more cautiously when they are traveling on the same road as husbands who are transporting their pregnant wives to the hospital. Remember, we think we have the *right of way* and what is ours we take!

A Message Received

God will never let anything come to you that He and you cannot handle together

—*The Complete Book of Zingers*

When we arrived at Dr. Hanson's office, the waiting room was full. Fortunately, within a short time, two patients were called back leaving two empty seats on opposite sides of the room. Sitting across the room from Sara Belle, I could see that her pains were getting more severe. I could see her tense up and watched her face as it was drawn with each contraction. I looked around the room and observed all the other women looking relaxed. Most were either enjoying the novel or magazine they were reading or were involved in pleasant conversations with the person next to them. Finally the nurse called my wife's name and escorted her out of the waiting room into the professional care of the doctor.

As I waited with the other ladies in the room, I randomly picked up a magazine and flipped through the pages in an effort to pass time as well as to calm my nerves. The article I turned to that caught my immediate attention was titled, "What If Your Child Is Born with a Birth Defect?" We never doubted our baby would be born any other way but full term and healthy. At that moment, I had a very sobering experience. For the first time I had to think, *What if...?* My unfounded worries about getting Sara Belle to the doctor on time, or fears of a baby delivery without the assistance of a doctor seemed ridiculous and immature. I never took the time to read the article but focused all my energy on the message of the article's title. As an after thought, I realized having this article in front of me was not a happenstance. It had to be a message, an awakening from God. I had a feeling go over me that is indescribable. I will never forget it. As I waited for Doctor Hanson to complete Sara Belle's examination I sat in the waiting room composed, sober, and deep in thought reflecting on the article's title. In a short time, Sara Belle entered the waiting room with Dr. Hanson beside her. His words to us were, "Go on to the hospital. Everything is going to be all right. See you later this afternoon." Sara Belle was happy and exceptionally radiant. I did not share the article with her or how it had affected my thoughts about possible problems our newborn baby may have to face.

As we left the doctor's office and walked across the parking lot to our car, Sara Belle turned to me and joked, "When the nurse comes out to tell you about the baby, you'd better ask how I am before you ask how the baby is."

Laughingly, I assured her I would.

A Special Gift from Our Father

God never sends a burden to weigh us down without offering His arm to lift us up.

—The Complete Book of Zingers

When we arrived at the hospital emergency room at approximately twelve thirty there was a nurse waiting for us with a wheelchair to transport Sara Belle to the maternity ward. This would be the last time I would see her until after the birth of the baby. After I parked the car, a nurse's aide directed me to the father's waiting room. She was very kind and made sure that I was comfortable. She stated that my wife was well into labor and had been taken to the delivery room. She assured me as soon as the baby arrived, a nurse would come out and let me know. Oddly enough, Sara Belle was the only expectant mother in the hospital at the time. Therefore, I had the waiting room all to myself.

It was a small room with five or six overstuffed but well-used chairs lined up around the perimeter of the room. There were several old magazines and one poor, almost dead plant on a coffee table in the center of the room. On the wall there was one pay phone next to the single curtainless window overlooking the back parking lot. There was little to do but wait. Some time was spent making phone calls to my mother, Sara Belle's mother, my sister, and a couple of our close friends to let them know Sara Belle was okay and waiting for the delivery. Time went by slowly since there was little or no activity in that part of the hospital due to the low census and no other expectant fathers in the room at the time. I can't help but wonder if this quiet time was not planned to give me time to think about the article I saw in the doctor's office. Throughout the afternoon my mind would not let me escape from thinking about the meaning of the article and its possible affect on our family. During several periods of the afternoon I reflected on how God had touched us and showered His patience and love on Sara Belle and me. I prayed for Sara Belle's comfort and wellbeing and the health of our soon to be newborn baby.

It was now 3:05 p.m. The afternoon seemed to be passing by at a snail's pace. However, it was a short time considering we arrived at the hospital around 12:30 p.m. and Sara Belle was immediately prepared for delivery. In retrospect, I must say that Sara Belle and the doctor should have listened to me earlier in the day. I knew things were moving fast, but no one would listen. From my perspective, we made it just in time.

At approximately 3:30 p.m. a nurse entered the waiting room. Looking around at the empty room she asked if I was Mr. Larmore. A little nervous and anxious, I said, "Yes."

She said, "You have a little baby boy."

Remembering what Sara Belle had teasingly told me and while I had a witness at hand I thought I had better ask how she was before asking about the baby. So I asked, "How is my wife?"

"Fine," she said.

"How is my son?"

The nurse hesitated for a moment giving me an immediate sinking feeling, perhaps as a result of the article.

She responded, "The doctor will be out to talk to you shortly."

I can still vividly see her lower her head, turn from me, open the door, and leave the room without another word. My heart sank, tears began to fall on my cheeks, and instantly my mind focused once again on the article. This truly had to be a message to us from God. He was certainly taking steps to prepare us for what was to come. I prayed and immediately told myself to straighten up and be prepared to face Sara Belle. I had to give her the strength and support she would need. Time passed slowly, making it feel like hours before the doctor entered the waiting room around 4:00 p.m. I was pleased to see it was Dr. Gallaher, who was a friend of ours, and also the one who delivered our son. After a brief moment of greetings, Dr. Gallaher told me that Sara Belle was doing well. I could see her shortly. He further stated that he felt pretty sure the baby was going to be okay. However, there was a small spot at the base of his spine he wanted Dr. Davis, the neurosurgeon on staff, to see.

"When do you think Dr. Davis will be able to see him?" I asked.

"It will probably be later this afternoon or early evening." He assured me that as soon as I could see Sara Belle either he or one of the nurses would be out to take me to her.

It wasn't more than ten minutes before a nurse came out to get me. As we started down the hallway, we met Sara Belle as she came out of the delivery room door on a gurney. Dr. Gallaher and Sara Belle were joking about something as they started down the hall. It did my heart good to see Sara Belle was not over anxious about the baby. The first thing she said to me as she passed in the hall was, "Did they tell you about the little spot on David's back?"

I told her that Dr. Gallaher told me about it, but not to be worried. Immediately, I realized that we had called the baby David, the name we had picked months earlier if the baby was a boy. I couldn't help thinking, *Wow! What a great feeling.* Goose bumps jumped out all over my arms. I thought, *David is here!* What a wonderful feeling to be a parent. What a miracle! It was not long, however, before I had to face reality again. The thoughts generated by the article began to surface. I knew in my heart there was a reason for me to turn to that article in the doctor's office. I was determined not to share this with Sara Belle at this time. I had to remain positive and upbeat to support her and to give her time to heal. After Sara Belle was comfortable in her room, I visited with her until she began to show signs of drowsiness. I rubbed her arm for a while then kissed her and told her to rest. I explained I needed to make contact with family, friends, both schools, and I would return in an hour or so.

On my way home I began to realize that David was facing serious problems. It was as if God was telling me to brace myself for news about David's condition. Not knowing what we were facing, I vowed that Sara Belle and I would conquer whatever needed to be. The feeling of something terribly wrong was so overwhelming I couldn't wait to be by myself. Once inside the house, I began to cry uncontrollably. After a good fifteen to twenty minutes, I pulled myself together knowing I had to make several phone calls to relatives and friends announcing David's arrival. With God's help and deep breathing exercises between calls, I was able to pull off what I thought would be an impossible task.

Everyone on our list was contacted. The message basically was David has a little spot on his back that needs to be examined, but he and Sara Belle were doing fine. One of the first phone calls I made was to our priest, Father Robert Varley. I told him that we were parents of a baby boy and Sara Belle wanted him to be one of the first to know. I shared with him that David had a problem. All I really knew was there was a spot on his back. Dr. Gallaher was going to have the neurosurgeon look at him later in the day.

"Sheldon, I have a meeting at church this evening, but as soon as it's over I will check in on Sara Belle and see what I can find out about David's condition," he said.

Father Varley had a gift for comforting others and at this moment, I was most appreciative of this gift. After resting an hour or so, I returned to the hospital to find Sara Belle in good spirits. I asked her if she had seen the doctor and if she knew when we could see David.

SHELDON LARMORE

"We can't see David yet. He's in isolation. Do you know what's wrong with him?" she asked.

"I don't know any more than you do. Has anyone said anything about when we might see Dr. Davis?"

"No one has said anything to me about Dr. Davis."

The remaining visit was spent just holding hands, talking, and laughing about the events of the day. Still having an unpleasant feeling about my earlier premonition, I concentrated on being optimistic, upbeat, and looking happy. It was well after 8:30 p.m. We still had not heard from any doctor, specifically Dr. Davis. Sara Belle was getting tired. She was fighting to keep her eyes open. I took this opportunity to kiss her good night and assured her I would try to get in contact with Dr. Davis. I rubbed her forehead lightly until she fell asleep.

I left the room with full intentions of finding out where Dr. Davis was that evening. I made several attempts trying to find a nurse on the floor that could tell me how or where to find Dr. Davis. Finally, I was put in contact with the nurse supervisor on duty. I explained to her that Dr. Gallaher informed us that Dr. Davis would talk to us about David today or tonight. She pulled a file from the nurses' station and studied it for a minute or so. Shortly afterward, she said Dr. Davis was in the hospital and she would try to contact him for me. It wasn't too long before she appeared again to inform me that Dr. Davis would be on the floor around 10:30 p.m.

"He will see you then if you can wait," she said.

Glancing at the clock in the hallway I had about one hour to wait. I thanked her and told her I would be glad to wait. At this point, I really was anxious to talk to Dr. Davis alone. I felt if I knew a little more about David's condition and prognosis, I could help cushion any unpleasant news for Sara Belle.

Fortunately, unlike other times of the day, ten thirty seemed to roll around pretty quickly. Dr. Davis was on time. After the nurse introduced us, she stated she had cleared the conference room if we would like to use it. Entering the room, we each took a seat at a round table in the middle of the room. My first impression of Dr. Davis was a positive one. He was easy to talk with, and he readily displayed a compassionate tone in his voice and mannerisms. Even though the hour was late, he did not appear rushed. He seemed willing to listen and share.

"What do you and your wife know about your son's condition?" he asked.

"Very little," I said. "We do know that he was born with a small spot on the lower part of his back. However, we've been told not to worry too much about it."

Dr. Davis looked at me a second or two before commenting further. This was a definite clue to me to brace myself for what would follow.

"Your son was born with Spina Bifida." There was a noticeable concern in his voice.

"What is Spina Bifida?" I asked.

"Spina Bifida is a birth defect in which part of the spinal column is exposed. In many cases it causes multiple congenital problems such as paralysis, brain damage, inability to speak, urinary infections, bowel and kidney damage, et cetera."

"I've never heard of it." I said.

Dr. Davis informed me that Spina Bifida was the number two birth defect, second only to mental retardation. He further stated he was soon to be a new father for the first time as well. One of his major concerns was having a child born with Spina Bifida.

In our conference, Dr. Davis continued to show concern for David's condition as well as a sincere sensitivity for me. Obviously, he was trying to ease me into a basic understanding of the magnitude of problems and crisis we might face in the future. My major concern at this point was what we, as parents, could expect from David and what his future would be like.

"We cannot predict the severity of David's problems until we do a more thorough examination," he said. "However, we must operate within twenty-four hours to close the open area on his back. This surgery will only mend the hole, not fix the damage. To prevent brain damage or further brain damage, I will also implant a shunt deep into his brain to drain fluid. His present condition, if not corrected, most likely will cause a malformation that will begin to dam the flow of cerebrospinal fluid from the ventricles in his brain, causing hydrocephalus, or water on the brain. Currently, the spinal column is exposed with many nerve endings on the outside of his lower back. Without this operation he will not survive. I have ordered for him to have a constant flow of water on his back until we operate. This will prevent the growth of bacteria and infection."

"When will we be able to see David?" I asked.

"David is in isolation, and we will keep him there until we are ready to operate. He has an open area on his lower back about the size of his fist. He is extremely susceptible to any germs in his immediate environment. As soon as the operation is completed and David is stable we certainly will want both you and your wife to be with him. He will need the comfort a mother can give and the love both of you can share."

Letting Dr. Davis know how appreciative I was of his time and patience, I left the hospital and returned home. I sat at the kitchen table for what felt like hours, stunned from the day's events. After a half hour or so of just staring in space and letting my mind race, I realized I needed to make preparations for the next day. I knew I could not handle too many phone calls in the morning. I also realized I had to concern myself with the daily operations of two schools as Sara Belle and I learned to deal with this initial crisis in our lives. I composed a letter to each of my assistant principals reviewing the day's events and explaining that I would be in and out of school office over the next couple of days or until David was stable and Sara Belle was home. I included a few instructions of what I thought needed to be taken care of in my absence. At approximately 2:30 a.m. I drove to the intermediate school in Hebron, Maryland, and the primary school in Quantico, Maryland, to leave the letter on each of the assistant principal's desk. Arriving back home shortly afterward, I walked straight to the bedroom. I set the alarm for 6:00 a.m., laid across the bed fully dressed and some time later, completely exhausted, I drifted off into a light sleep.

SHELDON LARMORE

LEARNING THE WAITING GAME

If God sends us on stony paths, He provides strong shoes.

—Corrie ten Boom

I was awake when the alarm rang at six o'clock. After a quick shower, I hurriedly dressed for the day. Soon I realized it was too early in the morning to call anyone or go to the hospital to see Sara Belle. I had little to do that I felt like doing, so the next hour or so was spent reflecting on the last twenty-four hours. I got on my knees beside the bed to pray, cry, and pray. I walked from room to room just to keep moving. I looked out the windows aimlessly. About ten minutes after 7:00 a.m., my mother called. She wanted to know if I had heard from Sara Belle. Mother worked at Montgomery Wards and was ready to take the day off to be with Sara Belle and me if we needed her. I encouraged her to go to work and assured her I would contact her as soon as I found out what was happening. I felt it would be much better for Mother to be busy at work than sitting in the hospital waiting for news. As I experienced many times since David's birth, a few hours of waiting in a hospital soon began to feel like an eternity. Shortly after talking to Mother, the phone rang again.

"Hello?" I said in a guarded tone.

"Hello, Sheldon. This is Bob Varley. Have you heard from Sara Belle this morning?"

"No, I haven't. I thought I would wait until eight or so before calling her in hopes she is resting."

"Do you know when David's operation is scheduled?" he asked.

"No. Dr. Davis said he was going to have to check with the operating room and he would let us know sometime this morning. He was pretty sure it would be early afternoon."

"I am going to the hospital this morning and I will check on Sara Belle," Father Varley said. "Let me know as soon as you find out when the operation is scheduled. I will be there."

"Thanks, we would really appreciate it."

I could not stay at home any longer without knowing what was happening at the hospital. My mind was racing, my legs were jumping, and my stomach was turning. I had to get to the hospital. When David was born, visiting hours were from 1:00 p.m. to 3:00 p.m. and from 6:00 p.m. to 7:30 p.m. I was a little concerned about how I was going to get to the third floor of the hospital to visit with Sara Belle so early in the morning. Having some thinking skills still intact, I called the hospital and asked to speak with a very dear friend of ours, Ms. Doris Hammond. At the time she was director of nursing at Peninsula General Hospital. She contacted the maternity ward and cleared the way for me. When I arrived in the hospital lobby I was surprised to find Doris waiting to personally escort me to the third floor.

As I entered Sara Belle's room, I found her wide-awake and surprisingly in good spirits. During the night there had been another delivery. The mother of that baby and Sara Belle were sharing the same room. Sara Belle introduced me to her roommate, Barbara. She was about our age and lived in Laurel, Delaware. She knew my sister and was as outgoing and as enthusiastic about life as Sara Belle. Shortly after the introductions, a nurse came into the room with Barbara's newborn baby. We watched as Barbara held out her arms to receive her son, Michael. We could feel the love and warmth between the mother and her newborn. At that moment, Sara Belle was as happy and as radiant as Barbara. She watched in awe as mother and child began to bond. I could only imagine what must have been going through Sara Belle's mind as she watched and listened to Barbara cuddling and playing with her baby. I had to turn my back and use every bit of the fiber in my being to prevent tears or, worse, a total emotional breakdown. What I knew and was hiding from Sara Belle was David's life might not be as promising or complete as Michael's. She was not as aware of the severity of David's problems as I was. I knew I needed to begin to prepare her for Dr. Davis's visit. I also knew I was going to have to struggle with how to control my own emotions as we talked. David's condition, Spina Bifida, was so new and foreign to me I felt uncomfortable in sharing too much information for fear of upsetting her.

I leaned down, kissed her, and asked if she had talked with the doctor. She said no, but shared that her nurse said David was to remain in isolation until the doctor made a decision about the spot on his back. She wanted to know if I had talked with the doctor or if I knew any more than she did. My prayer as I prepared to share with her was, *Oh, God, please give me the strength to do this. Please help me.* I started praying the doctor would enter the room at any time to relieve me of this task.

"I met with Doctor Davis around ten thirty last night. You will like him. He's very pleasant and really took lots of time to talk to me about David. He said that David was born with Spina Bifida."

"What's that?" Sara Belle asked.

"I'm not quite sure but he said mental retardation was the leading birth defect followed by Spina Bifida."

"Is it serious?"

"I think it is serious. But after talking to Dr. Davis I feel much better. He can't really be sure about David's condition until he examines him more thoroughly. You know he has a spot on his back. That spot is really a hole. Dr. Davis is going to operate on David this afternoon to close the hole." Watching Sara Belle as

I spoke, I could see her changing from a happy new mom living with the hopes and dreams for the future to a concerned, somewhat confused mother with growing fears and many questions.

"Will he be okay after the surgery?" she asked.

"I don't know. Dr. Davis said something about putting a shunt, a tube of some sort, in David's brain to drain off fluid to prevent his head from swelling. He said in many cases Spina Bifida can cause multiple congenital problems."

"What did he mean by multiple congenital problems?" she asked.

"I really don't know," I said. "When he comes in this morning let's ask him. I want him to explain to you what Spina Bifida is instead of me trying to tell you. I'm just not sure exactly what he said."

Spina Bifida, shunts, multiple congenital problems, malformation, cerebrospinal fluid, hydrocephalus, etc., were all foreign terms to us. The more we heard them spoken in relation to David's condition, the more frightened we became of his future or even his survival.

I sat by Sara Belle's bedside holding her hand for some time without either of us speaking to the other. We were both obviously absorbed in our own thoughts and questions. The quiet crying of the baby in Barbara's arms brought us back to reality. About that time, the nurse came into the room to check on Barbara and baby Michael. In such a short period of knowing each other as roommates, Sara Belle and Barbara quickly bonded as mothers. Sara Belle told Barbara she wanted to see Michael closer. Barbara handed him to the nurse and asked her to take him over to Sara Belle so she could hold him. I watched from the other side of the bed. Neither one of us had seen or held David since his birth. I'm sure, without sharing our thoughts, both of us were beginning to question if we would ever have the chance to hold our newborn. At that moment we heard a welcoming sound.

"Hello, my friends. How are both of you doing?" Father Varley asked in his deep, confident voice as he stretched out his arm to shake hands with me. He bent over to give Sara Belle a kiss on the cheek.

"We are doing okay," we both said almost in unison.

Father Varley, noticed Michael in Sara Belle's arms. He took time to admire Michael and tried to open up a line of communication between them using baby talk and babbling sounds. The nurse, who had finished the routine blood pressure and temperature check with Barbara, came over to take Michael back to his mother, freeing us to talk with Father Varley.

"I just left Dr. Davis," Father Varley said. "He asked me to give you both his apologies, but he will not be able to meet with you before he operates on David. He's getting ready to do an emergency operation now. After that surgery, he will then go right into David's operation. He has talked to the nurse in charge about David's case and the need to get your permission for the operation. He said she should be in sometime this morning. She will attempt to answer any questions you may have."

"Do you know when we will be able to see David?" I asked.

"I'm sure Dr. Davis will see you as soon as he completes the operation. I'm almost willing to bet you will be able to see him after he leaves the recovery room and the doctor feels he is stable," Father Varley said.

Sara Belle and I were becoming more and more aware of what was being said. Each hour we did not see David or hear from the doctor, we became a little more apprehensive. We began to read into words and phrases such as the ones just spoken by Father Varley, *I'm almost willing to bet*. What did he mean by *almost*? Was there any doubt? Was there a greater concern we needed to worry about as the doctor begins this operation?

As Father Varley prepared to leave, he assured us he would be in contact with Dr. Davis. "As soon as I find out anything I will let you know." He waved and disappeared into the hallway.

We were left again unsure about how David was, what Dr. Davis had found out about David's condition after further examination, or what we were supposed to do or think during this time void of answers to many questions. While we were involved with Father Varley, Barbara's husband, Bert, had entered the room for a visit with his wife and son. The four of us engaged in general conversations about joys of being new parents. We joked about how our lives would change with diaper changes, early morning feedings, and other parental responsibilities we were foreign to at this point in our marriage. Having overheard conversations with the nurse, Father Varley, and others visiting us they were becoming aware that David had problems. They were sensitive to our feelings and wanted to be as supportive as possible.

"How is David?" Barbara asked.

We responded by saying that we really didn't know for certain. We were hoping things were not as serious as we were beginning to think they might be. Bert and Barbara shared with us they would be glad to help us in any way they could. They assured us they would keep us in prayer and put David on their church's prayer list. Bert kissed Barbara good-bye and left to return to work. Minutes passed like hours as we waited for Dr. Davis's visit. Just as Sara Belle was beginning to dose off, lunch arrived. I helped her adjust in bed and pulled the lunch tray close to her. Making sure she had everything she needed, I left the room in search of a strong cup of coffee. I returned to Sara Belle's room to find her sleeping peacefully. Within fifteen to twenty minutes she began to wake up just as the nurse entered the room.

"Dr. Davis is in surgery now with David," she stated. "As soon as the surgery is over I'm sure he will be up to talk with you."

"How long do you think the surgery will take?" I asked.

"I'm not sure," she responded. "I would give him an hour and a half." With that she smiled warmly and touched Sara Belle lightly on the arm and left the room. Hospital routines and waits were all new to us. We knew little about what kind of questions to ask. We soon learned hospital staff did not share information freely and openly with patients or families. There was no way we could fully realize or understand that much of the next thirty-two years of David's life would be spent in waiting, questioning, and conferring with doctors in and out of hospitals.

At approximately 2:45 p.m., the nurse entered the room and stated that the operation was over and successful. She let us know that David would be in isolation and monitored closely for a period of time. She said Dr. Davis had left a message at the nurses' station saying he had another emergency and would have to talk with us later in the day. With such little experience dealing with hospitals and operations, we accepted this situation thinking it must be routine and typical in the day and life of a doctor. We took some relief and solace in knowing the operation was behind us. In reality, we had no idea what a successful operation of this type meant. We were totally oblivious of what was ahead for David and us. Did this mean things were greatly improved now? Did this mean the three of us would be leaving the hospital within the next day or two as a happy family ready to face the future? Were our wonderful dreams of David growing into a fine, productive, and successful young man about to begin?

Presently, we had nothing to do but wait patiently for the promised visit from Dr. Davis. As time lingered, we became more concerned and fearful. Every time we heard a male voice in the hallway we listened intensely in hopes it was the doctor preparing to visit us. As the afternoon slowly drew to a close, daylight gave way to darkness outside the hospital window. The evening nursing staff was beginning to make its rounds on the floor. Yet still no doctor in sight. The night nurse assigned to Sara Belle knew little about David or his condition. Her primary duty and concern was Sara Belle's general health and recovery. We briefly explained to her the events of the day and our endless waiting to hear from the doctor. She promised to see what she could find out for us after she completed her assigned rounds.

After another fretful and fearful hour and a half, the nurse re-entered the room to let us know what little she was able to find out. She stated that David was in isolation and still in critical condition. Hearing the word *critical* alarmed us greatly. It was a word we had not heard all day in describing David's progress following the operation. We asked her when we could speak with the Dr. Davis. She informed us that she had tried to contact him in the hospital before she came to our room. She was told he had left for the night. He was not expected to return until mid morning the next day. Totally perplexed, saddened, exhausted, and greatly disappointed, we tried to comfort each other before I had to leave for the night. We agreed that I should go to work early in the morning. It was nearing the end of the school year and there were many, many issues, reports, and other responsibilities that required attention. I was fortunate to have two capable assistant principals who were self-motivated. Once I laid out a plan of attack and a schedule of tasks to be completed, I could depend on them to follow through successfully.

THE REALITY OF UNCERTAINTY

God will take care of what you go through; you take care
of how you go through it.

—*The Complete Book of Zingers*

It was extremely hard leaving Sara Belle and David in the hospital that night. As I was leaving the room she gave me one of her big smiles, threw me a kiss, told me to not worry, and to get a good night's sleep. On the verge of breaking down in tears, I moved swiftly through the halls of the hospital. Once outside, I ran quickly through the parking lot to our car. My body and soul were filled with volumes of smoldering, raging emotions I had stored far too long. For the last two days my thoughts were, *I'm a man. I'm a husband. I'm a father now. I must be strong*. Once securely in the car, I broke into an uncontrollable convulsive cry. I could not stop the violent, involuntary spasms of my muscles. Through my tears—so many I could not focus my eyes—I looked through the windshield of the car into the heavens above. I prayed for God to be with David and surround him with His love and healing powers. I reminded Him that David was first His. I thanked Him for being so kind to loan him to us to raise. I told God again we wanted David more than anything in the world.

After I collected myself well enough, I drove home. I entered the house in a daze, walked to the family room, sat in the nearest chair and prayed until I fell asleep from exhaustion. I woke at

5:00 a.m. Like a mummy or a person with little or no feeling, I prepared myself for work. I arrived at school around 6:30 a.m. I scanned the mail, phone notes, memos, and correspondence from the previous day left by my secretaries, assistant principals, teachers, and parents. I mustered up as much energy as I could to write responses to each. I made a list for my two secretaries and assistant principals of things I wanted done during the day. I wrote a couple of memos to the faculty and had time to make coffee for the office staff before they arrived. I made great effort to project an air of calmness and friendliness as the office staff and teachers began to arrive. I strongly felt this sign of professionalism and strength was important for them to see. It made it easier for all of us, even though they knew and I knew my heart was aching terribly. So many of them wanted to express their concerns and offer help whenever needed. It was hard getting through the morning.

However, once the students began to arrive, the pain and self-pity I was feeling lessened somewhat. For a break from the early morning hustle and bustle of the school office, I walked out on the bus platform. As I watched the children depart from the buses, one little second grader walked up to me and cheerfully said, "Good morning, Mr. Principal. Have a good day!"

Anyone who loves and has had the privilege of working and relating to children knows how much their smiles, hugs, and eagerness to please serve to lighten the day and put things in perspective. They can make a dreary day into one filled with sunshine and rainbows. Children are like a healing medicine to those of us who have left our childhood and are now burdened with the complexities of life. As a young adult the *very, very, very* last thing I wanted to do with my life was to become a teacher. It's evident I did not believe or know just how much God had planned for my life on earth. Now, I thank God every day for guiding me into the teaching profession. The teaching profession, even though challenging and frustrating at times, has been by far one of the most pleasant and rewarding experiences of my life.

With a degree of accomplishment, or at least with a feeling the ship was beginning to sail again, I was able to leave school just before noon. I could not wait to see Sara Belle and help support her through the day. Well, really, she was the one who supported me. Her love and her strong, steadfast faith gave me the strength I needed to face each day, each new challenge. After greeting each other, we settled down to talk about the *what ifs* in our immediate future. We looked at this time as a new day with a new beginning. We were confident we would hear from Dr. Davis by mid-afternoon. Shortly after my arrival, the nurse entered the room to check Sara Belle's vitals. We asked her if Dr. Davis was in the hospital. She said he was and would be making his rounds on the floor soon. Upon stressing our urgency to her in wanting to see him, she assured us she had already placed a note in a prominent location at the nurses' station where he would see it. She also said she had alerted her two nursing buddies to let him know we wanted to confer with him. This gave us a degree of comfort as we began our day of waiting.

The remainder of the afternoon dragged by at a snail's pace. We passed time with small talk about the events of the day, reading the newspaper, and trying to rest when possible. Dinner arrived for Sara Belle. Our concerns and anxieties began to build once again. We realized it was almost 5:00 p.m., and we had not had the expected visit from Dr. Davis. While Sara Belle tried to eat her dinner, I went to the nurses' station to find out when they were expecting Dr. Davis on the floor. The nurse at the desk was very surprised we had not seen him. She stated she knew for a fact he had received the message twice by two different nurses reminding him that we wanted to see him. She informed me that Dr. Davis had left the floor an hour earlier and would not be returning until late in the evening. The rest of the evening lingered unmercifully without any word of or from Dr. Davis. To make matters worse, David was still in isolation. Even though we had been assured that David's condition was stable, it was beyond belief we had not been able to see him or hold him since his birth.

The next morning was Friday. I went through the same routine as I did the day before. Waking up at 5:30 a.m., I quickly readied myself for the day and left for work by 6:15 a.m. Once at work I opened mail, jotted down to-do lists for both of my assistant principals, and prepared a faculty bulletin outlining information about the forthcoming county-wide spring tests, school announcements, due dates, and other tidbits to help teachers in planning each day. After the school day was underway, I left for the hospital. I was determined I was going to make some kind of contact with Dr. Davis *that day*. Upon arriving at the hospital I stopped at the nurses' station and asked if Dr. Davis was in the hospital. I was informed that he had already made his rounds earlier in the morning. He would not be returning until the evening.

Distressed over missing Dr. Davis again yet determined to make every effort to talk with him personally, I asked for his office phone number. Afterward, I went to Sara Belle's room for a brief visit. I shared with her the events of the morning and my plan to somehow see Dr. Davis. At approximately 11:00 a.m., I went to one of the payphones in the hospital lobby and made a call to Dr. Davis's office. Not much to my surprise, I found out he was not in the office but he had returned to the hospital. This was getting well beyond exasperation! After a sympathetic and pretty exhaustive search and several phone calls made by a couple of nurses on the floor, one of them was able to locate Dr. Davis. He was involved in surgery. Later, through a doctor friend, we learned the patient was a victim of an automobile accident. The surgery had lasted a little over six hours.

Early in the afternoon, Dr. Gallaher entered the room to check on Sara Belle. We were pleased to learn that he was releasing her from the hospital the next day, which was Saturday. As a friend, he took time to sit beside the bed to talk with us about how we were really feeling. He was utterly surprised we had not had any contact with Dr. Davis since the day of David's birth, May 6, 1970. He was further amazed that Sara Belle had not even met the man during her stay in the hospital.

Observing our level of anxiety and our growing fear about David's health issues and prognosis, Dr. Gallaher showed us much compassion. He assured us he knew Dr. Davis and, in his opinion, he was a fine and competent physician. However, he admitted he was as puzzled as we were why Dr. Davis was not keeping us informed. He left the room promising to try to locate Dr. Davis, and he promised to check on David's progress. Within thirty minutes or so, Dr. Gallaher returned with news that Dr. Davis had again left the hospital. At this point the situation, though distressing, was becoming a joke! Through further inquiries with nurses on duty, Dr. Gallaher found out that Dr. Davis always made his evening rounds in the hospital between 9:30 p.m. and 11:00 p.m.

Knowing this, Dr. Gallaher and Sara Belle's nurse strongly urged me to stay in the hospital through 11:00 p.m. with hopes I could meet with Dr. Davis during his rounds. I agreed! She explained our situation to the nursing supervisor and got permission for me to stay beyond the normal visiting hours. Before leaving, Dr. Gallaher let us know he had seen David and his condition remained stable. He assured us he was getting excellent round the clock care.

The evening hours dragged as Sara Belle and I waited anxiously for the time we could talk with Dr. Davis. At the stroke of 9:00 p.m. I began walking the halls of the hospital looking for the doctor. I made several trips around the halls between 9:00 and 11:00 p.m. I'm sure I made a nuisance of myself by frequently checking at the nurses' station in my efforts to locate Dr. Davis. Hoping against hope as 11:00 p.m. approached, I still expected to see Dr. Davis walk down the hall any moment. Dr. Davis did not return to the hospital that evening.

Early on Saturday morning, 1 hurriedly got up, dressed, and left for the hospital. I was going to bring my wife, David's mom, home that day. When I arrived at the hospital Sara Belle was packed and waiting for me. Sadly, however, there still was no word from the neurosurgeon, Dr. Davis. Shortly after I arrived, the nurse came in the room to give Sara Belle last minute orders from the doctor and to check her vital signs before releasing her. Before we could leave we had to go to the nurses' station to verify our son's name, David Jefferson Larmore, on the birth certificate. As we stood waiting, one of the community's well-known pediatricians walked up to the desk. After placing a chart on the counter, he turned to us and said this regarding David, "You should expect nothing and appreciate anything. I would not bond with him. In fact, I would encourage you to institutionalize him."

We were dumbfounded. We just looked at him and walked away. If I had it to live over again I can promise you that is *not* the way that conversation would have ended!

As she had promised Sara Belle earlier in the morning, her nurse took us to the nursery so we could see David before leaving. What an overwhelming moment! David was in a small, enclosed incubator in a room marked "Isolation." Before entering the closed room we had to put on a paper hat and gown, rubber gloves, and cover our mouths with masks. As we entered the room we saw that he was so small and fragile. He looked helpless. We stood watching David sleep. We held our breath in anticipation of each breath he breathed. As I stared at the incubator, my mind raced through many thoughts, mostly of the future. *What if, what if, what if* were the only two words that initially seemed to surface. I tried to calm my innermost thoughts and fears. Surprisingly, the more we watched David, the more at peace we felt. It was this realization we both shared that kept us going. With God's help we knew we would conquer and overcome whatever we needed to do to make David healthy and safe.

After spending a few more minutes with David, we headed down the hall to the elevator. Another mom with her newborn baby cuddled in her arms was already waiting at the elevator to begin their journey home. As the door closed on the elevator, I had a moment of sadness sweep over me. Leaving our newborn son at the hospital was not actually the plan we had in mind. However, we both knew David needed extra care to survive.

CHURCH, FAMILY, AND FRIENDS

If you expect God to stay at your house during the week,
you ought to visit His house on Sundays.

—*The Complete Book of Zingers*

After arriving home, Sara Belle soon was ready for a light lunch and an afternoon nap. I spent time making phone calls to my assistant principals to catch up with happenings in both schools. Later, I worked on a grant project that was due in the central office by the end of the following week. One of our neighbors and best friends, Ruth Twilley, prepared fried chicken with all the trimmings including mashed potatoes, green beans, garden salad, and hot homemade rolls for our dinner. She and her husband, Floyd, brought it over, set the table, and served it to us as if we were the king and queen of the neighborhood. For dessert, she made an apple cobbler and topped it with ice cream. We were so appreciative and humbled by this act of kindness we had to share a little cry and a few hugs before sitting down to our first home cooked meal since David's birth. After dinner, Ruth and Floyd cleaned up the kitchen and placed the leftovers in the refrigerator. Before they left, they made us promise we would call them anytime day or night if we needed help or just wanted to talk.

After the Twilleys left, we became anxious again and felt the need to check on David. Even though Sara Belle was tired and still frail from the week's ordeal, she wanted to go to the hospital to be with David for a while. Concerned for her wellbeing, I tried to talk her into calling the nurse's station to ask about David. However, she was persistent. I reluctantly took her to the hospital. As we entered the nursery area, we were greeted by one of the many nurses we had gotten to know over the last three or four days. She walked with us to David's room and helped us get *gowned up*. Once we entered the isolation room, we found David sleeping peacefully on his stomach. As we stood by the enclosed crib we noticed it had a circular opening with a door on each side. These were used by the nurses and doctors to gain access to David without taking the top off of the crib. Just being with David gave us comfort. However, we couldn't help but feel uneasy at seeing oxygen being administered to him, and numerous tubes and wires leading from his small, frail body to various machines surrounding his enclosed crib.

At the time we didn't fully understand, but this visit to David's bedside was truly a gift from God. As anxious parents searching for positives, we couldn't help but notice David was sleeping with the thumb of his right hand under his chin. It appeared as if he was pushing his chin upward. It seemed he was saying to us, "Don't worry, Mom and Dad. Everything is going to be okay." With his eyes closed, we saw a small circle on each of his eyelids. Sara Belle reached for my hand and held it, saying, "It looks like God is gently closing David's eyes giving him a chance to rest." As we prepared to leave the room, Sara Belle leaned over, kissed the plastic enclosure, and whispered a quiet prayer.

Before leaving, we *again* felt the need to find out if Dr. Davis was anywhere in the hospital. This routine of inquiring about Dr. Davis was becoming as normal with us as breathing. Again, we got the same kind of response. No. Again, we were assured a note would be left for the night supervisor letting her know we desperately needed to talk with the mysterious Dr. Davis. This seemed to be a replay of many earlier conversations. I guessed constant reminders to Dr. Davis wouldn't hurt. *Well, anyway the note messages were free. Hopefully, they were not being charged to our insurance.* We had to have some sense of humor or gentle sarcasm about the "missing" doctor to help us get through some of the daily stress.

We woke up to a warm, bright Mother's Day Sunday. We regularly attended the 8:00 a.m. service at St. Peters Episcopal Church. This day, however, I got out of bed quietly, thinking Sara Belle would want to sleep a little longer. However, she woke with a start saying, "This is Sunday. We've got to get ready for church."

I knew trying to convince her to stay home was useless.

"We need to be in church," she said. "God has been so good to us. We can't let Him or David down."

I truly will never forget how emphatic she was that morning. Sara Belle's love for her church was unquestionable. Her faith before the birth of David was strong. Since David's birth it was growing stronger and stronger each day. We both can honestly say we never questioned God's love for us. We praised Him for giving David to us to care for and nurture. To us, David was perfect.

Following church we visited David. He seemed to be resting well. He was holding his own. He appeared to be waiting for the rest of the world to make some decisions so he could move to his new home permanently. After leaving the hospital we went to my grandmother's for dinner. Grandmother loved Sara Belle dearly. She accepted her as if she was one of her own granddaughters. My parents, my mother's brothers and sisters, and an assortment of cousins always met at grandmother's house every Sunday for dinner. What a wonderful, joyful time we always had at these family gatherings. This day was no exception. The excitement of being together and the laughter shared made these special times with family memorable. We knew by the hugs and kisses my family showered on us that we were truly loved. They had us foremost in their thoughts and prayers.

As we prepared to leave grandmother's house after dinner, we were besieged by aunts and uncles willingly and unselfishly offering us support and money to help us with our expenses. We appreciated their generosity but assured them we were okay at the moment. Later their financial gifts were gladly accepted and greatly appreciated. Grandmother *always* insisted on giving us a little piece of money to help with our expenses. The little pieces usually came in the form of $30.00 or $50.00 every time she saw us.

Early the next day we tried to keep busy tending to a stack of three to four days of mail, paying bills, doing the wash and laundry, and giving the house a quick "lick and promise" cleaning job. Like cockeyed optimists, we remained confident Dr. Davis would call sometime that morning. Just about the time we could not stand the stress of waiting any longer, the phone rang. Anxiously and with much hope, Sara Belle answered it on the first ring.

"Hello," the voice on the other end said. "Just checking in to see how you are doing." It was Father Varley. "I'm on my way to the hospital and will check on David. Have you heard from Dr. Davis?"

We regrettably had to say no but asked if he would try to make contact with him. The next two or so hours we walked the floors or sat in chairs staring at each other. The phone rang again. It was not Dr. Davis. It was Father Varley with a message from Dr. Davis. Father Varley stated he had just met with Dr. Davis. David had to have another shunt operation that afternoon since the first one had shut down, causing the brain to swell as a result of a build up of cerebrospinal fluid within the head. Surgery was imperative. The time for the operation was uncertain since it had to be worked in with those already scheduled. Dr. Davis sent his apologies to us for not making contact sooner. He assured Father Varley he would contact him or us after the surgery. Father Varley encouraged us to stay home while he attempted to find out about the operation.

Again, we waited and waited. In the early evening the phone rang once again. Anxiously expecting to hear the voice of Dr.

Davis, we heard instead Father Varley say, "Hello. Everything went fine. David is back in isolation. All his vital signs look good according to the nurses. Dr. Davis will be in the hospital until nine p.m. or so. He said to have him paged, and he will try to find time to meet with you."

At 7:00 p.m. we were on our way to the hospital. On our arrival we requested one of the nurses to page Dr. Davis for us. We then immediately headed toward David's room. Two nurses were adjusting all of the apparatuses connected to him in an effort to make him as comfortable as his little body could be. Other than having the top and sides of his head totally wrapped with gauze and white bandages, he still looked like our beautiful little angel. We spent the remaining hour visiting with him, watching him sleep peacefully with his tiny chest rising and falling with each little breath. We expected to hear from Dr. Davis most any time now. By 8:30 p.m., we kissed David good night through his plastic enclosure and headed to the nurses' station. They told us Dr. Davis had not responded to the page but they would try again. As they paged him we could hear it through the speakers in the hallway. A few minutes later a phone rang at the nurses' desk. Unbelievably, it was a message saying Dr. Davis had left the hospital for the evening. We resigned ourselves to the fact we would never be able to make contact with Dr. Davis again. Our one glimmer of hope was that David seemed to be making progress.

DOORS OPEN TO NEW DIRECTION

Lord, we don't know how you are going to solve our problems, but we know you have something in mind and we thank you for it.

—Unknown

For the next week and a half we journeyed to the hospital each afternoon and every evening to sit with David. David rarely opened his eyes or gave us any indication he felt our presence. But we never, *never* gave up! We expected any day he would be released from the hospital into the caring arms of his loving parents. What a surprise when Sara Belle received a call from a friend of ours who was a respected gynecologist in the community.

He said, "Sara Belle, it is none of my business, but, as a friend, I want to encourage you to seriously think about transferring David to Mercy Hospital in Baltimore. I have stopped by David's room three or four times this week and have talked to the nurses in charge. In my humble opinion, they are doing nothing for David. They don't know what to do with David. All they are doing is keeping him comfortable and alive. I think you need to talk with your pediatrician. I know he has worked extensively with Dr. Crosby, an internationally known pediatric neurosurgeon, who practices in Baltimore. Our families are close, and we just felt the need to share our concerns with you and Sheldon."

The next day Sara Belle contacted David's pediatrician, Dr. Chester Collins, and pointedly asked him if he thought we needed to transfer David to Baltimore. Without hesitation, he stated he was about to contact us with the same idea.

"If David was my child, I would do it without second thought. Our hospital has never treated infants with Spina Bifida. David is the first one to remain locally since we now have a neurosurgeon on staff. Infants in the past with such birth defects have immediately been transferred to Baltimore. I have a personal relationship with Dr. Crosby in Baltimore, and if you would like, I will make contact with him and follow through with the transfer. However, we have to have Dr. Davis release David from his care. You, as David's parents, will have to obtain this before we can officially proceed."

When I arrived home that evening from work, Sara Belle shared with me her conversation with David's pediatrician. She told me Dr. Davis had to release David from his care before steps to transfer him could be initiated.

"Oh well, that is *certainly* a task simple enough to handle! Did you tell him how many times we have tried to contact Dr. Davis?" I asked.

The remainder of the evening was one filled with mixed emotions. We had lengthy discussions about what we thought would happen if David was transferred to Baltimore. How could we see him as often? How serious really was David's condition? How long did we have to wait for this transfer to take place? How would we ever pay for all these mounting bills that were beginning to trickle into our already over taxed budget? We went to bed with some anxiety but with a feeling of relief, knowing something more was going to be done to help us get David home soon.

The next morning after the school dust had settled, all the morning pleasantries were exchanged with staff and parents, and all the buses had delivered their children, I met briefly with my assistant principals to outline our day. Afterward I entered my office, closing the door behind me. I was determined to make contact with Dr. Davis even if it took all day and half of the night. Having Dr. Davis's office number at hand I took a deep breath and dialed the number. One ring, two rings, three rings, then, "Sorry, this number is no longer in use." *What?* Thinking maybe, out of anxiousness, I had dialed the wrong number I tried again. One ring, two rings, three rings, then, "Sorry, this number is no longer in use."

By this time I really began to think I was in some kind of twilight zone. Without hesitation, I called our friend at the hospital, Doris Hammond. With some surprise I got Doris on the first ring. I shared with her my dilemma about not being able to contact Dr. Davis to obtain a release from him so we could move swiftly in transferring David to Mercy. She was surprised to find out his office phone had been disconnected. She stated she would do some investigating and get back with me shortly. Doris worked fast. Within minutes Dr. Davis called.

"I understand you need to talk with me." *What an understatement!* However, being so grateful to hear from him my anger melted. I told him we wanted a release from him so we could transfer David to Baltimore. He willingly agreed to the release. He promised to sign the necessary papers while in the hospital later in the morning. When I expressed surprise his office phone had been disconnected, he explained he had closed his office and was currently working from the hospital. Later that week, we found out through our sources at the hospital he had discontinued his practice in Salisbury. He had already, supposedly, moved to the West Coast. As we reflect on David's first days, we can't help feel a degree of respect, satisfaction, and admiration for Dr. Davis. To this day we know he saved David's life! It was most frustrating not to be able to communicate with him; however, we were blessed the hospital had employed him as the first neurosurgeon to ever practice in our area.

Even though his stay in Salisbury was short, he was there for David's birth. Dr. Varley told us Dr. Davis left the area for whatever reason the same week we transferred David to Baltimore. When Dr. Crosby did the initial examination on David, he was surprised and most complimentary about the expert job done at birth in closing David's open spine. The method and type of shunt used to drain the spinal fluid from the brain to the abdomen was the latest and most efficient at the time. He was surprised this type of shunt was available in Salisbury since patients with these types of needs were transported to hospitals in metropolitan areas. We still can't help but wonder what miracles we experienced the first few days of David's life without even being aware they were happening. Our faith tells us God was present, and He was in charge of these precious days. Even though we forget at times, we learned we must be quiet and listen to the messages God sends us to help us through each day.

UNEXPECTED COMPLICATIONS

Those who see God's hand in everything can best leave everything in God's hand.

—The Complete Book of Zingers

After receiving the release from Dr. Davis, David's pediatrician, Dr. Collins, arranged for us to transfer David to the care of Dr. Crosby at Mercy hospital in Baltimore. The initial plan was for us to drive David to Mercy. This was exciting, yet a little frightening for us as brand new parents who had not held our son in our arms for even a second. When we arrived at the hospital on Friday morning, we were eager to accept this challenge. To our pleasant surprise, we discovered that a nurse friend, Katherine Middleton, had been assigned to travel with us. She was to take care of David during the journey. One can only begin to imagine how relieved we were not to have that total responsibility! The trip to Baltimore was happily uneventful in spite of ninety-degree weather in a car without air conditioning.

We arrived at Mercy just before our scheduled appointment with Dr. Crosby at 1:00 p.m. Our first impression of Dr. Crosby was a positive one. He was a soft-spoken gentleman who seemed to radiate compassion and love for his patients.

After exchanging warm greetings, his first comments to us were, "I'm so sorry you had to travel up here from the shore on such a hot day in all the beach traffic. But you're here, and now let's talk about David." At that point he introduced us to his assistant who was interning at Mercy. We followed Dr. Crosby to a small room down the hall where he began to examine David. As he did he asked us many questions including pre natal care, family health issues, diets, circumstances of David's birth, and care in Salisbury. He asked what we had been told or knew about Spina Bidfa. He more specifically questioned us about what we knew about David's condition and his chances of surviving to adulthood. The assistant was rapidly taking copious notes.

After approximately two and a half hours with Dr. Crosby, he took time to summarize what he could tell us from this very brief examination coupled with the information we provided. In a nutshell, he told us of the many different kinds of abnormal defects both mental as well as physical David may face or have to overcome in his short lifetime. He wanted us to be aware that a majority of children born with Spina Bifida did not reach their teen years. With this news we were beginning to feel the inward cascading of silent tears. Our quiet prayers were, *Oh God, please take care of David. Please make him healthy. Please, please God!* At the end of our appointment, Dr. Crosby stated he would order a series of tests for David. Afterward, he would begin to map out a program for treatment to best meet his needs. He made sure, in his gentle way, we realized the seriousness of David's birth defect and assured us he would get the best of care. He asked if we could return on Monday for a conference. He wanted the weekend to complete and analyze the tests. On Monday he could give us a more accurate picture of David's prognosis.

Shortly after our meeting with Dr. Crosby, we were introduced to one of the nurses on the pediatrics floor. She gave us a brief tour of the area, taking us to the infants' ward where David would be placed. This area seemed to be well equipped with monitors of all kinds throughout the room. It was obvious the floor was well staffed as nurses, assistants, and interns traveled in and out of the areas tending to the needs of the patients. Making sure David was asleep, we were comfortable to begin our journey home.

Once home on Friday evening, we felt disconnected as a family for the first time. David was in Baltimore, and we were some 130 miles away in Salisbury. Even though David was still under a twenty-four-hour intensive-care treatment, we felt the need to be with him on Saturday and Sunday. Without a second thought we began making plans for the weekend. Sara Belle addressed the things that needed to be taken care of at home while I went to the school office early on Saturday morning to make plans for my staff for the first of the week. Being principal of two schools gave me little slow time. To make matters even more challenging, it was the middle of May. This was a time that always brought much added work and responsibilities to all of us in schools. So much work had to be completed before the school year ended. Once ready, our plan was to travel to and from Baltimore both days. The cost of staying in a motel and eating out just wasn't in our budget.

By mid morning Saturday we were on the road to Baltimore. It was a beautiful day for the trip. As we traveled the countryside we were frequently treated to the Eastern Shore fresh smell of newly plowed fields, and lots of recently dumped manure being emitted in the gently blowing breezes. The weekend was basically uneventful until our return trip to the hospital on Sunday morning. When we arrived in the hospital lobby we each went to the restroom before visiting with David on the seventh floor. As I started to exit the restroom, I broke the zipper on my fly. This was just the kind of excitement I needed on a Sunday in the city with all the clothing stores closed. Since it was a good eighty-five humid degrees outside I didn't have a sweater, jacket or even a large handkerchief to conceal the accident. Sneaking out of the restroom, I quickly spotted Sara Belle on the other side of the lobby. By this time, to me, the lobby looked like what I expected Grand Central Station might look like on Christmas Eve.

In reality there were probably no more than five or six people moving about. But my eyes magnified the number to be fifty to one hundred. I beckoned for her to come over to me. My luck, she just didn't seem to understand. There was no way I was going to sashay across that lobby in my condition or more like the condition of my zipper. Finally, she came to me. Explaining my dilemma we laughed and quickly moved toward the elevator with me following closely behind her. As the elevator door opened on the seventh floor, I reached for a sweater Sara Belle had in her hand and used it as a shield for the next seven hours. I'm sure no one thought it was odd for me to be carrying a bright pink lady's sweater in front of my pants all day long on a sweltering spring day.

On Monday morning before we left for Baltimore, I went to work for a couple of hours while Sara Belle made phone calls to family members and friends, keeping them abreast of the latest happenings in the Larmore household. She also made contact with Father Varley. He insisted we call him about our conference with Dr. Crosby as soon as we returned home that evening. Shortly after 10:00 a.m., I arrived home from work, picked up Sara Belle and began our trip to Mercy for our 1:00 p.m. meeting with Dr. Crosby.

As we got off the elevator on the seventh floor of the hospital, we were surprised to see Dr. Crosby walking toward us. He had just completed an operation and was on his way to check on David. His gentleness came through again as he put his arm around Sara Belle's shoulder saying, "I'm on my way to see David. You might as well come with me."

Entering the room David shared with five other infants, we found him peacefully content in the arms of a nurse's assistant. To us it was a picture of beauty. She was slowly rocking and singing to him while feeding him his formula. Dr. Crosby checked David's chart and questioned the assistant about his general condition and responses during the time she had been with him.

SHELDON LARMORE

We couldn't wait to hold David, but we knew it was time for our conference with Dr. Crosby. We both bent over and gave him a kiss on the cheek. With tears from mixed emotions, we followed Dr. Crosby across the hall for our meeting.

Dr. Crosby started the meeting by explaining to us again in greater depth the seriousness of David's condition and the complications associated with Spina Bifida. As the conference continued, his manner became more of one of concern.

"As you know we examined David pretty thoroughly over the weekend," he said. "We gave him several tests to determine the degree of his birth defect. We needed this information to help us map out a plan for his treatment. As you are aware, the reason for David's shunt is to provide a passageway for the spinal fluid to circulate through the brain and down the spinal column and back. In an effort to find out the extent of the blockage we attempted to run dye through his brain. This procedure was unsuccessful and gave evidence of a more serious problem than we expected. David has a rare condition where all the cerebral ventricles and arteries are blocked. There are only five other cases of this type of condition caused by Spina Bifida recorded in medical records. We must operate as soon as possible. The longer we wait, the chances of severe brain damage increase greatly. In addition, there are signs that the shunt is quickly shutting down. With your permission, we can operate tomorrow morning. The operation is a tricky one and will take several hours to complete. Without the operation his life is in jeopardy."

Even though this news was a shock, we somehow had prepared ourselves for the worst. We were not giving up! With God's help and guidance we were ready. As long as David was willing to fight, we were ready to surround the three of us with our armor of faith, love, and prayer, and move ahead. From that moment we knew God had us in His care. We just knew from all of the blessings we had experienced that there was a greater power standing with us. The many prayers sent above by our family, friends, and members of the community helped to brace us for this next level of the battle. Without hesitation, we signed the necessary papers for the operation. Dr. Crosby assured us he would have the expertise of his associates, all the necessary staff, equipment, and supplies needed to guarantee the success of the operation.

THE MIGHTY STRENGTH OF PRAYERS

When fear knocks at the door, send faith to open it, and you'll find no one there.

—Ray Cross

Before leaving for home, we went to say good night to David. His little body was so still we could hardly detect any breathing. We stood quietly by his crib for some time, each of us lost in our thoughts about tomorrow, the future, and life in general. If only we could hold him in our arms. We were sure if we had asked one of the nurses or assistants they would have made it possible. However, David was hooked up to so much equipment with tubes for this and tubes for that hanging everywhere, it would be a real feat to accomplish for the short time we would be allowed to hold him. With tears running down both of our cheeks we each kissed our fingers and placed them on his forehead and I whispered, "We'll see you tomorrow. We love you. Remember, Jesus is with us. Good night, Bunky."

Stopping for a quick dinner we arrived home by 7:30 p.m. We were drained from the emotions of the day, yet awake with many unanswered questions and thoughts spinning around in our already taxed brains. We knew we needed and wanted to touch base with Father Varley. We needed to hear his voice. We needed to know he was praying for David and us. We needed his reassurance that tomorrow was going to be okay. When Sara Belle called him at home, Beverly, his wife answered. Since Sara Belle babysat for the Varleys while she was in college, Beverly and she had become close friends. Beverly knew we wanted to talk with Father Varley but first she had to know how David was. After a brief discussion, she told Sara Belle that Father Varley was expecting us to call. He told her to have us call him at church. When we contacted him he said he was going to be in a counseling session at church until 9:30 p.m. or so. As soon as it was finished he would call us. Around 10:00 p.m. the phone rang and it was, as expected, Father Varley. He stated the session had lasted longer than he had thought. He wanted to meet with us at church.

"Now?" Sara Belle asked. "You're sure it's not too late?"

"No, if it's not too late for you," he replied. We were in the church office within fifteen minutes. As usual, we found comfort being in the presence of Father Varley. It was obvious he was sincerely interested in learning about our day with Dr. Crosby. He truly was becoming like a father to us. He was compassionate, always ready to listen, and willing to give advice if it was asked of him.

After sharing with him the events of the day and our concerns for David, Father Varley opened the church sanctuary and led us to the altar. He began praying for David's healing. We prayed for God's presence in the operating room. We prayed for His guidance in directing the skilled hands of the surgeons, for peace and understanding among our family and friends, and for our safe journeys to and from Baltimore. Prayers were also lifted up for all those in the medical profession who give of their time and talents in helping others. During the hour or so at the altar rail we prayed, we talked, we cried, and we knelt quietly as a gentle spray of peace and comfort seemed to encompass us. What a feeling of God's presence we experienced that evening. It was as if the heavens had opened above, showering rays of triumph and beauty down upon us. We felt safely surrounded in a warm comforting mist of peace and an abundance of His gentle love.

That night we truly witnessed the glory of God's kingdom and received many blessings. It was clear Father Varley was a devoted servant to his Father. The love he had for shepherding his flock was most evident. We slept well that night mostly because of the peace we received from our communion with God. That evening with Father Varley rejuvenated our souls and provided us with the courage to deal with our future.

By mid morning of the next day we arrived at Mercy Hospital. We were to meet with Dr. Crosby before David's scheduled 12:30 p.m. operation. We were informed that Dr. Crosby was still in surgery but was expected within the hour. This delay gave us time to visit with David. As we approached David's crib we were again overwhelmed with the numerous tubes and machines connected to his fragile, little body. Through all this he continued to be resting peacefully. We stood by his side rubbing his tiny arms and quietly praying. We truly did not know what to pray for, only that we wanted God to watch over him and make him whole. We were filled with the miracles of birth and parenthood. We were far too naïve to understand what our future together might hold. At times we would glance at each other, squeeze hands and share a smile between us as tears rolled down our cheeks. Inwardly, we knew these smiles spoke of how pleased we were to have David as our son. Just his presence in our lives had strengthened the love we had for each other. Without question we knew the three of us would survive and grow as a family in God's love.

After twenty minutes or so a nurse came in the room and said Dr. Crosby was ready to meet with us in the conference room. We were led across the hall to a brightly decorated room overlooking the city. The sun was brilliant that day as it shined through the windows providing a cheerfulness that seemed to fill us with an unexplainable calmness. Shortly the door opened as Dr. Crosby and one of his interns entered. We had prepared ourselves to hear about the severity and consequences of the operation.

Dr. Crosby said, "In preparation for today's surgery I wanted once again to study and confirm the plan I had developed for the operation. We will not have to operate today." Sara Belle and I tried to absorb what Dr. Crosby just said and looked at each other in utter disbelief. "When we ran the dye test this morning the dye ran through all the arteries and veins without a problem," he said. "We did not find any blockages anywhere." We were stunned beyond belief. Emotions took over. We cried, laughed, cried, and thanked Dr. Crosby over and over. With a moment of hesitation and a fatherly smile dampened with a noticeable tear, he said, "Don't thank me. I had nothing to do with it. A much greater power than any we know here on earth"—he pointed above—"was at work here." This confirmed to us that Dr. Crosby was a man of God. From that moment on, we put David's medical care and our trust totally in Dr. Crosby. This was truly another of many blessings we had and would continue to experience throughout David's life.

After this wonderful news Dr. Crosby spent some time explaining to us that David's second shunt was closing down and he would have to replace it that day. He reiterated the seriousness of David's condition still existed and made sure we understood he was far from being out of the woods. As our conference ended, Sara Belle gave Dr. Crosby a big hug. We both expressed to him again how thankful we felt having him watch over David. At the time I'm sure Dr. Crosby was a little surprised with the hug he received from Sara Belle, but this was only the beginning of many, many hugs both of them would readily share. Dr. Crosby was not only David's neurosurgeon, over time he became a friend and told us to consider him David's godfather. Following David's shunt operation in the afternoon we stayed with him until the end of the evening visiting hours. With the events of the day so fresh on our minds we were able to float the two and a half hours

SHELDON LARMORE

home. We had just witnessed again the power of prayer and the unwavering and unquestionable love from our Father above.

David remained in Mercy for another two weeks as he continued to be monitored and to gain strength. One of the happiest days of our lives happened on Friday, June 19, 1970. David was released from the hospital to travel home for the first time. Initially, we had doubts as we thought about the beach traffic and traveling home with a new baby for the first time by ourselves. Those thoughts lasted about three seconds. The joys and excitement we were about to encounter as we started our life as a family of three overrode any anxieties. By the time we were indoctrinated about medications, the care of the shunt, skin irritations, and other medical necessaries we were somewhat overwhelmed but more than ready to accept the responsibilities. David was discharged just before noon. Fortunately we were able to travel across the bridge to the eastern shore with only moderate traffic and without any baby incidences that required brand new, inexperienced parents to handle.

Blessings
Continue to
Abound

The three grand essentials to happiness are: something to
do, something to love, and something to hope for.

—Joseph Addison

Our first afternoon and evening at home were pure joy. After settling David in his bassinet in our family room, we opened the windows to let the gentle summer breeze flow into the room. We turned on soft easy listening music and sat back to watch our son as he drifted further into a peaceful sleep. The weekend was filled with family and friends, good food, fellowship, and many blessings. David was a trooper. He handled all the comings and goings, the *ahs* and *ohs*, and the kisses and hugs just like a veteran celebrity. The days that followed were always filled with new discoveries of parenthood. The excitement of watching David grow and adjust to his new environment was our pleasure and entertainment. To us, like all parents, he was the most beautiful thing we had ever hoped to cast our eyes on.

During the summer months and into the fall, David seemed to be progressing well in spite of his many physical problems. He enjoyed being outside, riding in the car, and watching activities around him. We were so blessed. David rarely cried or gave any indication of discomfort. Later we found out this was not necessarily a good thing. Doctors explained to us that David might be in trouble physically and not show any signs of distress since many of his nerve endings in his legs and back were dead due to his birth defect.

Church continued to be a focal point in our family life. Not wanting David to be exposed to any more germs than necessary, we divided our time in church. I went to the 8:00 a.m. Sunday service and stayed home with David while Sara Belle went to the 11:00 a.m. service. We continued this routine through mid fall. At that time we began attending the 9:30 a.m. service and David adjusted well. We were so proud of him. It was a rare time if he even made the slightest peep during the service.

In late fall 1970 we began to notice David having signs of irritability. After a couple of days we made an appointment with his doctor, Chester Collins. Following a complete examination, he informed us David's shunt appeared to be malfunctioning. He further stated he would be better satisfied if Dr. Crosby saw him as soon as possible. While we waited in the examining room he called Dr. Crosby, explained David's condition, and made an appointment for us to meet Dr. Crosby at Mercy Hospital the next day. After examining David, Dr. Crosby confirmed what Dr. Collins had suspected. His shunt was beginning to shut down. The operation to replace the shunt for the fourth time since birth was scheduled for December 8.

David had not been baptized. We felt it was important to take care of this before he faced another operation. Within the week the ceremony was scheduled for Sunday, December 6 during the 9:30 a.m. service. This was a special time in our lives. Family and friends were invited, food was prepared for a buffet following the service, and a fresh Canadian Spruce Christmas tree was set up and decorated in our living room. The reception in our home following the baptism was filled with laughter, joy, and love.

The next day we traveled to Baltimore with David for his operation. This time we were not so sure what the outcome might be. In our discussion with Dr. Crosby he stated even though not

SHELDON LARMORE

necessarily unusual, replacing a shunt four times in less than six months was a concern. New worries began to surface. *Is this a condition that will have to be addressed every three or four months? Is there a blockage or another type of physical problem that prevents the shunt from functioning as it should?* Our worries were put to rest following the operation. Dr. Crosby assured us everything went well. However, he put in a second shunt leaving the old one in place. He stated he would remove it in February when he repaired an aqueductal obstruction. He assured us following this surgery David should not have to have another shunt revision for some time. Obviously the tubing would have to be lengthened as his body grew.

Whenever David was in a hospital out of town Sara Belle would pick me up after work on Tuesdays and Thursdays with a packed sandwich to eat on our way to the hospital. We would stay with David until the end of visiting hours. Even though he slept most of the time we were there, it gave us satisfaction knowing he was okay. The important thing was that the three of us were together. After a period of a week or so we began to expect a call from the hospital saying he was being discharged. Instead we received a call from Dr. Crosby saying David had developed a low-grade fever. He needed to stay in the hospital for further testing. Within a couple of days the fever broke. However, there was no sign David would be released. This uncertainty continued into Christmas week. On December 23, we began to make plans to spend Christmas Eve and Christmas Day in the hospital with David. Throughout the week we prayed relentlessly for David's recovery and his return home. We so much wanted him to share his first Christmas at home. Prayers are answered! Late in the afternoon of December 23, Dr. Crosby called. His first words were, "Would the Larmores like to have a Christmas present? How about picking David up in the morning?"

After many, many words to express our thanks we assured Dr. Crosby we would be there early in the morning. We looked at our sad Christmas tree. It had been up for at least four weeks with little care or water. It was as dead as could be. When we walked across the room we could hear the needles by the truckloads falling on the hard wood floor. We agreed this would not do for David's first Christmas. So we proceeded to untrim the tree, go out, buy a new one, put it up and re-trim it. Before we went to bed we made sure every little detail related to gifts, phone calls, house cleaning, laundry, and food for Christmas day was taken care of to our satisfaction. All we wanted to do was totally enjoy David and smother him with our love.

The next morning we raced across the bay faster than Santa and his eight tiny reindeer would circle the earth that evening. As we prepared to leave the hospital with David we met Dr. Crosby in the lobby. He had just finished his hospital rounds and was on the way home to enjoy his family. He was excited that all four of his children would be arriving during the day to spend the holidays at home. As he helped Sara Belle in the car with David he asked us to call him the first of the year for an office appointment. At that time he would talk to us about scheduling the surgery to correct the obstruction and the removal of the shunt.

Surprises Continue to Unfold

Contentment is not found in having everything, but in being satisfied with everything we have.

—From the teachings of Dr. Kenneth Boa

Our trip home was filled with the excitement of celebrating our first Christmas as a family. We had just picked up the most precious gift of all. What else could we ever want! Oh, what a wonderful, unforgettable time it was for all of us to be nestled in a home filled with warmth, happiness, love, and hope. Unbelievably, a group of carolers sang throughout our neighborhood on that blissful eve before Christmas. Unexpectedly our first special Christmas night was topped off with six or more inches of snow. Truly, it had to be a gift from the heavens.

Early January, we called Dr. Crosby's office for a follow-up appointment per his request. The earliest appointment we could schedule was in mid February. We were informed that Dr. Crosby would be out of the office most of January due to a reoccurring illness.

The months of January and February were fortunately uneventful. It was a time we grew stronger as a family while enjoying the many opportunities to share in activities of our family and friends. The latter part of February we met with Dr. Crosby for a regular check-up. He took much of the morning examining David. Afterward, he questioned us about David's activities and the growth patterns we had observed over the last couple of months. Following the exam, Dr. Crosby commented that David seemed to be a contented little man; however, his body size continued to be quite spectacular. To us, that meant we were blessed to have a cheerful, chubby baby. At the end of the appointment, Dr. Crosby scheduled time in March for the pending operation to correct the aqueductal obstruction which was, in essence, a blockage preventing the normal flow of cerebrospinal fluid through the mid brain area. During the same operation the old shunt was to be removed. It was Dr. Crosby's hope that the new shunt would function effectively and eventually David would be shunt independent.

The operation was not as simple as planned. Once Dr. Crosby started the operation it became more complicated. The suspected aqueductal obstruction turned out to be a severe Arnold Chiari malformation with kinking of the aqueduct. From what we understood in layman's terms, there was an abnormal opening in the spinal column. This opening caused the brain stem, cerebellum, and cerebella brain tissues to be squeezed downward through an opening at the bottom of the skull. Basically, part of David's brain was lodged in his neck. The operation was quite tedious and time consuming. The method used was called decompression surgery, which involved moving the brain slowly back up into the skull. After several hours the surgery was completed and successful. A week later, David was released from the hospital to return home to the good old Eastern Shore of Maryland.

Each time hospital stays separated David from us it seemed to make our love for each other grow stronger. Words will never be found to describe the feeling of security and comfort we felt as parents as we journeyed home with David on that day. It was one of those typical March days when the sun shines hot and the wind blows cold. It was like summer in the sun and winter in the shade. As we drove home I couldn't help but recall a quote I had read recently in one of Sara Belle's daily scripture pamphlets. It was written as a message from God: "Good morning. This is God. I will be handling all of your problems today. I will not need your help, so have a miraculous day." There is nothing that brings peace to a soul any quicker than to know God is in His heaven and He loves and cares for each of us.

Spring was a beautiful time for the Larmore family. This is the time of the year that seems to bring a sweetness of new beginnings and endless possibilities. It's like God created hope the same day He created spring. It was a time spent watching David grow and blanketing him with our love. It has been said that babies fill a hole in our hearts that we never knew existed. How very true!

With the arrival of April we celebrated our fourth wedding anniversary and counted the blessings that had been showered upon our family. We took David on little outings in the car or we strolled through our neighborhood enjoying the green grasses, plowed fields, chirping of the birds, and the bursting leaves on the trees. David was recovering nicely from his stays in the hospital. We noticed each day a new development in his personality. He was becoming more aware of his surroundings and beginning to communicate verbally to us his needs and feelings.

On May 6, 1971, I awoke with David in bed between Sara Belle and me.

"Dad, do you know what today is?" Sara Belle asked.

"It's David's birthday," I said.

Sara Belle looked down at David. "David, show Dad how old you are."

With that David stuck up one finger to his nose. I was amazed!

"How did he know that?" I asked.

Sara Belle laughed and had to tease me a little about not knowing just how smart David was. Then she told me she and Joann, a neighbor, thought it would be fun if they could teach David to hold up one finger for his age on his first birthday. They proudly accomplished this somehow by constantly putting David's finger to his nose and saying, "How old are you?" Eventually, most every time they said, "How old are you?" David would move his finger to his nose.

SHELDON LARMORE

A TIME TO GROW

Life is hard by the yard—by the inch it's a cinch.
—*The Complete Book of Zingers*

I recently read in a newspaper article a wise saying that seemed to characterize our lives as a family, especially during David's first years. The saying was, "Spend time, not money, on your children." We're glad it didn't read in reverse since money was scarce. However, time was plentiful, and love was in abundance in our family. These certainly seemed to be necessary ingredients for making homemade happiness in our daily living.

The beginning of David's second year marked a time when we settled down to a normal life. Consciously, we knew we would be facing setbacks and additional surgeries as David grew. However, it was our choice to live each day to its fullest. We agreed to let the future take care of itself. We had enough to concern ourselves with the present. Shortly after David's birth a family friend shared with us that one of the kindest things God ever did was to put a curtain over tomorrow. Many people miss much happiness because they never stop to enjoy it while they have it. This was not our case. David's presence in our lives brought us so much joy that we couldn't help but count our blessings each day. As in all families some days were more challenging than others.

Each day I could hardly wait to arrive home after work to find out what new things David had done or learned in my absence. One evening as I walked in the door, Sara Belle greeted me with David in her arms. Her first words to me were, "Here! You take him for a while." I looked puzzled as she put David in my arms. "He has been crying for a solid hour and a half and I can't quiet him down."

As I held David on my shoulder and lightly patted his back he soon stopped crying and fell sound to sleep. "I don't know what your problem is," I smugly said. Well! That was not necessarily what she wanted to hear at the time. So I had total charge of the situation while she collected her wits and prepared dinner. Once again this reminded me of how awesome the job of a full-time mom is trying to keep the house "running" and tending to the every need of an infant. Men have it easy. Most times they are able to come home from work, play with their children, and help put them to bed. The next day they return to work to carry on normal adult conversations with their colleagues.

There was the time when we most definitely learned never to leave David to his own devices. As we were finishing dinner one evening the phone rang at the same time the doorbell sounded. While I went to the door, Sara Belle answered the phone. Within moments we heard a loud crash in the kitchen. We both ran to the kitchen with our hearts in our throats. There we found David with his eyes wide open as if in a state of wonderment, banging his spoon on his highchair. On the floor running everywhere was a half-gallon of spilled milk. Obviously, somehow it was knocked off the table by David's flinging arms. It was so much fun for the next half hour cleaning up David's *entertainment*.

It was always fun to feed David and watch his expressions as he tasted the various kinds of baby food. One day at noon, I was able to break away from the office and have lunch at home with my family. Dressed in a suit, white shirt, and a new tie just bought the past weekend I decided I was going to feed David his lunch. For lunch David was going to taste test his first jar of squash. With his bib tied securely around his neck, the jar opened and the spoon in hand, I proceeded to feed him. Holy cow! I soon learned I was the one who needed the bib. Within seconds

SHELDON LARMORE

of tasting the delicious squash, it ended up, with torpedo speed, all over my suit jacket, shirt, and brand new tie. Following two or three seconds of initial shock, I broke into laughter and enjoyed the moment. For fun I continued to *torture* David by feeding him spoonfuls of tasty squash. The more he reacted and spit out the squash the more I laughed, and the more he seemed to grin as if he knew what was happening. Since David, the highchair, and I were already a mess, why stop the fun? Fortunately for David, Sara Belle soon put a stop to my foolishness and sent me back to work after I had changed by clothes. Oh well, another lesson learned and another dry cleaning bill.

When David was about two and half years old we went shopping in one of our town's first discount stores, Nichols. As Sara Belle shopped, I carried David in my arms and played all kinds of silly games with him. We would go from aisle to aisle hiding from Sara Belle. For fun I began to make funny faces and crazy sounds to entertain David. Shortly, David was mocking me and returning crazy, loud noises and funny faces. This became a contest between us—who could be the craziest. As we turned the corner of one of the aisles, we ran into two very distinguished, seemingly straight-laced elderly ladies. They stopped and looked at us as if puzzled about what they had encountered. We hurriedly vacated the area in search of our safe haven, Sara Belle. Afterward, I realized this was one of David's first adventures shopping. It occurred to me that some people in the community who knew us and knew about David's struggles at birth might be wondering just how alert or functional David was or would be as he developed. As I explained the situation to Sara Belle we both laughingly agreed there would not be any more wondering. This single act spoke volumes and sealed any doubt. With the gossip flowing from these women the whole community would learn that neither the father nor child is normal. We would be perceived as *just not right!*

Poor little defenseless David had to endure some strange experiences with his mother as well. David had a difficult time speaking in his early years. As a result he did not attempt to talk until he was three or four years of age. His means for communicating with others was through making sounds or using hand movements. When he did start to talk it was usually one word, never a simple sentence. One day Sara Belle and David left home to visit with her parents in Milton, Delaware. On the way, for whatever reason, David started to talk to his mother in sentences asking where they were going, telling her he loved her, wanting to know if I was at work, etc. This change in David's efforts to communicate floored Sara Belle so much she got caught up in the moment.

The longer she drove the more he talked. They were just having the greatest time of their lives. Soon Sara Belle came upon a traffic light where she didn't expect to find a traffic light. Stopping, she thought, *Where in the blue blazes am I?* She tried to find a landmark or something that looked familiar. Driving a little farther she came upon a sign that read, "Welcome to the Town of Bridgeville." With that surprise she realized she had traveled up Route 13 missing the turn off to Georgetown, Delaware. To those of you who know Sussex County in Delaware, Bridgeville is a far cry from Milton. This day will always remain close to Sara Belle's heart. It was filled with the love and laughter that can only be enjoyed and understood between a parent and child, a time of joy, a time for bonding and a time for healing.

Shortly after one of their weekly trips to Milton, Sara Belle and David spent one afternoon grocery shopping. On their return home David again opened his mouth and began to spout out all kinds of wisdom as his mother was driving. Fortunately, she was in control and was able to maneuver the car in the right direction home. However, when they arrived home, Sara Belle backed the car into the driveway while talking with David at the same time. She was so intrigued with what David was saying she forgot to put on brakes. The foundation of the porch suffered many bruises as the car came to rest, knocking loose one of the pillars holding up the roof. Needless to say that evening after dinner I had to sit both of them down at the kitchen table and have a heart to heart discussion with them about talking while driving!

OH, THE JOYS OF SURGERIES

Loving Father, I entrust myself to your care this day;
guide with wisdom and skill the minds and hands of the
medical people who minister in your Name.

—*The Complete Book of Zingers*

Shortly before David's second birthday Dr. Crosby expressed concern regarding David's head size. He felt it was a little big for his body. He explained this was due to the failure of normal body growth in a child with a severe Myelomeningocele (a birth defect in which the backbone and spinal canal are not closed before birth). He also was not happy with David's development of large motor skills. He wanted David enrolled in some sort of exercise program to make him stronger and more active than he was currently. As a result he arranged for us to become a part of the Myelomeningocele clinic at Kernan Hospital. This clinic was a godsend and one we attended every two or three months until David was eighteen years of age. It provided us with the services of orthopedists, urologists, neurosurgeons, physical and speech therapists, brace makers, nutritionists, pediatricians, as well as social workers and chaplains.

One of the first acts of the clinic was an agreement to place David in a set of full-legged braces. This enabled him for the first time to stand upright in a standing box. David adjusted to this new way of life quickly and seemed to enjoy being able to participate in and watch activities around him in a standing position.

This soon led to Dr. Collins directing us to Deers Head Hospital in our hometown for a program of physiotherapy. These twice a week sessions helped in strengthening David's muscle tone, improving his coordination, and building his self-confidence. Life with David continued to be one of pure joy. Even though there were days, sometimes weeks, of anxiety we chose to dwell on the pleasant times we shared.

A couple of months after David's second birthday it was decided he needed an eye operation to correct his severe strabismus or cross-eyedness. This surgery was scheduled as an over night stay at the Wilmer Eye Institute at Johns Hopkins hospital in Baltimore. Once in the room we spent time getting David acclimated. In the process he wanted his electric bed lowered.

"Oh, David that's easy," I said. "Dad can do that just by pushing this button." I did just that and the bed started down but began to show some resistance. "Wow! David, this bed should go down farther than this." I began to investigate. To my surprise I found the problem. One of the metal posts involved in raising and lowering the bed had *totally* penetrated our brand new Samsonite (still to be paid for) luggage. I had placed the luggage on the floor and it obviously got pushed or kicked under the bed in the process of getting David settled. When I attempted to raise the bed so the post would come out of the luggage, the luggage was stuck to the post. I had to literally separate the two by hand. Oh well! Just another experience and another expense! Picture me at the end of visiting hours walking through the hospital lobby with a piece of *see-through* luggage in tow. I bet this sent lots of people to the department stores the next day looking for a piece of this *very fashionable, exquisite luggage.*

In the fall of 1973 David had his first hip operation at the James Lawrence Kernan Hospital in Woodlawn, Maryland. Due to David's multiple birth problems the surgery proved to be a little more involved than usual. However, it was a success, and David adjusted well to his hospital environment except the times we had to leave him after visiting hours. We were fortunate the hospital had an assistant named Mickey who was truly an angel. As we prepared to leave after each visit, she would take David in her arms and walk him about the room as he cried and screamed knowing we were leaving. Mickey would always insist we call her when we got home so she would know we made the nearly three-hour trip safely at night. This also gave us a piece of mind that David was okay before we went to bed.

During this period when David was in the hospital we traveled back and forth on Saturday and Sunday of both weekends and on Wednesdays after I got off from work. On one of these dark, windy, chilly evenings in mid October we were walking from the parking lot to the hospital when we met a pleasant gentleman walking in the opposite direction.

"Hello, how are you?" he said.

"Fine. Have a good night," I said. Then I immediately turned to look at him again as he continued to walk to his car. A light bulb began to flash! I stopped Sara Belle in her tracks and said, "Do you know who that was that just passed by us?" She was clueless! With all of the excitement I could muster I said, "That was Johnny Unitas!" My enthusiasm would not be retained. With Johnny a city block and a half away I shouted, "Hi, Johnny! Best of luck Sunday!"

Fortunately, for my thrill he answered, "Hi. Thanks a lot." After telling about my surprise of seeing Johnny Unitas to Mickey, she shared that the Colts football team used the physical therapy department at Kernan on a regular basis when in town. It was old hat for the staff to see the various team members roaming the halls.

Two weeks following surgery we brought David home. This was on my birthday, October 30. What a wonderful present until…! David was in a total body cast and lying on the sofa in our family room. The three of us were celebrating with ice cream, cake, and soda. In the process of drinking from a glass David evidently bit down too hard and shattered the glass into what seemed like a thousand pieces. Glass was everywhere! Within seconds I gathered all the broken pieces I could find and reassembled the glass. All the pieces matched with one small piece missing. Fearing David may have swallowed the piece we immediately called our pediatrician. Unfortunately our least favorite doctor was on call. Explaining to him our dilemma he stated in a very irritated manner, "All kids eat glass. He won't die."

"Is there anything we should do?" I asked.

"No, he will pass it," he replied. Afterward we called our friend Doris Hammond. She told us to have David eat pieces of bread. If he did swallow glass it would attach itself to the bread and ease the bowel movement. Would you believe after settling down from all this *lively* trauma in the Larmore household, David asked for another sip of soda? After searching through all the cabinets in the kitchen we finally found one of his old, much-used plastic cups.

Just before David's fourth birthday he was scheduled for his second hip operation. We took him to Kernan a couple of days before the planned surgery to meet with Dr. Decker, his orthopedic surgeon. The day of surgery we arrived at the hospital at 8:30 a.m., just minutes before they took David down for the operation. Previously, Dr. Decker told us the operation would take two and a half hours. We went to the waiting room, which overlooked the parking lot. After an hour or so I got up from my seat and walked over to the window. To my surprise I saw Dr. Decker walking to his car and watched as he drove off. I shared with Sara Belle that the operation must be over. It seemed odd Dr. Decker did not come to the waiting room to talk to us before leaving. We went to the nurses' desk to see if they could tell us anything about the operation or the whereabouts of David. After checking with the operating room they reported to us that the surgery was still in progress.

"That's odd. I'm sure I just saw Dr. Decker leave the hospital in his car," I said. They assured us David was still in surgery. One of the nurses said, "It must have been someone that looked like Dr. Decker."

I was 99 percent sure it was him but we took our seats and waited, and waited, and waited. At 12:30 p.m. we could wait no longer. We asked at the desk again if the operation was over or if they could give us any information that would ease our minds. They checked with the operating room again. The message they received this time was quite different from the first one. They reported to us the operation could not be done due to the difficulty in preparing David with an intravenous tube. David had very small and *rolling* veins. After several attempts to place the needle in his veins the staff felt he had been through enough and stopped the procedure. David was sent to the recovery room just before 9:30 a.m. The nurse in charge was surprised we had not been told. It seemed Dr. Decker received a call from Mercy hospital about one of his patients and had asked a nurse in the operating room to explain the situation to us and the need to reschedule the surgery. The nurse either forgot or was called to an emergency. We obviously did not get the message.

"Where is David?" I asked. The nurse again placed a call to the recovery room asking about David and his condition. The reply was, "We don't have a David Larmore." As parents, we were beginning to panic. It was obvious the nurses at the desk were registering real concern. Shortly, the phone rang at the nurses' desk. The recovery room had found David in the corner of the room behind drawn curtains. He was placed there after his attempted surgery and somehow forgotten or overlooked. Through this series of errors we survived. We look back on this experience, still with questions, but one we can find humor in today. As a side note, it just proves these kinds of experiences can and do happen in any hospital regardless of their status or records of excellence.

This hip operation was rescheduled a month later. To make sure the same difficulty would not occur again, Dr. Decker made the necessary arrangements for us to stop by the University of

Maryland Hospital to have the needle properly inserted. Then we continued to Kernan where the operation went off without a hitch. Within eight or nine days we brought David home with both legs in a cast separated by a bar between his knees. He remained in this cast for six months. The day we took him back to have the cast removed he developed a fever. Dr. Decker felt we needed to admit him so tests could be done to rule out any serious problems such as a shunt malfunction, or any type of infection that may be developing. The cast was removed on a Friday. We could just see the relief and the appreciation of freedom David was feeling. We visited him both days of the weekend. On Sunday, we noticed that every time we barely touched his leg he would let out a scream or start to cry. This concerned us greatly. We requested that a doctor on duty examine him to see what may be going on. We left after Sunday evening visiting hours without any answers to why David was having such a negative reaction by us touching his leg.

On Monday morning Sara Belle got a call from a house doctor. Very apologetically, he stated, "David has a broken leg. We will have to recast him."

"How in the world did that happen?" Sara Belle asked.

"After the legs have been casted for such a long period of time as David's were, the bones become very brittle. A nurse's assistant turned David over on his back and accidently struck his leg on the metal side rail. This caused the break," he explained.

Poor David! The next evening Sara Belle picked me up from school and we traveled the three hours to Kernan. When we arrived we were greeted as if we were the King and Queen of the Medical World on an official visit. We assumed why. They were afraid of repercussions. However, this was not the Larmore style. We put them at ease and assured them this could happen to anyone. We were just so pleased that it wasn't worse.

BEGINNING OF ELEMENTARY SCHOOL YEARS

A child who knows how to pray, work, and think is already half-educated.

—*The Complete Book of Zingers*

When David turned five years old he was eligible to attend kindergarten. However, as parents and educators we took time to really objectively evaluate his progress and felt strongly we should wait until he was six before entering him into school. Based on this decision we enrolled him in Asbury Nursery School for a year to give him a chance to mature more and become familiar with a school setting and routine. As we look back on this period in time we realize this was a blessing in disguise. David adjusted well to school and most days could not wait to be with his new friends. However, during the year David had several bladder infections. We also had another scare that his shunt was beginning to malfunction again. As a result he did miss periods of school. During the spring of that year Sara Belle was diagnosed with a serious melanoma. Her doctor stated that if it had advanced to her lymph nodes she had six weeks to six months to live. After extensive surgery with the removal of numerous lymph nodes, skin drafting, and plastic surgery we had to wait ten days for the lab reports. These reports would determine her future. God blessed us once again when all reports came back negative.

However, David and I had our own issues at home during Sara Belle's hospital stay. David, at the time, was wearing long-legged braces, which seemed to have every possible mechanism invented for bracing attached to them. It was my job each morning to learn, without the guidance of Sara Belle, how to put these contraptions on by carefully monitoring the language that would like to flow from my mouth and at the same time keep my cool in front of David. Fortunately, I had a great superintendent and co-workers to work with who understood my need for flexible hours in the morning during Sara Belle's recovery.

For the first four or five days while she was in the hospital, I would get up between 5:30 a.m. to 6:00 a.m. first getting myself ready for work then approaching the task of getting David ready for nursery school. By the time I delivered David to school and got to work it was usually around 9:30 a.m. I tried and I tried to improve my timing. I was getting up earlier and earlier. Over a period of a week I had cut my time down so I was getting to work by 8:30 a.m, which was still a half hour late. Finally, I began to climb out of bed at 4:30 a.m. Surprise! After the third day of up and at 'em by four thirty in the morning I had delivered David to Asbury and I was at work by 8:00 a.m. With great joy and cheerful applause from my office staff, I was truly pleased with myself. At 8:05 a.m. my secretary's phone rang. Dot Maddox, my secretary—one of the best secretaries in the world—handed me the phone saying, "It's Sara Belle."

I greeted her with, "Surprise! I made it to work on time today. It's the first time since you have been in the hospital. How are you today?"

"I'm fine. I have been discharged. I'm ready to come home," she said.

"Now?" I said jokingly, "Honey, this is the first day I've gotten to work on time since you've been in the hospital and you expect me to come get you now! All right, I'll be right there."

Once home Sara Belle had numerous problems stemming from her extensive surgery. After being home a couple of days we had a real scare. During the night as we slept, her incision opened wide draining pus and blood and ruining the bed sheets. This necessitated packing David up with all his needs and traveling to the emergency room for treatment of the surgical site. Later, Sara Belle developed an ongoing low-grade fever that needed to be treated with antibiotics. Her recovery was slow but sure. We were blessed with the love and care from our many friends and family throughout this period. By mid summer Sara Belle was ready again to tackle the world and whip David and me back in shape.

As we approached the beginning of the school year our excitement of David entering kindergarten grew. One morning at work our school superintendent called me into his office and expressed his concern for David in a public school setting. Being a close personal friend as well as a distant relative he had known David since birth. He had been in our home and in David's company numerous times over the last six years. He stated he just wanted our lives as stress free as possible while we dealt with David's adjustment to the outside world. He shared with me the option of sending David to a special handicap school in the county. Without thought I told him we were not interested and we were going to place David in the public school system. If things did not work out, then we would consider other avenues.

As David grew and continued to become the very center of our existence, we learned the importance of living for the day with a focus on tomorrow. As parents, we would be remiss if we were not concerned for David academically as well as having some doubts about how well he would adjust physically to the school environment. We discussed David's welfare many times in the privacy of our home and prayed for guidance and help.

In the summer just before David was to enter kindergarten, Congress passed a special education law known as Public Law 94-142. This law was designed to improve opportunities in education for all handicapped children and adults ages 3-21. They were guaranteed a free public education in the least restrictive environment. In essence, handicapped children were no longer to be housed in a special education facility but were permitted to attend classes in a regular school setting, receiving special help from a teacher or assistant as needed. This event in our lives proved God again works in so many mysterious ways. He does truly answer prayers if we give Him time and we have patience to wait. Just as we needed it with David entering kindergarten, God provided us and other families such as ours with help in assuring handicapped children receive an equal opportunity for an education. This is the reason this book is entitled *Be Quiet and Listen*. We, like so many others, have learned to pray and step back quietly in our daily lives and *listen* for answers from God. They may not come as soon as we would like. We like to think of God as He is—our parent in heaven just waiting, evaluating, and thinking about us and our circumstances before deciding the best way to answer our request in prayer. Isn't that what *we* do when *our* children ask us for assistance or favors?

David's elementary school years were showered with many wonderful friends, teachers, memorable events, and happenings. There certainly were enough challenges he had to face that helped build his endurance as well as his character. From the beginning, his teachers and the many friends he gained helped him bridge the gaps between loneliness and fellowship, frustration and confidence, despair and hope, setbacks and success. David was able to walk about the classroom during his early school years with the help of heavy braces and quadruple canes. However, his chief mode of transportation was a little red wagon we purchased for his school use. Teachers would assign children on a daily basis to pull David about the school. Other than a few dumps here and there, and some cracks and scrapes in the walls and door frames their journeys through the hallways were successful.

As parents, we are proud to say we never heard David say a negative comment about any teacher or personality in the school. He could always find something nice to say or he would say nothing. David enjoyed school and woke up every morning by 6:00 a.m. ready to start the day. There was not a time throughout his school career that he didn't want to go to school. He just simply loved life to its fullest. He never complained about what he couldn't do because of his handicaps. He spent his time finding things he could do and would enjoy doing with family and friends.

On Labor Day just before David entered second grade, the three of us were invited by Ronnie and Margaret King to go on a picnic to Assateague State Park near Ocean City, Maryland. It was a beautiful day for the beach. Chris and Ronnie, Jr., sons of Ronnie and Margaret, were really neat boys who were very attentive to David and full of fun. When we went anywhere with the King family we were sure to have great fun and more than enough delicious food. Ronnie wanted to spend some time fishing, so we moved quite a distance down the beach away from other campers and beach goers. Once we had everything unpacked and set up we decided to sit by the water and relax before we swam or fished.

Our previous visits to Assateague State Park had always been pleasant. However, our feelings for Assateague were about to change. The boys were first to run down and jump into the ocean. Soon after, David wanted to go in the water. I picked him up in my arms, placed an inner tube around him and carried him in the water. We played for a while in knee deep water with me bending down letting him get wet up to his waist or above. We did this several times having great fun and lots of laughs while his mother and Aunt Margaret watched from the beach. He had gotten used to the water during the summer by taking swimming lessons from Julia Taylor, a good friend and neighbor. He loved the water and had no fear if his face got wet or head went under for a second or two.

Without warning as I bent down allowing him to submerge to his waist, I stepped into a hole the same time a large wave hit us both. I held on to David as we both went under water. Thinking I still had a tight grip on David, I struggled to my feet and realized I only had the inner tube in my hands. David was gone! I stood for only seconds surveying the massive ocean in front of me. As the waves hit the beach and rescinded again to the ocean there was no David in sight. Even now, the scene is so real it still brings waves of tears rolling down my cheeks. I dived into the water frantically searching for him. I came up again. No David.

I looked to the sky and screamed out, "Oh, God! Help! Help! Oh, God!" Just then I felt David's body hit my leg under water. I quickly reached down to grab him and missed. "Oh, God! Oh, God!" is all I could say or think. I dived again. I came up. No David! For what seemed like minutes but in reality was only a second or two, I looked out over the ocean again with great panic and fear we had lost David. In that moment I was knocked down by a wave as I stepped in the hole again but this time I was hit hard with David's body. I grabbed him with great force and determination and pulled both of us to shore the whole time crying, "Thank you, God! Thank you, God!"

Once on the beach I laid him on a blanket. He began to choke, shake, and spit water. I picked him up and hugged him, perhaps harder than he had ever been hugged, as I cried like a baby. After David gained his breath and could speak he expressed his feelings about his ordeal, "Wow! That was some swim." He wanted to go back into the water. I didn't want him to be afraid of the ocean so I regained my composure and faith and carried him to the water's edge and stood about ankle deep. We will always credit Julia Taylor for her part in saving David's life. She is the one who taught him not to fear water and how to breathe underwater.

SHELDON LARMORE

During the whole time Ronnie, the boys and I were searching the waters for David, Sara Belle and Margaret, panic stricken, watched helpless from the beach. In a way it was worse for them because they could do little but look out over the wide span of the ocean seeing nothing but water, water, and water. God was with us on the beach the whole time. We realized to even a greater degree that God's hands are truly everywhere.

After that experience Sara Belle and I were more than ready to go home. We were so shaken by the thought of losing David we could hardly function. However, this was to be a fun day for the Kings and us, so we pulled ourselves together, put on our happy faces, and did the best we could to enjoy our time together. For the next couple of summers I couldn't and didn't want to look out over the ocean. I got little pleasure walking on the board-walk in Ocean City or Rehoboth, Delaware, since the ocean was so visible. That experience of thirty-five years ago had such an impact on us we have not returned to Assateague Island and have no desire to do so.

As David continued through his primary grades in school, his health seemed to be pretty stable. He worked hard to achieve the best he could. He was a real people person and a pleaser. He would arrive home from school and after an hour or so he would begin work on his homework without any prompting from his mom or dad. Friday nights were always set aside for family time. We would go out to dinner, usually walk through the mall, which was a favorite of David's, and then be home by 8:00 p.m. to watch *The Dukes of Hazzard*. Afterward, if he was still awake, we most likely would play a game before bedtime.

From birth, David had many wonderful and caring people in his life. One couple that played a major part in making him feel good about himself and his accomplishments was Walt and Erma Thurston. He called them Uncle Walt and Aunt Erma. He loved them like grandparents and was always glad when they came for a visit. However, there was one Sunday evening the

Thurstons stopped by near David's bedtime. This was fine since David always got great pleasure playing on the floor with his Uncle Walt. This particular night the playing continued into overtime. We could see David was getting sleepy. Shortly, David had had it. He stopped playing and looked up at Uncle Walt and said, "Uncle Walt, I wish you would go home so I can go to bed."

Immediately, Uncle Walt jumped up from the floor and said, "Erma, get your coat. We're going home. We've been kicked out of better places than this." With that they winked at us, gave David a big kiss, and left. The four of us had many laughs about this as time went by.

Uncle Walt was a professional photographer and owned a successful photography business in the community. He became David's free, on call personal photographer. Whenever David was in a school play, church pageant, or any other event he would make sure he was there to take his picture. When he got a new camera in the store he would come by the house or have us over for dinner so he could test the camera out on David. As a result, we are fortunate to have many, many wonderful professional pictures in our possession that bring back fond memories of the past. The Thurstons were truly gifts from God.

Easter Sunday of 1978 was a special time with the Thurstons. Uncle Walt had a new camera and he was going to take several pictures of various poses of the Larmores. For Easter, Sara Belle bought David a black suit identical to one I had. David wanted both of us to dress alike for Easter Sunday church service with his mother wearing matching colors as well. We went shopping for two identical ties, identical tie tacks, and two new bright white shirts. Man! We were set. We were going to be the Larmore twins.

Saturday evening we got a mighty meal from English Grill, which consisted of David's favorite foods: fried chicken, mashed potatoes with gravy, and coleslaw. When we sat down to eat I took one bite of chicken and immediately felt a funny hard piece of something in my mouth. Upon investigating I found the hard object was a false tooth that had broken off of my partial plate, squarely in front of the upper row of teeth. In shock initially, I opened my mouth to show David. His reaction—the little devil—was a surprised look followed by a healthy belly laugh. He laughed so much I became less concerned about my tooth and more concerned he was going to choke.

The next day I could not disappoint David by staying home from church just because I had a gap in my mouth wide enough to stick a broom handle in with room to spare. So I went to the neighborhood Seven-Eleven and got a pack of chewing gum. Just as we prepared to leave for church I chewed and chewed and chewed all five sticks of gum. Then I carefully molded the gum around my partial plate and expertly pressed the loose tooth in the mold. A miracle! It stayed in place. Once in church I learned to display a stiff, plastic-like expression just wide enough to resemble a half smile. Any more of an effort might make my tooth fall out. With great trepidation I approached the church altar to take Holy Communion. My fear was Father Johnson was going to put the cup to my mouth, hit my tooth, and it would fall into the wine. Quickly I took hold of the cup as he neared my mouth, shut my mouth tight, and let the cup lightly touch my lips then like a flash of lightning pull the cup away. Done! I survived the morning in church with my tooth intact. That afternoon Uncle Walt took many pictures. One of the best portraits he made from those pictures is hanging in our dining room. All of our mouths are open with full sets of teeth. Another miracle! David never let me forget that day!

Shadows of Darkness Turn to Sunshine

Faith hears the inaudible, sees the invisible, believes the incredible, and receives the impossible.

—From *The Complete Book of Zingers*

In early March of David's fourth year in school he was beginning to experience a lack of energy. At times he was lethargic at home as well as in school. His was exhibiting poor writing skills and his ability to recall information was a concern to us as well as his teacher. We made an appointment with Dr. Collins. We were fearful these symptoms could be an indication of his shunt malfunctioning. Dr. Collins was unable to determine a reason for David's lack of interest or his regression in school performance. However, he stated he would feel more comfortable if Dr. Crosby examined David further in case there was some underlying cause that may be affecting the shunt or spinal fluid.

Two days later we met Dr. Crosby at Mercy Hospital. After a thorough examination that included various measurements of David's head, blood and urine tests, and much prodding and poking, Dr. Crosby could not find anything related to the shunt that may be causing David's change in performance or attention in school. He changed his medication and asked us to keep a log of David's behavior for a period of time. Sara Belle was already doing this and had been for some time. However, we did attempt to monitor him even more closely. We tried to determine if there were any changes in his environment or general behavior that might be triggering these behaviors.

David's lack of interest and his poor performance in school continued. About three weeks after our visit with Dr. Crosby we experience a new development in David's behavior. At the dinner table one evening we were carrying on a relaxed family conservation as the three of us shared the events of the day. David started to share his day and simply stopped in the middle of a sentence. We both looked at him waiting for him to continue. Immediately we realized he was having some kind of a seizure. It was as if he was frozen. He stared into space, not moving a muscle or making any type of facial expression. He became very rigid. We could not get him to respond. We were frightened! After what seemed to be an hour, which in truth was perhaps less than a minute, he woke up. At first he did not know where he was or who we were. At this point it was seven o'clock at night.

Extremely concerned, we had three choices. Knowing that Dr. Collins was out of town that week, we could call his answering service. However, I thought sarcastically, with our luck, we would most likely find that our very favorite and most compassionate pediatrician was on call. Our two other choices were to take David to the emergency room or monitor him at home. Since he seemed fine after the seizure we decided to keep him home and observe him through the night. The next morning we contacted Dr. Crosby and explained what we had experienced. From our description he stated he was sure David had a petit mal seizure. However, he wanted to see him the next day.

After an examination, Dr. Crosby could not explain to his satisfaction what may have caused David to have the seizure. Once again all of David's vital signs, measurements, blood tests, etc., appeared to be normal. On the day of this visit David was not having any difficulty and really felt quite well. In Dr. Crosby's words as he joked with David, "David, I don't know what we are going to do with you. You are making my job difficult. You know, David, you and your body are not following the picture perfect textbook model for the development and diagnosing of Spina Bifida." He turned to us and reiterated that it was difficult to determine if the shunt was beginning to malfunction since David never exhibited the normal symptoms of severe headaches, chills, and vomiting.

"This young man is a mystery." He smiled as he patted David on the shoulder. Laughing, he shared that he and Dr. Decker agreed David was a challenge during operations. In surgery, they had found nothing was quite where it should be according to the books. It was either a little to the right, a little to the left, a little higher, or a little lower than where it was normally found.

We left Dr. Crosby's office with prescriptions changing medications and with an assignment to document any unusual behaviors we noticed in David's daily activities. For a couple of months David seemed fine. However, in mid May he began to experience a series of petit mal seizures again. This condition continued through the summer months. Each time we would consult with Dr. Collins or Dr. Crosby keeping them abreast as to what was happening. Office visits to both physicians still led to an unsolved mystery. For short periods of time he would become rigid with eyes open wide, staring in space as if unaware of anything or anyone around him. Each time we would shout his name repeatedly and gently shake him. Soon he would snap out of it and continue whatever activity he was involved in as if nothing had happened.

Late one afternoon during the first week of school I was conducting a meeting with my office staff and supervisors when over the public address system came a loud, firm voice from the office receptionist, "Sheldon, go home immediately. Sara Belle needs to take David to the doctor." To say the least, I was stunned. I guess out of disbelief I stood frozen for a second or two. I was snapped out of this second long stance by my coworkers shouting, "Go, Go!" I faintly heard some saying, "Let me, let us take you." However, by that time I was racing through the parking lot. On my mile-and-a-half drive home all I can remember saying or thinking was, "Oh, God! Help! Oh, God! Help!" I couldn't help but think the worst. It had to be a real emergency for Sara Belle to leave a message with Sandy, our office receptionist, instead of asking to talk to Dot, my secretary. As I pulled into the driveway I could see the back door was open and Sara Belle's car was gone. Racing into the house, I entered our family room and found it in disarray with a small end table turned over with a broken picture frame lying on the floor next to a cushion from the sofa. A blanket from David's bed was scattered across the room. The phone with its receiver off the cradle was also lying on the floor. The buzzing of the busy signal was deafening to my ear. I panicked! I raced out of the house and drove directly to the doctor's office, which was less than half a mile away.

As I entered the parking lot from the highway I was greatly relieved to see Sara Belle's car. My initial thought was at least she made it to the doctor's office with David. Entering the reception area I was greeted by a nurse who was familiar with our family. She led me to the examination room where Sara Belle and David were waiting for Doctor Collins. My immediate focus was on David who said without any great display of an unpleasant ordeal, "Hi, Dad. I'm surprised to see you."

"I raced over here when Mom called the office," I told him as I reached down to give him a big hug. Puzzled, I turned to Sara Belle.

"He seems fine now," she said. "When David came home from school he sat in the kitchen while I prepared a snack for him. As he ate his snack we talked about the day and what we were going to do over the weekend. Shortly, he told me he wasn't feeling well. I suggested he should go lie down for a little bit while I started dinner. I helped him to the sofa. Just as he sat on the sofa he let out a deep breath and his eyes opened wide. His

SHELDON LARMORE

body became very stiff like it's done before. He just stared into space. I kept yelling his name and shaking him but he just didn't respond. That's when I called Sandy. He started to come around. I just couldn't wait for you. I picked him up the best I could, pulling and dragging him to the car. When I got here two people helped me bring him into the office."

"David, how are you feeling, Bunky?" I asked him as I studied his movements, eyes and his general awareness.

"I'm okay, Dad. I don't remember what happened." I sat on the side of the bed as Sara Belle and I talked about the day and kidded with David. We made every effort not to show any alarm or anxiety around him.

Within ten minutes or so, Dr. Collins entered the room with his ready smile and comforting manner.

"Well! What a pleasant surprise. What brings you here today, David?" he asked.

What a wonderful way to put David and us at ease even though we knew he had been briefed by his nurse before entering the examination room. He proceeded to ask Sara Belle what had occurred at home. After several questions and conversations between us, Dr. Collins examined David thoroughly. The results: nothing, except the pupils of his eyes seemed slightly dilated. He had no fever. His blood pressure was normal. His shunt seemed to be working fine. Eyes, ears, nose and throat were fine. His complexion was clear and rosy. At the end of the examination Dr. Collins said, "I think it is time for the Big Man (meaning Dr. Crosby) to see him again. I'll call him first thing on Monday and make an appointment." As he jotted down his home phone number, he strongly stressed to us, "Call me anytime if you need me over the weekend."

Saturday and Sunday were, fortunately, normal days for the Larmores. We had dinner at home Friday evening and laughed our silly heads off watching the *Dukes of Hazzard* on TV. Afterward, we watched a short VCR of Bud Abbott and

Lou Costello. Saturday was spent doing laundry, cleaning house, and all those other wonderful family chores while David relaxed watching the Saturday morning cartoons. In the afternoon we grocery shopped, and spent a leisurely evening at home. Sunday we went to church followed by lunch out. The real fun part of any weekend we put off until Sunday evening. That time was spent helping David do his homework and study for a math test.

Monday, David went to school feeling well, and I went to work feeling concerned for David's future. We left Sara Belle home to anxiously await a call from either Dr. Collins's or Dr. Crosby's office. At mid morning the call from Dr. Collin's came. He stated he had made an appointment for us to meet with Dr. Crosby on Wednesday at eleven o'clock at Mercy Hospital. He told us we might want to prepare David for the possibility of being admitted to the hospital for a couple of days. Dr. Crosby may want to do more extensive testing.

On a bright sunny, warm Wednesday in the middle of September we found ourselves on the seventh floor of Mercy hospital waiting for our appointment with Dr. Crosby. It wasn't long before we saw him cheerfully strolling down the hall toward us. Just being in his presence was consoling. Hearing him speak in such a calming, reassuring voice gave us the peace necessary to cope with uncertainties. Following our informal discussions about David's most recent episodes and a general discussion about his progress, we were not surprised to hear Dr. Crosby suggest that David be admitted for a couple days for tests and observation. He said he would call us on Friday to give us an update on his findings. David, as usual, was okay staying at the hospital. As long as he knew he could keep in contact with us and the outside world by phone, he was satisfied.

That Wednesday evening we left David in the hands of the excellent nurses, doctors, interns and staff of the seventh floor of Mercy Hospital. Little did we know they would soon become like our close-knit family away from home. Since I felt I could

SHELDON LARMORE

not afford to be away from the office on Thursday and Friday, we kept in contact with David frequently by phone. Without a doubt, we probably were in phone contact with him at least five times a day. In addition, his Aunt Faye, my sister, encouraged him to call her anytime he wanted to talk. This privilege was unlimited. Unfortunately, we had to try to curtail some of these phone calls since my sister was a single parent doing her best in raising two teenagers. She worked diligently to provide them with as normal of a life as she possibly could. To her credit, she did an outstanding job without ever complaining. She was always, always there for us or David whenever and however she could be of help.

On Friday, Dr. Crosby called as promised. He discussed the fact that David obviously had been shunt independent for at least five years and things seemed to be doing well. However, tests indicated for some unknown reason David was experiencing increased intracranial pressure. That condition could only by lessened by repeated aspiration of spinal fluid from his shunt. Therefore, it would seem that his shunt was shutting down.

He continued by stating, "This gives us the answer to why he may be experiencing increased seizure activities. As we well know, David likes to make our jobs interesting by not exhibiting the outward signs of a malfunctioning shunt. Therefore, it is difficult to always know what really is going on in his body. Let's plan to operate on Monday. Once we revise the shunt, I feel David's condition will improve almost immediately."

We agreed without hesitation. Dr. Crosby stated he was on his way to see David and wanted to know if it would be okay to tell him about the operation. We most definitely encouraged him to tell David. Who else was more qualified to prepare David for this operation? Before we had a chance to call, David called us with his news.

"Hello, Mom," David said. "Did Dr. Crosby tell you I was going to have an operation on Monday?"

"Yes, he did, David. How do you feel about it?"

"It's okay," he replied. "What time are you coming up tomorrow?"

"As soon as the roosters wake us up!" she said.

"Mom, we don't have roosters," he said as he chuckled.

Our hospital visits with David on Saturday and Sunday were pleasant ones. David, as usual, was up beat and enjoyed the frequent visits and attention he received from the nurses and the interns who constantly stopped by to say hello. Saturday afternoon our friends Will and Shirley Mahaffey visited with David and stayed to have dinner with us in the hospital's cafeteria. They were the brother and sister-in-law of Royd Mahaffey, a very close friend and former, much-respected superintendent of schools in Wicomico County. Whenever we had to spend time in one of the hospitals in or around Baltimore, we could always depend on them checking in with us. We will always cherish the love and support the Mahaffeys and their extended families showered upon us over the years.

Early Monday morning we started our oh-so familiar trip to Mercy. We arrived about ten o'clock so we would have time with David before his scheduled one o'clock operation.

Entering David's room we found him bright eyed and bushy tailed if not a slight bit sarcastic, saying with a devilish grin on his face, "Oh, I see the roosters did wake you up in time." He didn't get this sarcasm from me for certain. It must have come from his mother! Surprisingly, the time we had with David before they began to prep him for surgery went by rather fast. At ten minutes of one, his nurse and one of the interns arrived to take him down to surgery. After several hugs and kisses they began to roll him out of the room with David saying, "See you when I get back." In the emptiness of the room we turned to each other, hugged, and shed a few tears. This was David's eighth or ninth major operation in his short life. They just didn't seem to get any easier. It seemed as if he got one thing fixed there was always another that would surface or break down.

A little over two hours Dr. Crosby found us in the waiting area on the seventh floor.

"David is doing fine," he said, "but we were not able to complete the operation. We had trouble regulating his blood pressure. We stopped the surgery and will finish it in the next couple of days."

"What exactly does this mean?" Sara Belle asked.

"It is nothing to be alarmed about. This happens in these kinds of cases. He will be fine until we finish the procedure. I left the old shunt in place since it will be doing the work until it is completely replaced."

"What do you have to do to complete the surgery?" Sara Belle asked.

"Basically, we need to run tubing from the new shunt to the stomach so the fluid can flow properly," Dr. Crosby replied. "At present, the new shunt is not operational." As Dr. Crosby prepared to leave, he told us David should be back in his room within the hour.

While waiting, we went to the gift shop looking for something to keep David busy the next couple of days. Once David was stable and comfortable we needed to travel home so I could return to work. Fortunately, I had the total support and understanding of my superintendent, Harold Fulton. He strongly urged me to put David and Sara Belle before the office in these difficult critical times. He insisted the office would survive. However, it was not my style to take advantage of his kindness.

As we searched the gift shop, Sara Belle said, "Look, I've found just the right thing."

"What?" I replied.

"It's a cute cartoon puzzle of an operating room. He will enjoy looking at it and seeing all the crazy things going on in the picture," she said excitedly. "It has fifteen hundred pieces."

"Fifteen hundred pieces! In all our married life we haven't tried to put together even a hundred piece puzzle," I said.

"Oh, well, maybe it isn't a good idea. But, you know, people visiting and stopping in his room could help put it together," she said.

Well, we walked out of the gift shop and up to David's room with the 1,500-piece, impossible-to-put-together, cute cartoon puzzle.

Soon after we arrived in David's room he was wheeled in by his nurse with the help of an assistant. Instead of being drowsy and in pain, David was wide-awake, happy, and ready to entertain. After a time of welcoming him back with hugs and kisses Sara Belle pulled out the puzzle to show him. To my utter surprise he was happy with her purchase. I thought with a smile on my face, *Right! He can be happy, but who in the heck is going to put this sucker together?* Well! Surprise again! Shortly, two of the young interns, one male and one female, came into the room to check on David. The female spotted the puzzle and immediately started admiring it.

"I really enjoy putting puzzles together. It's my favorite pastime," she said as she examined it closer.

"Tell you what, David, as soon as we finish our rounds we will come back, won't we Josh?" She nudged her counterpart by poking him in the ribs. "We'll find a little table somewhere and get you started on your puzzle." David was in seventh heaven having a girl in his room helping him with the puzzle. David *always* liked his girls!

David had a great time watching and laughing with his new friends as they periodically stopped by the room to work on the puzzle. This was therapeutic for both David and us since visits from them helped pass the time of the day. Since Mercy was a training hospital there seemed to be an ample number of interns on the floor regardless the hour of the day or night. They all were very conscientious in carrying out their responsibilities and addressing the various needs of the patients.

Before we realized it was early evening and the busy hallways were beginning to quiet down as the staff and patients were preparing for the night. For a period of time all three of us were silent as we rested from the day watching news on TV. Shortly, Sara Belle got my attention and whispered to me to watch David. Observing him, we both noticed he had fallen asleep but was twitching his body involuntarily while making faces and little throat sounds. We both got up and moved to the side of his bed and gently woke him up. He just seemed to stare as if he didn't know where he was or who we were. Within a short time, he seemed to wake up more fully and acknowledged our presence. We stood by his side and rubbed him back to sleep. Almost immediately, he began to have the same reactions.

Alarmed, I went out in the hallway and found one of the interns. He immediately came in, checked David, then went to the nurses' station to page the doctor on call. Both returned and stayed with David for some time checking his vital signs, examining the area of surgery and simply watching him as he drifted back to sleep. They could not give any explanation as to why he reacted the way he did but promised they would keep close tabs on him. When they left they assured us they would be on the floor all night and to call them if we needed them. At this point we gave up the idea of traveling home that night. Once we were sure David was okay and stable, we would ride out on the beltway to find a cheap place to spend the night. Blessed be credit cards at times like this.

A good hour had passed since David's little episode. He seemed to be sleeping peacefully and breathing with case. We were beginning to feel a bit more comfortable and considering leaving for the night in search of a motel. Once at the motel we could call the seventh floor and give them the address and phone number of where we were in case they needed us during the night.

As we sat beside David's bed each drifting off into a light sleep we were abruptly awakened by a terrible rattling and shaking coming from David's bed, followed by loud unrecognizable noises from his throat and rapid fits of breathing. It frightened us to death. This was the first time we had ever witnessed anyone having what we thought was a grand mal seizure. We stood by David's bed in shock. I did have enough wit about me to yell, "Help!" Within a second or two there were three doctors in the room. Immediately, they rolled David down the hall to another room and closed the door.

A fourth doctor led us down the hall to an area outside of the room where they had taken David. He knew us from the afternoon he spent in David's room trying to make sense of the puzzle. Immediately, he stood between us and put his arms around both of us. He calmly explained to us that the reason they moved David into another room was because there was more equipment available to assist them as they helped David. He guided us to a little quiet area off the hallway in view of the room where they had taken David. He offered us coffee or something cold to drink and stayed with us for a short time. I'm certain this was to make sure we had gained some sense of composure before leaving us.

"I'm going to be with David but will return shortly. Are you okay?" he asked, as if *he* was our second son.

We sat across the hall facing the closed door where our son was. Horrible things were shooting through our minds as seconds of waiting dragged on for an eternity. Periodically a nurse or an assistant would appear to see if we were okay or needed anything. A good hour passed. No one had left the room. The only movement was people going in taking supplies or instruments or machines. We died a thousand deaths as we sat stunned, lifeless, speechless, just holding hands and praying.

SHELDON LARMORE

Finally, the door across the hall opened widely. Two doctors exited and made their way to us. Their faces were grim but for whatever reason that brought a degree of calmness to our otherwise shattered bodies and souls. An older doctor who we had not seen before spoke first.

"David is stable. However, he is not conscious. To be honest with you we cannot be sure at this point if there has been any brain damage." In the midst of this conference, his pager went off. He responded to it and abruptly excused himself saying he had an emergency and would return.

"Dr. Donaldson will be able to answer your questions."

"What caused this?" Sara Belle asked.

Dr. Donaldson, the doctor who led us to the waiting area responded, "We don't know. At this point it's hard to determine. We have contacted Dr. Crosby and will wait for his directions before initiating any other procedures. At this time we will continue to monitor David around the clock and make sure he is not in any difficulty. We have transformed the room where he is into a temporary intensive care unit."

"Can we see him?" I asked.

"Yes. Definitely. Give us a little time to straighten the room. We made a mess of it as we worked to stabilize him.

"By the way, let me introduce myself," he said, "I'm Ed Donaldson. I'm currently serving my internship here at Mercy and have the good fortune of working closely with Dr. Crosby. Please call me Ed."

"We will, only if you call us Sheldon and Sara Belle," I said.

"Okay," he agreed with a smile. "Sheldon and Sara Belle. I will be here all night. If you need me and I'm not on the floor, tell whoever is at the desk. They will get me. When we have a chance we catch a snooze in the physicians' lounge down the hall." From that point on he was a true blessing to us.

After the room was cleaned, Ed took us in to see David. He was lying very still. His body looked drawn and more fragile then ever. From past experiences we were not totally shocked to see such an overwhelming display of equipment, wires, tubes, and numerous machines making gurgling, gushing, bubbly sounds in the stillness of the room as they moved fluids in and out of David's body and the attached equipment. We stood. We watched. We prayed. And we prayed. Both of us could feel the presence of Ed beside us. He too was standing silently watching David as if he was a member of the family. Eventually, we turned to him and shared we were going to spend the night in the hospital. We asked, and he readily agreed for us to stay in the room with David.

The first hour or so was quiet. David continued to rest peacefully. Each of us took turns sitting next to his bed touching his hand and rubbing it lightly. To our dismay, suddenly David began to have a major seizure again much like the original one. We called for help. Three or four nurses and interns came running. We stood to the side watching in disbelief. Soon the seizure action began to subside and when it appeared his condition was back to normal we were left with him alone again.

Within fifteen minutes, he had another seizure. We called for help again. The staff came running. This time it took them a little longer to quiet David. One of the nurses remained with us for a short time afterward just to be sure David was breathing okay and his seizure activities had abated. It wasn't more than ten minutes after she left that David had another violent seizure. Again, the army of medical personnel came. Again, they succeeded in calming David. The fourth time within twenty minutes of the last, Ed arrived as part of the group. He had been on his dinner break and missed the prior action. After settling David down for a fourth time, Ed contacted the doctor on call and got permission to change some of David's medications. This obviously did not work since David suffered ten more of these seizures during the night, each as violent as, or more than, the previous ones. Fortunately, David was not conscious and hopefully was unaware of what was happening.

Early the next morning Dr. Crosby appeared in David's doorway with Ed by his side.

"I understand you had a rough night," he said. He walked over to David, placing his hand on David's forehead, rubbing it gently. He stood by David without saying a word for a couple minutes. He left the room with Ed saying, "Let me go and check his chart. We'll be back shortly." They returned just in time to witness the sixteenth seizure since surgery.

After this ordeal Dr. Crosby felt David needed to be on a life support system to aid his weakened body. "His body is just working overtime and needs to rest," he said.

After Dr. Crosby made several adaptations to the medical equipment in the room and revisions to his medications, we took our places beside David's bed watching him sleep and breathe. Ed told us Dr. Crosby had to leave for a seminar he was conducting at the University of Maryland Hospital. However, he left orders to contact him immediately if David's condition worsened.

By this time it was approximately nine in the morning. Things were beginning to settle down somewhat on the seventh floor. Ed and another intern arrived at the door with a cup of coffee and a donut for each of us. He said he wanted to make sure we were comfortable and to see if we needed anything. After a few minutes of talking about the weather and sharing with us that his wife had called him telling him to be home early because her parents were coming over, he left stating he would return later to check on us.

From morning through early afternoon minutes and hours moved slowly but fortunately they were uneventful. We sat in this small room overcrowded with medical equipment and an abundance of medical supplies. When we asked Ed why there seemed to be so much equipment and other things in David's room he explained most of it was used initially when they were working on David trying to stabilize him. Dr. Crosby had ordered some of the machines to be placed in the room. He wanted to make sure they were on hand without having to search throughout the hospital in case there was an urgent need for them. Curtains at the windows had been drawn, cutting out light from outside. The room was cool and quiet with just the constant, monotonous sound from the life support machines, *beep, beep, beep.* Sitting by his bedside and hearing this steady, droning sound was not necessarily a pleasant experience. However, it helped in reassuring us David was clinically alive and stable. It provided us hope. Our level of anxiety and stress coupled with little or no sleep for forty-eight hours was rapidly turning us into sitting, walking zombies. Ever so often one of us would have to stand, leave the room, and walk around the halls to keep awake.

Shortly after three o'clock in the afternoon Sara Belle touched my arm as she stood up signaling she was going for a little walk. As she tiptoed out of the room the sounds of *beep, beep, beep* continued. Even though they were soft sounds, they were becoming almost deafening. I turned in my chair and closed my eyes again. All of a sudden I heard, *beep, beep, beepbeepbeepbeep* in rapid repetition and then nothing. Scared speechless I looked at the monitor. It had flat lined! At that second I looked at David. His eyes were wide open, and he was drooling.

"Help! Help! Ed! Ed! Oh, God! Help!" I shouted. Within seconds people were rushing into the room from everywhere. By this time Sara Belle was by my side at the doorway. Literally, we were pushed from the room into the hall as the door of David's room slammed shut. We stood in total, absolute shock as we watched. In a matter of seconds people rushed in the room, dashed out, grabbed this and that, shouted this, ordered that, etc. We were paralyzed! We couldn't move. This was David they were working on so franticly. This was our only son, our only child who now was fighting for his life. He had come so far and been through so much in his short lifetime we *couldn't* lose him now.

As we stood frozen and helpless, we witnessed our Ed, our angel from heaven, open David's door and walk over to us.

"We are still working on David. He's still unresponsive. I will let you know if there is a change. I'm going to take you around the corner to the physicians' lounge. Too many people know you and are finding out about David. They mean well, but you don't need to be questioned or have to talk to people. This is not the time."

We thanked Ed for his consideration and support. However, we told him we wanted to go to the chapel. Immediately he checked to find out if the chapel was open. It wasn't, but he called security, and had them unlock the doors for us. He had one of the interns escort us. Once in the chapel we noticed the beautiful evening twilight shining through the numerous stain glass windows surrounding the interior of the room. The chapel provided us with an unexplainable kind of serene peacefulness, a safe haven where we could talk with our Lord. We both found seats in the middle of chapel. We sat for some time squeezing and rubbing hands without uttering a word. Our only thoughts were of David. There were many unanswered questions steadily floating through our minds as we cried, prayed, and talked openly to God.

The longer we sat the harder it was to hold back our emotions and tears. Finally, the gates to our souls broke. I dissolved into an uncontrollable cry. Giant tears rolled aimlessly down my cheeks. My body trembled and my heart felt as if it was tearing out of my chest. I cried out, "Oh, God! Please help. Oh, please. Help David. Oh, God. Be with David. We can't lose him."

I felt Sara Belle's soft, gentle hand rubbing my back and tenderly pulling my head over to rest on her shoulder. I looked up into her eyes. They were flooded with tears flowing freely as she tried to console me. I cried so hard I experienced difficulty breathing due to the strong contractions in my chest. Sara Belle was my strength, my rock. Even though grieving deeply and crying softly, she remained in control for my sake.

Once I could speak in broken sentences I turned to Sara Belle and said, "I can't believe we are in a Catholic hospital with nuns and priests all over the place. Now that we need them they are not anywhere around." As soon as I said this, the door in the back of the chapel opened. We both looked and realized another prayer had been answered. Walking toward us was a priest.

"You are David's parents, Mr. and Mrs. Larmore?" he asked.

"Yes," we answered with a mixture of relief and fear. We were fearful he was bringing us news that David had passed away.

"Do you mind if I give David his last rites?" he asked.

"No, please do. Thank you." We responded in unison. With that he moved closer and touched both of us on the shoulder.

"Your family will be in our prayers. God bless." He turned and left as quietly as he entered.

The visit by the priest served as a calming affect on us. We probably sat in the chapel listless and speechless for another two to three minutes lost in our thoughts. Leaving the chapel we went back to the seventh floor where we met Dr. Crosby in the hallway.

"I came over as soon as I got the call."

Looking for any positive signs of hope from Dr. Crosby, which we didn't get, we asked, "How is he?"

"It doesn't look good. But we're not giving up hope yet."

"Should we contact family?"

"I'm sorry to have to say this, but yes, it's time," he said.

At this point we were so shell-shocked and empty we accepted what he said without emotions. We moved as robots down the hall to make our first call. My call was to my sister, Faye. I was not looking forward to this because I knew the news would upset her. I also knew if I allowed her, she would ask me questions I either didn't know the answers to or I just did not want to think about.

"Hello?" Faye said.

I braced myself as I spoke my first words in a very deliberate, monotone voice. I was determined not to break down on the phone.

"Don't ask me any questions. Listen. David may not live"—I had to pause—"through the night. Go tell Mother. Prepare her. Call whoever you need to." I had to stop again. "I will call you later. Love you."

One phone call was all I could handle. As we started down the hall to David's room, we were met by Ed. As he walked toward us we couldn't help but notice he was beginning to cry softly. Immediately we braced ourselves for the news as his tears turned to a joyous smile and then to an emotional laughter as he said, "David is awake. He seems okay."

We were so overwhelmed by emotions we had no idea how we ended up standing beside David's bed. As Sara Belle started in the door, Dr. Crosby put his arms around her giving her a much, much needed hug. As we looked at David he seemed to be unbelievably rested, bright eyed, and energized. Using every minuscule fiber in my being to hold back the tidal wave of tears and emotions that were about to erupt, I praised God and looked upon His latest miracle. Just as if nothing had happened, David asked, "Dad, where have you been?"

"Right here, Bunk. Where have you been?" I asked.

"With Jesus," he stated in an unassuming manner.

Controlled tears had to flow now as I looked down on him and leaned over to give him the biggest hug possible while fighting with all the apparatus, tubes, and machines still connected to him. When I told Sara Belle what David said she was elated to say the least. However, she was not surprised. Since birth she and David had prayed together, shared thoughts about life and heaven, and in general had served each other well in constantly strengthening their faith and their love for Jesus. My wife, Sara Belle is a saint! David and I are fortunate to have her in our lives.

After returning home David had absolutely no recollection of this hospital stay. This total time at Mercy was completely wiped from his memory bank. He did not remember the operations, the puzzle (even when we showed it to him), Ed Donaldson or anything else about this month and a half at Mercy. Eventually, realizing this, we never questioned him further about this time in his life. What we and others did witness however was his rejuvenation in the things of God. He read his Bible more, he craved quiet times listening to gospel and praise music, and spoke more of his love and faith in his Father.

A Period of
Emotional Rest
and Reflection

Peace rules the day when Christ rules the mind.

—Wilkie Collins

After things settled down later that evening, Dr. Crosby and Ed insisted we join them for a cup of coffee in the physician's lounge. They said this would give them an opportunity to share with us the events of the day that led to David's recovery. After minutes of friendly badgering between Ed and Dr. Crosby, and a general conversation about the Eastern Shore of Maryland, which they both dearly loved, Ed stated, "As soon as I saw what was happening with David I ran to the phone and called Dr. Crosby."

"I immediately left the seminar and raced over here. It took me by total surprise," Dr. Crosby said.

"And do you know what he did with his car when he got here?" Ed asked us with a laugh. "He stopped it in the middle of street, jumped out, ran into the lobby, and elevated it to the seventh floor." He turned to Dr. Crosby and asked, "Doctor, do you know where your car is now?"

"No, as a matter of fact I hope the doorman heard me when I asked him to get someone to move it off the street and put it in the garage."

When we got down to the serious part of our conversation, Dr. Crosby stated he was really perplexed about David's condition. "Nothing was done during the operation or afterward that would justify such violent seizures. After I saw David I knew some type of immediate action had to take place if we were going to save him. Puzzled, I took my assistant aside, and we rapidly began to throw out ideas that might lead to a solution. From nowhere I got a brain storm."

"I thought what would happen if I simply injected a needle in David's brain. Would that release any build up of fluid? We raced to his room. We were greeted by a priest leaving his bedside after administering his last rites. I prepared the needle and inserted it into his head praying the whole time. Fluid gushed out all over the place. David opened his eyes. Obviously, the dye we injected into David's arteries had inadvertently traveled to his brain and caused the problem. A miracle! I should say so. Someone far greater than me solved this problem. I only served as His instrument."

Wow! Wow! We could have said lots of wows that evening. It was such a blessing and so wonderful to have doctors who actually believed in God and who realized God used them to help do His work instead of having doctors who actually think and act as if they *are* God. As we continued to talk, Ed made an observation that seemed to pull everything together.

"You know, isn't it an amazing coincidence that while Sheldon and Sara Belle were in the chapel praying and the priest was giving David his last rites, you had the brainstorm about inserting the needle?"

"That was not a coincidence. It was a God-incidence," Sara Belle said.

"It's so wonderful. It was truly God at work," Dr. Crosby said.

As we began to depart from our coffee hour, we remembered Dr. Crosby sharing with us after David's operation that he was not able to complete the surgery as planned. At the time he stated within two or three days he would have to finish replacing the old shunt.

"Does David still need the second part of the surgery?" I asked.

"Yes," was his expected reply. "We will plan to do it Thursday. No later than Friday."

Our concern was if David would be strong enough so soon. Dr. Crosby felt pretty confident he would be but also stated it was a risk we would have to take. He reminded us David had shown that he, unfortunately, was again shunt dependent. The present shunt was practically non-functioning. Therefore, we might have been running against time. If the current shunt stopped working before the new one was operational, then we would have created a serious problem.

As Dr. Crosby left the room he told Ed he wanted David to remain in the makeshift intensive care unit as a safety precaution until the operation. Stopping mid stream, he turned to us and said, "Let's shoot for Friday for the operation. I will be in touch."

Walking toward David's room with Ed we reminded him he needed to go home. His wife was expecting him for dinner with her folks. He stated he had called her and everything was on schedule. He would see us later in the evening when he returned.

"You're coming back?" I asked with uncertainty.

"Yes," he answered. "I want to keep check on David through the night."

This act of devotion and compassion for David and us left no doubt he truly was our special angel sent from heaven. He watched over us as if that was his only responsibility as a physician.

David slept most of the early evening as we sat by his side watching, praying silently, and thinking of the blessings we had received during the day. Around nine o'clock Ed appeared at the door. He briefly checked David's condition then pulled up a chair to sit beside us. At our request, he shared the events of his evening at home. He talked with great enthusiasm about his wife's delicious spaghetti meal spiced with much humor as he described his in-laws whom he quickly mentioned he loved dearly. Ed was always alert and knew just how to put a shine on our day.

Laughingly he said, "I have to tell you a joke my father-in-law told at the dinner table. A guy goes into a doctor's office. There is a banana stuck in one of his ears, a carrot stuck in one nostril, and a cucumber in the other ear. The man says, 'Doc, this is terrible. What's wrong with me?' The doctor responded, 'Well, first of all you're not eating right.'"

What a great way to close the evening. What a wondering sense of timing and compassion Ed possessed.

Amazed about how alert he seemed to be after the stress of the last forty-eight hours, we had to ask him, "Ed, how do you keep going?"

"Sheer determination with an eye on that doctor's degree," he responded with a laugh.

"When do you ever see your wife?"

"Oh, I sneak home every once in awhile," he stated with a twinkle in his eye. "The life of an intern around here belongs to the hospital. We take turns cat napping wherever we can. You learn to survive." Shortly, Ed left us to check on other patients. He shared he had enough paper work to do to keep him busy all night.

It wasn't long before Joan, one of the many nurses we were becoming to know on a first name basis, appeared.

"You both are spending the night with David?" she asked.

"Yes," we answered.

"We have located an empty room on the eighth floor. You are welcome to use it tonight. It's yours with the understanding that if during the night we need to use it for a patient we will have to ask you to leave."

We were so weary from the lack of sleep, the stress, and the anxiety of the last couple of days we accepted the offer immediately. Joan stated she had a couple of patients to check on but would take us to the room when she returned.

In a few moments, Ed returned to tell us there was a small shower room around the corner. If we wanted to use it we could. Without much hesitation we jumped at the offer. It had been well over forty-eight hours since we had washed or even had anything but coffee with a cookie or two to eat. I took advantage of the shower first. Without much thought I entered the shower room, eager to experience the warm, refreshing water cascading over my tired body. It felt absolutely wonderful. Turning the water off I reached around to grab the towel. Oh, my! What towel? In my haste to enter the room I forgot to get a towel. So there I was soaking wet, in a small room filled with steam from the semi-hot shower. I had no way to dry off enough to get dressed. I couldn't open the door, enter the public hallway, and travel down to David's room to get a towel. Well! I had to use some ingenuity. I used my undershirt as a towel, patted myself with my shirt, and after a few moments of shaking my shirt all around my still damp body, I got dressed. I entered the hall carrying my wet undershirt in my hand just like it was the most normal and fashionable thing to do. Sara Belle, the thinker in the family, was better prepared. She had her towel, a comb, a brush, a hospital issued toothbrush, toothpaste, and deodorant. She was all set to enter the shower room in style.

After our showers, Joan took us to our room for the night. She introduced us to the nurse in charge telling her our situation. She explained we would probably be up and down throughout the night visiting with David on the floor below. The room was a small one with one single bed.

We were so tired we just stretched out on the bed fully clothed with Sara Belle laying her head at the top of the bed and me with my head at the foot of the bed. Within minutes we both fell into a deep sleep. Sometime between 12:30 p.m. and 1:00 p.m. we woke up with a start. In the darkened room with the blinds closed, we saw images of what appeared to be tall figures surrounding our bed, all draped in glowing white gowns and heads covered with white caps.

Sara Belle, with great alarm, sat up in bed and said, "It's David, isn't it? What's wrong? Tell us!"

I sat frozen on the side of the bed in this darkened, sober place waiting for a response. The figures surrounding the bed seemed to grow in number. It took us a few moments to actually realize they were nurses dressed in their white uniforms. For what seemed like an eternity they stared at us without responding to our questions. The deafening silence was broken when one of the nurses asked, "Who are you?"

Puzzled, Sara Belle said, "We're David's parents."

Rather sternly the nurse asked, "Who's David?"

Almost immediately it was evident to both of us that they didn't know who we were or why we were in this single hospital bed together in the psychiatric area on the eighth floor of Mercy hospital. As we began to explain who David was and why we were in the room, they immediately apologized.

One of the nurses shared with us as she started to laugh, "Oh, I'm so sorry. I had no idea who you were. I was on my rounds checking on each patient. When I opened the door to your room I got the surprise of my life. I knew from our census there wasn't anyone assigned to this room. But there you were. Two bodies lying asleep. Recently, we've had a few problems with street people coming into the hospital to find hiding places to rest or get out of the cold. My first thoughts were, *Oh, my God! We have vagrants on the floor.* I rushed back to the desk, told my supervisor and gathered up as many nurses and staff members as possible. The whole army of us marched down to your room, armed with our pagers ready to call security, if necessary."

We all joined in on the amusement of the moment, some teasing others and all laughing about all the what ifs. Really, what if, in fact, the security or police had been called and we had been threatened with an arrest? The head nurse explained that it was

SHELDON LARMORE

a routine thing for the hospital to offer an unoccupied room to out-of-town family members of critically ill parents.

"However, no one from the previous shift had mentioned or left a note stating you were using the room for the night." With the hospital's recent invasion of homeless people they were becoming more vigilant of visitors roaming the halls at night. As a result of this rather unexpected, yet humorous fiasco we were accepted by the eighth-floor employees, shown where their break room was, encouraged to use it any time, and to eat the cookies available. Before returning to our room for rest we decided to go down to the seventh floor to check in on David. Entering the area we found Ed sitting at a table in a room adjacent to David's thumbing leisurely through mountains of paper. He greeted us in his usual friendly manner, offering us a Coke as we joined him at the table for a few moments of light conversation. I was beginning to experience an unexplainable soreness on my right side whenever I sat down or stood up. We all agreed it was coming from stress and a lack of rest. As we parted for the night he assured us he would let us know of any changes in David's condition.

As we entered David's room early on Thursday morning, Ed had opened the curtains letting the bright sunshine flow in and throughout the room. David was sitting up. He and his room seemed to glitter with golden, refreshing rays of warmth and hope. The day was developing into a very pleasant one. However, the soreness on my right side was much more pronounced. I was having some difficulty breathing because of the pain. With the persistence of Sara Belle joined by the forces of Ed and David's day nurse, Judy, I went to the hospital's emergency room. Ed went home for a much needed rest. He stated he would be returning at midnight. He wanted to be in the operating room on Friday when Dr. Crosby did his surgery on David.

Down in ER the X-rays indicated I had two broken ribs. How in the world did that happen just by sitting in the hospital the last four days? After reviewing the week and thinking of all the possible ways I could have broken the ribs it most likely happened while I was in the chapel. The doctors in the emergency room stated that the uncontrollable muscle spasms and contractions I encountered were obviously powerful enough to crack my rib cage.

Even though David was alert throughout the day, he drifted in and out of sleep. His strength was improving. All his vital signs were consistently good. All indications were he was going to be strong enough to face surgery in the morning. As his parents, it helped us to know he was ready for his big event mentally, emotionally, physically, and most importantly, spiritually.

He wanted to get this over with and return home. As he said in a half joking way, "Enough is enough. It's time to move on."

Even though our week at Mercy had been a hectic, disquieting, and worrisome one, the friendly surroundings and the sincere treatment we received from the staff and professionals helped us cope with the almost impossible. As one reads about our stay one may get the impression we were being treated like royalty. Well we were, and so were all the other families. The hospital staff was well-trained and demonstrated great compassion and care for all who entered their doors.

Friday, the day of surgery, we followed behind David as attendants rolled his bed to the elevator door. While waiting for the elevator four or five nurses and some members of families we had met during the week began to gather around David's bed wishing him luck and sharing hugs. The elevator doors opened. As they pushed David in, his words to us were verbatim (I will never forget), "I'll be okay, Mom and Dad. Don't worry. See you when I get back." With that the elevator doors closed. Instantly, we collapsed into a quiet stillness with noiseless tears running down our cheeks.

SHELDON LARMORE

About two hours later, Dr. Crosby and Ed greeted us in the seventh floor waiting room. "David's fine" were the first words Dr. Crosby cheerfully shared. "Everything went as scheduled. If he continues to improve he just might be ready for the Eastern Shore the middle of next week."

That evening the hospital found a room for us on the fourth floor. Saturday, David seemed to be doing so well we decided, with David's knowledge and blessings, we needed to go home to catch up with our *other life*. I had missed a week from work. I really felt the need to spend some time over the weekend in the office. I had so much unused vacation time I could have stayed out of the office for almost half of the year; however, schools were in session and unfortunately problems, paper work, grants, budgets, long-term planning, etc., don't take vacations.

We returned to Mercy mid-afternoon on Sunday after I spent over six hours from five thirty in the morning to noon on Sunday in the office trying to catch up with the events of the previous week. David's condition was improving by leaps and bounds. He was sitting up in a chair and entertaining two new interns we had not had the pleasure of meeting. Surprisingly, David was back in his original room and the wonderful, amazing 1,500 piece puzzle had been resurrected.

Throughout the day David was entertained by people coming into the room trying to put a part of the puzzle together. What a great way to entertain and be entertained! By the time David left the hospital the puzzle was finished. To keep it in place for the journey home, one of the nurses painted it with puzzle glue she brought from her home.

Waiting for the Other Shoe to Drop

When we do what we can, God will do what we can't.

—Unknown

Sunday evening after visiting hours we headed home feeling comfortable David was on the mend and was in good hands. We left with the idea we would stay home Monday and Tuesday keeping in touch with him by phone. Wednesday evening after work we headed for Baltimore, stopping in Easton to get coffee to have with the sandwiches and cookies Sara Belle packed for the journey. We couldn't wait to see our son. Once we arrived we were able to relax after seeing him in such good spirits and looking so well. However, he did have some sad news to share with us.

"Guess what?" he said. "Ed is not here anymore."

"Why?" We were most disappointed.

"He said he was going to another hospital for a while. He gave me his phone number to give you."

Later that evening we called Ed. He told us his transfer to the University of Maryland Hospital was part of his obligation for fulfilling his internship. He asked us to keep in touch with him about David's progress. We talked with him on two other occasions but eventually lost contact with him. Later Dr. Crosby shared with us Ed had graduated with a degree in orthopedics and moved his family out west to be closer to his ailing parents. Was his presence in our lives another "God-incident?"

We visited with David until almost 10:00 p.m. getting home around 1:30 a.m. after stopping for a bite to eat. The way things were progressing we had great hopes of being able to bring David home Saturday or Sunday.

I arrived at work at six on Thursday after three to four hours sleep. The morning was packed with meetings, all so wonderfully stimulating. The afternoon was scheduled for visits to schools. Just as I was preparing to leave the office shortly after lunch, Sara Belle called.

"David's taken a turn for the worse. Dr. Crosby wants us to come up immediately," she said as she cried.

"I'm on my way home. Be ready," I said without expressing alarm, hoping to calm her. I literally ran out of the office saying to my secretary, Dot, and for others in the office to hear, "David's taking a turn for the worse. We are on our way. I'll be in touch."

Traveling to Baltimore was a tense, quiet time. We each prayed silently and out loud. On purpose and in control, I broke the speed limit going 70 to 80 miles an hour on straight stretches of road. I stayed focused and slowed down in areas of pending traffic. If I got stopped I prayed the officer would believe us and give us an escort. We arrived in the parking garage of Mercy hospital in just under two hours. We ran through the parking garage and into the hospital lobby. By luck we were able to enter an open elevator.

When we arrived in David's room we expected the worst. The worst is what we got. Dr. Crosby and a nurse were standing over him adjusting tubes that had just been placed in his mouth, through his nose, and in various parts of his body. David was not responding. We were in shock. We just stood, watching, and waiting for Dr. Crosby to speak. It was as if we were in another world in another time. How could this be happening when less than a few hours ago he looked so healthy, happy, and ready to restart his life?

Dr. Crosby turned to pick up a tool of some kind from a nearby sterile table and acknowledged we were in the room as he turned back to David. Within seconds, he turned back facing us and spoke.

"David is suffering from severe peritonitis. His condition is grave."

We were frozen. Between the two of us we couldn't gather enough consciousness to form a question or make an intelligible response. Eventually, Sara Belle was able to communicate in some sort of broken language.

"What's going to happen?" she asked.

"As soon as he is stable we will need to operate. This was caused by having the draining tube that leads the fluid through the shunt to empty into the stomach. We felt it was just too risky to place the tube in the heart. But now we don't have a choice. The tube has to be drained into the heart." This is basically what we understood Dr. Crosby to say in layman's' terms.

It was really difficult watching David lie in bed so still again. It brought back many unhappy moments and nurtured such tremendous feelings of anxiety. His breathing seemed normal, but his complexion was ashen in color. When we began to gather some degree of existence we realized that for the first time ever we didn't question Dr. Crosby about what each of the tubes or machines were or why they were necessary. We had no idea about how they served to support his life or how they provided him comfort.

We spent the night at David's bedside. This was the first of many times we missed our lifeline, Ed. Throughout the night, nurses came and went checking this and checking that, doing this and doing that. They were all very pleasant, but they could not feel the loneliness, the emptiness, or the helplessness we were drowning in, not knowing again what the future held for the three of us. We were truly living through a lifeless, endless nightmare with little hope.

✝

The rising sun began to bring life to the seventh floor as the hospital personnel changed shifts. Steams of bright light reflected on the walls of the room while sounds of horns, garbage trucks, and sirens from the outside world filled the air. We watched David begin to stir.

He hesitantly opened his eyes and looked up at us. In the quietest voice he whispered, "Good morning."

We spoke back and moved close to him on either side of the bed and rubbed his arms.

"David, honey, you're going to have an operation this morning to make you feel better."

"Good," was his only response as he slipped back into a peaceful sleep.

We couldn't help but wonder what the day would bring. Some answers came soon. Bill, one of the new interns we were beginning to become acquainted with, entered the room with news that David's operation had been scheduled for ten o'clock.

Just before nine, they arrived to take David to surgery. Again, we had to transform our battle scarred faces into an artificially cheerful smile so we could project a feeling of security to David. We stood weak and powerless once again as they wheeled him away. This time when he entered the elevator he was not awake enough nor had the energy to tell us, "Don't worry. See you when I get back." Something surely was missing. It left us with a feeling of uneasiness as we settled into a long morning's wait. Our little world at Mercy was changing. We no longer had Ed. A few other interns we had grown to know and love were also moving on to continue their training elsewhere. We had a whole new group of promising young men and women on the floor anxiously awaiting their turn to become full-fledged physicians.

SHELDON LARMORE

On this particular day, daybreak was brightly filled with promise. However, in just a matter of a few hours the view from David's hospital window changed as dark thundering rain clouds began to move over the city. The hospital halls were darker than usual. There seemed to be an unusual quietness and a kind of chill in the air that we had never experienced at Mercy. Speechless, we turned to walk to the end of the hallway where there was a comfortable, inviting, small waiting area with large windows overlooking the city. We sat. We prayed. We aimlessly watched people move about. We couldn't talk. Sara Belle reached over and took my hand into hers. We looked at each other with a faint smile and a squeeze of the hand. We prayed. Off in the distance we heard the rumbling of thunder as the day darkened into almost night. The blackness in the sky was interrupted with frequent flashes of bright lightning. Watching from the windows we could see the storm moving angrily over Baltimore, slashing out with high winds and torrents of drenching rain. As suddenly as the storm started, it ended.

Almost instantly the deep gloominess changed into a multitude of brilliant rays of golden sunshine. It was as if God was saying, "Peace be on Baltimore," as He reconnected the trillions of electrical wires snapped by the bolts of lightning. It really made us think again of the wonderful power of God and His healing grace. I couldn't help but think, *Did God do all this just to prove to us that He heard our prayers and that He is answering them?* Laughingly, I thought would He actually disturb a whole city just to prove to the Larmores that He was by our side? You know, I had to come to the conclusion He definitely would, not just for the Larmores, but for anyone who believes. God is good!

With the sun shining so brightly through the halls we could not immediately make out the figure turning the corner and walking toward us. It was Dr. Crosby followed by his new intern, Jake.

"It's over!" Dr. Crosby said with a big grin on his face. "Everything went well. I want to keep David in recovery for some time as a safety precaution. Why don't you go have a good lunch? Our worries are over."

That we did. We took the elevator straight to the sixth floor cafeteria. We ordered the biggest hamburger sandwiches our almost last ten dollars would buy. We ate and enjoyed the sandwiches more than if we were having filet mignon at the Waldorf Astoria hotel in New York City. God is good! He does answer prayers.

✝

On Saturday, the day after David's operation, Sara Belle's brother Jeff and his wife, Jenny, traveled from Milton, Delaware, to visit with us in the hospital. Before leaving they asked to take us out for dinner somewhere in the city. With David's insistence and blessings we were guided by a couple of nurses to try the nice, little restaurant a couple blocks from the hospital. They warned us reservations were usually needed, but this early in the afternoon they may be able to seat us. We walked the distance to the restaurant. When we arrived we found what appeared to be a little cellar café. We had to take three or so steps down off the sidewalk. There we walked through a mahogany door with gold-plated handles. This should have instantly told us to get prepared.

Somewhat inquisitive, the four of us entered the restaurant with Jeff and me wearing our khaki pants and sport shirts. Sara Belle and I crossed the threshold of the restaurant first. We were greeted by the maitre d', who was as equally polished as the door.

"Good afternoon, monsieur. Good afternoon to you, madam," he said.

"How are you?" Sara Belle asked.

"We know we don't have reservations, but can you squeeze us in?" I asked.

The maitre d' carefully, but subtly, looked Jeff and me up and down. We knew we possessed the charisma, the charm, and the killer smiles any debonair patron would have to have in order to be accepted into a joint such as this, but we lacked the one thing the door bouncer, I mean the maitre d', was looking for: a suit jacket.

"I'm sorry sir. You must have a jacket. If you don't have a jacket with you we will loan you one from the restaurant's wardrobe." I looked at Jeff, Jeff looked at me, and we agreed to wear one of their hand-me-downs.

As the maitre d' handed each of us a jacket he said, "You know, we must uphold our dress code."

As I started to put the jacket on I immediately realized it was going to be way too big. I asked the gentleman if he had a smaller one.

"No. Our smaller sizes are at the cleaners," he said.

When we entered the dining room Jeff and I felt just as if we had stepped off the pages of *Esquire* magazine. No wonder so many people turned heads to view us make our grand entrance. Both of us were wearing either a size 46 or 48-inch jacket on a size 40 frame. At first glance it had to appear the *Barnum and Bailey* Circus had arrived. No wonder the jackets had to be sent to the cleaners so frequently. The sleeves were constantly being dipped into the wonderfully served cuisine.

We returned to this same restaurant with Sara Belle's sister, Eleanor, and her husband Bob in 2008 some twenty-eight years later. This time Bob and I were dressed in a suit and tie. The women were dressed in their finery. Wow! How things have changed. Now we were out of place! We were met at the door by a hippy type, long-haired, tattooed host. After telling him we would like a table for four his reply was, "No Problem. Right this way, guys."

No maitre d', no Madam, no Monsieur, just *guys*. *A new time!* Our fellow diners were mostly dressed in jeans with flip flops and baseball caps hanging cross ways on their heads, or in cutoffs and wrinkled dress shirts with button down collars worn outside their pants. A few of the wrinkled, gray-haired or bald patrons were dressed in old fashioned costumes such as we were. Can't imagine why they did not stop us from entering without having us borrow one of the restaurants latest outfits. We were surprised they even allowed us to enter their exquisite dining area without a baseball cap and barefoot, or cardboard sandals. One thing was constant, however; the prices listed on the menus *still* required a minor bank loan.

David's recovery was more rapid than Dr. Crosby or we anticipated. Within a week David was ready to be discharged. We happily made that wonderful journey once again across the bay bridge into the beautiful land of pleasant living on the Eastern Shore of Maryland.

David Puts "Work Clothes" on His Dreams

Whatever you do, work at it with all your heart, as working for the Lord, not for men.

Colossians 3:23 (NIV)

David had already missed a good portion of the first two months of his fifth grade in school. Dr. Crosby wanted him to stay out of school at least until January to build his strength. This would help him avoid contact with any unnecessary illnesses or germs since his immune system had been seriously compromised. A tutor was hired by our board of education to teach David at home daily until he was able to return to school following the Christmas holiday. This was a wonderful time for family growth and togetherness. No homework to do every night after dinner because it was done during the day with the tutor and in the afternoon after she left. No daily lunchtime trips to the school to take David to the bathroom. No worries about getting David ready for the school bus by a quarter past seven each morning. He could sleep in and take his time getting ready for home school since his tutor did not arrive until ten each morning. We made up for lost time and enjoyed life to its fullest. In fact, the Larmores always had fun as a family.

For us, January arrived too soon. But for David, January couldn't arrive fast enough. He loved school. Why? We didn't quite understand. Every day whether the sun was out or not, whether it was raining, sleeting, cold, hot, or snowing he had to get out of bed at six. As soon as he woke up he was ready to start the day, no more lying in bed. Many days we knew he was not feeling up to par. As hard as we tried to get him to stay home and rest, he was even more determined to force himself to go to school. Each day he arrived home from school he took a short time for a snack. Afterward, he would start his homework while Sara Belle cooked dinner. After dinner he would continue his homework without any prodding. At times it was painful for us to watch him do his work. He had little use of his left hand and had difficulty turning pages in a book with his right hand. His writing was agonizingly slow and deliberate. Every letter had to be formed to the best of his ability.

Early on Dr. Crosby told us David would never be able to do cursive writing. Surprise! David wanted to learn to write cursive like the rest of his friends, so he struggled and struggled and finally mastered the art of cursive writing. However, he printed much faster, so his teachers allowed him to print his homework and class work until David was in the ninth grade. He spent a good five hours (equivalent to one hour for a student without a handicap) one weekend printing an assigned report. We checked it over and praised him for doing such a great job.

A couple days later the teacher returned the graded papers to the class. The only mark on David's paper was a big fat red cross mark from one side to the other side of his front page. To add insult to injury the comment scribbled in bold red was, "Ninth graders don't print their work. Do over." Now, understand Sara Belle and I had an agreement from the time David first started school. Since I was in the central office of the Wicomico County Board of Education with the title of Director of Elementary Education I was not, unless absolutely necessary, going to person-ally question teachers about concerns in any areas we felt David was being treated unfairly. This agreement between us was made not because I did not want to be involved. It was made because I didn't want David's teachers to feel any unnecessary pressure in the conference because of me and the title I held. Many times I was indirectly involved in their annual evaluations. Besides, Sara Belle had been a successful teacher with a good reputation for fairness before David's birth. She was quite capable of handling conferences with David's teachers and getting to the bottom of any situation we felt needed addressing.

This incident unfortunately changed an easy going, compassionate, caring educator into a raging, angry parent. It took every ounce of fiber in my body to rein in my fury before I could even begin to think reasonably and professionally about how to approach this unreasonable act of stupidity. A time to meet with the teacher was scheduled. As the conference started I calmly, but deliberately, stated why I had requested time to meet with her. She listened in a condescending manner as if her body language was saying, "I'm a high school teacher. This is where we prepare students for life. You are only elementary trained." By this time I pointedly shared with her my total dissatisfaction about how she graded the paper.

After fielding questions to her such as: Why did you want to be a teacher? What pleasure do you get from being a teacher? If you had a handicapped child and this kind of irresponsible grading happened to him or her how would you feel? Tell me, have you taken time to read David's IEP which clearly states his work will be done in manuscript? Is it going to be necessary for David to redo this paper? I *think* she was beginning to grasp why I felt the urgency for this conference. David would not say anything derogatory about this teacher. In fact, he liked her. It always amazed me how accepting he was of anyone he met.

Our trip as a follow-up visit to Dr. Crosby in January resulted in his request for us to investigate the possibility of giving

David water therapy. He stated he was in desperate need of exercise. Water therapy would be a fun and easy way for him to strengthen muscles that had "gone to sleep" during and since his recent surgeries.

The next morning following our visit to Dr. Crosby, Sara Belle was on the phone seeking all the information she could about water therapy. Her chief goal was to find someone willing to provide David with water exercises. God knew David and I would not have survived without the energy, determination, care, and love Sara Belle gave us. When Sara Belle is given a task to complete or a challenge to face she is right on it! Me? I'm the world's second worst procrastinator. Don't ask me who the first one is. I don't know, but I'm definitely sure I'm not accepting that honor!

A friend directed Sara Belle to call a gentleman in the athletic department at Salisbury University. Upon contact, he stated he would have the physical education instructors share our request for help with their classes. The next afternoon Sara Belle received a call from the university. Our prayers had been answered. A student by the name of Dan Harris had expressed an interest in working with David. He wanted to meet with us, talk about our needs, and discuss what he thought he might be able to do with David. We met Dan at the Salisbury University pool on that Friday evening. This was a union made in heaven. Dan and David hit it off immediately. We asked Dan how much he charged.

"Let's wait and see first," Dan said. "I don't want to take up your time if I can't help."

"When do you want to start?" I asked.

"How about Monday at five here? I have permission to use the university's pool."

On Monday we met Dan. David was really excited. He did not seem a bit fearful of the Olympic-sized pool. The first session went well.

"How much do we owe you, Dan?" I asked.

"Let's wait. I'll let you know," he said.

I thought to myself half in jest and half in all seriousness, *Since we are rapidly getting ourselves head over heels in debt with incidental medical bills, you'd better let us know soon. We can't let this cost get out of hand. Hope we don't have to remortgage the house.*

"When do you want to see us again?"

"How about Wednesday at the same time?" he said.

"Okay, we'll see you then."

On Wednesday we went through the same routine. We asked, "How much do we owe you?"

We got the same response: "Let's wait and see how things work out." Dan asked to see David again on Friday. These sessions with Dan continued three times weekly until his graduation in May. He never accepted any payment for all the time and effort he devoted to David. His comments were always, "Forget it. We're having fun, aren't we, David?"

About a month into our friendship Dan introduced us to his girlfriend, Michele, who also was a senior at Salisbury University. We found Michele to be as caring, considerate, and lovable as Dan. What a great couple of kids we were adding to the Larmore household. Soon afterward, we had the privilege of meeting their parents. The love that both families demonstrated toward each other and those around them certainly gave evidence to why Dan and Michele had developed into such thoughtful and selfless people. Immediately, we informed both families we were going to adopt Dan and Michele as part of our family. From that point on they have played an important role in David's life as well as ours. We love them as if they were our own.

Another form of exercise Dr. Crosby and other physicians of the Spina Bifida clinic suggested for therapy was horse back riding. This astonished both of us. We have a son who can't stand alone or walk a step. He basically had no use of his left hand and was essentially paralyzed from his waist down. Were we hearing what we thought we were hearing?

The problem was Sara Belle heard the doctors make this suggestion and she was on it before the words had time to cool. *Anything* suggested to help David she was "in gear and ready to go." The following day she was on the phone in search for someone with a horse to give David lessons. In a couple days she located a lady with just the right horse. Charlotte Daugherty lived with her husband, Dr. Blox Daugherty, a veterinarian, on a farm between Delmar and Sharptown, Maryland. They had a couple stables of horses. Some were theirs and others they were boarding. Charlotte, seeing David's size, decided her pony Jelly Bean and David would be a perfect match. He was a small light brown pony with patches of white on his nose, forehead, and chest. With some prodding and lots of encouragement David quickly began to feel comfortable sitting on Jelly Bean. It did not take him long to learn how to use the reins to guide Jelly Bean around the farmyard. It may have been our imagination, but it seemed Jelly Bean lit up when he saw David approaching.

Charlotte shared that Jelly Bean must have sensed David's need because he was extra gentle when David was on his back. With Charlotte's patience, skill, and compassion, David entered and won first or second place in three of the four shows he and Jelly Bean participated in during their time together. These lessons continued until David's legs became so stiff it was impossible for him to stretch them far enough apart to mount Jelly Bean.

In the spring of 1981, as David completed his fifth grade school we were approached by Mittie Ring of the local March of Dimes. She asked if we would permit David to serve as their poster child. Sara Belle and I had been active in raising money for the March of Dimes by participating in its annual Walk-A-Thon from its conception in the mid 1970s. The first two or three annual walks were twenty miles in length as compared to those of today, which are six miles or less. When David accepted this honor little did we know how much it was going to change his life in a most positive and active way. For the next five years David served as the March of Dimes Ambassador for the lower Eastern Shore of Maryland.

His duties included participation in *all* lower shore Christmas parades, presence at several local events, the lead walker in the annual March of Dimes Walk-A-Thon, and attendance at numerous March of Dimes programs, dinners, and organizational meetings. One of the activities he really enjoyed was his appearance on the Jerry Lewis Tele-A-Thon program twice during his rein as ambassador. His most favorite duty was the crowning of the new Miss Teen Maryland each year at the Ocean City Convention Center. This was an event that required him to wear a tuxedo and to be surrounded throughout the evening by twenty-four beautiful, charming young teens competing for this prestigious award.

We had the opportunity to meet most of these young ladies each time. We were impressed with their sincerity and compassion in relating to someone like David in a wheelchair. At the end of the evening each year, the contestants and the production crew of the pageant would meet at a local hotel for a big party of pizza, hamburgers, hot dogs, and all the other heavenly stuff enjoyed by growing teenagers. David was always included in things such as games, interviews with reporters, and photo shoots with beautiful girls (which he dearly loved). As parents, we were always heartened to see how many contestants took the time to introduce him to their family and friends.

Until David entered his sixth grade in school his mode of transportation from place to place was me carrying him or with his mother or me pushing him in a lightweight baby stroller. Without our help his mobility was limited. At the time our insurance would not pay for a wheelchair for his use. We surely could not afford to take another dime from our budget to purchase a battery-operated scooter. Mittie Ring from the March of

Dimes realized David needed a better method of moving about his surroundings. Without our knowledge, she contacted the local Rotary Club asking if there were any funds available for the purchase of a wheelchair. They were interested in learning about David and most willing to finance whatever seemed to be the best for his needs. As a result, the members of the Rotary Club bought and presented him with his first Amigo. This was a three-wheeled, battery-operated scooter. The real plus of this scooter was that it could be disassembled into five parts making it easier to transport. Little did we know how much this new mode of transportation would change David's world. This one kind act by the collective membership of the Rotary Club of Salisbury helped turn our family's life around 180 degrees.

One of the first outings David had with his new wheels was a trip to his Aunt Faye's house for dinner. Once we got David and his Amigo into the kitchen, conversations about the day, families, and other topics ran rapid as they always do when we get together with Faye or other members of our closely knit family. All of a sudden we were interrupted by the excitement of David's voice, "Mom, did you know Aunt Faye has three bedrooms?"

"Yes," Sara Belle answered with as much excitement in her voice. "You've been exploring, haven't you?"

"I really like this scooter!" David stated cheerfully as he backed over my foot.

"Ouch!" I cried out. "David," I said jokingly, "I'm taking your license away from you if you run over my foot one more time."

David chuckled and with one of his famous mischievous smiles said, "Sorry, Dad. You're just going to have to watch out until I learn how to drive."

That night we had a real awakening! We witnessed David explore his world *on his own*. This was the first time we realized how sheltered and protected his life had been. He only saw things where we took him or sat him in our travels. Prior to this night I would have walked into Faye's house carrying David, looking for a place to sit him. As we moved from one room to another I would simply bend over, pick him up, and carry him to the next room and sit him down. Wow! What a great evening. David's life of independence was launched! Watch out world!

It was always great fun to be with my family enjoying excellent cooking, great conversation, and much laughter. We always took time to share memories and reflect on all the blessings God had showered upon us over the years. This night was no exception. David once again led us to the understanding that the happiest people don't necessarily have the best of everything. They just make the best of everything. This is perhaps why David's favorite verse in the Bible was Philippians 4:11, 13: "For I have learned, in whatsoever state I am, therewith to be content, I can do all things through Christ which strengtheneth me." This verse is inscribed on David's head stone.

David loved life. With his newfound independence, he ventured out to make the best of every day. His primary goals were to do God's work and share his happiness with others. It's been said if there is a smile in your heart, your face will show it. He certainly taught us a smile is more important than anything else you wear. As his parents we felt so special to have him as our son. In so many ways he reminded us of the story of the cross-eyed discus thrower. He didn't set any records in life, but he sure kept the crowds attention.

The summer before entering middle school, we arranged to send David to Camp Fairlee Manor, an Easter Seal camp for handicapped individuals in Chestertown, Maryland. This was not an easy decision on our part. David was not 100 percent behind the idea but agreed to give it a chance. Getting him ready to attend camp was an experience in itself. Before we were able to obtain blessings from his doctors for him to attend camp, we had to make sure all of his medical needs were able to be met along with numerous other requirements that normally are not issues when sending a child to a regular camp setting.

In addition to all of the necessary items that were packed for the adventure, we included fifteen self-addressed, stamped post-cards for David to send us, hopefully, each day during his two weeks at camp. We told him all he had to do was simply write something like, "Hi, having a great time." If that was too much for him to do we told him, reluctantly, he could just write, "Hi," letting us know he was still on the planet. When the day arrived to take David to camp we packed the car and started the two and a half hour jaunt to Chestertown. The closer we got to the camp the bigger the lumps in our throats got. Oh, good Lord, were we doing the right thing? Everyone kept telling us it would be a great experience for David. This might be so, but as overanxious parents we had to wonder if we would be able to handle the experience of having him so far away from home. Oh shucks! We had to realize he'd been that far away from home while in the hospital under much more stressful, life-threatening situations. We thought, *Relax! Enjoy the moment.*

Our arrival at camp was greeted by a well-oiled and ready to go team of camp counselors. As soon as we parked and started to get out of the car we were greeted by two young adults ready to begin David's stay at Camp Fairlee Manor in a royal manner. They introduced themselves to David first and then to us. Immediately, they helped unpack the car. They knew which cabin David had been assigned and guided us there. They helped us throughout the total registration process. In amazement we just stood by and left all the details to the counselors. We just followed them around as obedient parents while they helped us handle one task after another. It was obvious to us that David was going to be taken care of by an extremely well trained team of young men and women. Why should we worry so much!

When it came time for families to leave the camp we bravely pulled ourselves together and mustered up the strength and courage to bid our good-byes. It helped to see David fitting into camp life so soon. As we parted, his counselor was at his side and ready

SHELDON LARMORE

to take him and two others on a tour of the facility. We knew this was going to be a wonderful experience for David, but as parents it was hard to part with him without being able to visit him for two weeks. Surprisingly, we survived, and David made out like a champ!

On the day we picked David up from camp we were not sure he was ready to come home. It was quite evident he had had a blast in his two weeks away from home. Once again we had to remember the Lord reminds us numerous times, "Trust Him through our trials and worries. He's had thousands of years of experience and knows how to deal with our problems." This was another time in our lives we had to understand we had to get out of the driver's seat and let Him handle the wheel. As we packed the car with David's stuff I noticed one of the counselors nudging David and whispering something in his ear. David smiled. Again, the counselor nudged David trying to get David to say something. Finally, the counselor said, "Mr. and Mrs. Larmore, David has something to show you."

With that David handed his mom a plaque. Inscribed on it were the words, *David Larmore, One of Camp Fairlee Manor's Campers of the Year.* The counselor explained that after each camping session the team picks an individual who demonstrated the best leadership and citizenship skills as a camper. David was honored with that title for this session. With great excitement and pride, we grabbed David and gave him lots of hugs as we congratulated him. He really did enjoy camp. Obviously, we worried and fretted for nothing. By now we should know worrying doesn't give us anything but wrinkles; just something else to worry about.

David's middle school years were spent in Wicomico Middle School. This school was built as a three-story high school in the early 1930s. One year before David entered seventh grade the building was totally renovated. An elevator was included in the renovations so handicapped students could have easy access to all floors of the building. I have to think again. Was this a coincidence or a God-incidence? I graduated from that school in 1954 and vowed never to step another foot into *any* school building the rest of my life. Little did I know God still had my life under construction. I guess He knew I didn't like school, and He was determined to change my attitude. He did! Absolutely, through no desire or plans on my part, I entered the teacher training program offered at Salisbury State Teachers College in Salisbury, Maryland. I was in college at the time with no goal in mind. A degree in education was the only major offered at STC in the fifties. At the end of my sophomore year I had two choices: drop out and go to work full time or stay and enter the teacher training program. After little thought I decided, *What the heck? I'll stay.* Well, as a result the next forty-five years of my life were spent in the world of education. I thoroughly enjoyed every minute of it—well, with a few exceptions.

In the eighth grade David's teenage personality really began to develop. He decided it was about time to investigate the world beyond his protected home and school environment. Once we realized he was testing the waters by making little sly comments and checking our parenting skills by talking back when asked to do something, gears were put in action to bring that personality change to a sudden halt. We had several long talks over a period of time. Fortunately for us he soon realized the wrongs of his ways. If we had not nipped this experiment of uncontrolled independence we would have had greater problems than necessary. We explained to him there would be many wonderful opportunities in his life, but there would be temptations he would have to learn to deal with in time. We constantly took every chance to teach him right from wrong. His involvement in church from infancy apparently made an impact on his life and his development into a kind and productive human being. Thank you, God.

Middle school years for most parents are trying. This certainly continued to be true in our family's experience. On one weekend in the early spring of David's eighth grade all was not well in the Larmore household. On this particular Friday night I took off from work early. The three of us were going to have a date night out of town. I picked Sara Belle up at home, and we drove to Wicomico Middle to pick David up after school. Sara Belle went into the school to get David. On her way out she met one of his teachers. I could see that they were going to be involved in a conversation so I got out of the car to get David. We waited for Sara Belle to join us so we could begin our plans for the evening.

When the conversation ended I watched Sara Belle as she walked toward the car. It was not a pretty sight. I could see she was getting angrier the closer she got to the car. She opened the car door, sat down, and for a few seconds said nothing. Then in a controlled deliberate voice she asked, "David, do you have something to tell your dad and me about your math quiz?"

"No," he said.

"Where is the note from your teacher asking for a conference?" she asked. By now I was all ears.

"What note?" he mumbled.

"What's happening?" I asked.

Sara Belle responded with anger and disappointment in her voice, "David, got an *F* on his last math test. His teacher wrote a note home asking us to call her for an appointment so we could discuss his progress."

"David is that true?" I asked him as I watched him from the rear view mirror. There was no response, just a shrug of his shoulders.

"Well, that's the end of a wonderful night. We are going home and you are going to tell us exactly what all this is about young man!" I said.

When we arrived home we began to question David about the situation again. He just sat, folded his arms, and would not respond to any of our questions. This was a whole new David. It was so unlike him that it was frightening. I never dreamed I would be having, or trying to have, a conference with my son while feeling such a huge empty pit in my stomach. Honestly, we both were so taken aback by his attitude and indifference we didn't know or couldn't even think about how to approach this problem *or* him. We simply stood looking at each other and then him. Soon I said to him, "Young man, you go to your room and think about this. When you are ready to talk with us you let us know."

Without a word, David turned his Amigo around and with his head hanging went back to his room. I watched him roll down the hallway in utter disbelief. We both were devastated. Who was this person in the other room? It certainly couldn't be David! For a good half hour Sara Belle and I sat numb and speechless in the family room. Sara Belle was the first to get up. She walked down to David's room with me following behind. She saw that he was watching television. She quietly walked over and without a word turned the set off.

David made no response.

Looking at David she asked, "Are you ready to talk to us about what happened?"

"No." With that we walked out of his room without another word. As nightfall approached Sara Belle gathered enough energy to fix a dinner of baked beans and hot dogs. I took David a platter to his room, set it down, and left. This silent treatment was killing us. After we attempted to eat a tasteless dinner I went back to David's room to see if he had finished eating. He had taken one bite of his hot dog and had not touched his baked beans.

"Are you ready to talk?" I asked.

"No," he replied.

Disappointed, I told him he was going to stay in his room without television until he was ready to talk. I received no comment from him. I turned to walk down the hall, heartbroken and on the verge of tears.

"Sara Belle," I said, "are we doing the right thing? We can't force him to talk. There is no sense in yelling or losing our tempers. That's not going to help."

"Let's wait a little longer. We'll keep an eye on him to make sure he's okay," she said.

Later we returned to his room together. We asked him if he wanted to talk and his response was no. I calmly picked him up, placed him on the bed, and prepared him for the night.

"Good night," we both said as we left the room. There was no response from David. To make sure he was okay through the night, I decided to sleep in the living room on the sofa. This way I would be able to hear him during the night, and I could periodically check on him without waking Sara Belle.

Early Saturday morning David began to stir. I entered his room with a cheery "Good morning."

"Hi" is all the response I got. I got him up, gave him a shower, took care of all his personal needs, and made sure he had his medications on time. Afterward he returned to his room seemingly content sitting on his Amigo looking out the window.

I asked again, "Do you want to talk?"

"No."

We were long past trying to think who was being punished more, David or us. Saturday came and went without any change or willingness to talk about what happened in school. Every hour or so we would go in his room, check to make sure he was all right and then ask the same tiresome question while getting the same one word answer: No.

Sunday arrived with a heavy down pour of rain. David and I went through the same routine as we did on Saturday morning. Afterward, he seemed satisfied to return to his room and sit. Even though we had silently prayed throughout this ordeal it was now time for a serious, reaching out to the heavens, in-depth prayer. Throughout our married life, prayer has been important, even more so since David entered our world. In fact, Sara Belle has said many times in the past, "Prayer is the mortar that holds our house together." As witnessed and referred to several times already in David's life, prayer has always served as the pause that seems to empower us to face what life brings. We both prayed.

After another day of questioning, eating alone in his room, and several negative responses to our requests to talk, there was an abrupt change.

"Mom, Dad, I'm ready to talk," David said as he looked at us with tears in his eyes.

With a flash Sara Belle and I knelt beside David's Amigo surrounding him with our arms, hugging him tightly with streams of tears covering each of our faces.

"I'm sorry. I just thought you would be mad if I told you." David said as he cried.

"David, you know we are never angry with you for telling us the truth. We always want you to tell us the truth. We love you." Sara Belle said as we comforted him.

David shared again in a broken voice, "I'm sorry."

We have learned and truly believe prayer doesn't need proof, it needs practice. God surely has given us many occasions to practice our communication skills with Him. This little, yet very frightening situation helped us appreciate even more the thought that things begun in prayer usually end in power.

THE UNCERTAINTY
OF ANOTHER
OPERATION

In the face of uncertainty, there is nothing wrong with holding on to hope.

—O. Carl Simonton

From the time David was three years old, we took him four times a year to a Spina Bifida clinic housed at Kernan Hospital. This clinic was under the direct supervision of Dr. Scott Decker, David's orthopedic surgeon, and Dr. Robert Crosby, his pediatric neurosurgeon. For each session they were joined by a team consisting of a pediatrician, an urologist, an optometrist, a social worker, periodically a technician from their casting department, and always two or three interns. The exam room was pretty well filled by the time all of the team members were assembled. These visits consisted of a thorough examination of David by each physician present, discussions among them about their findings, and then a pretty comprehensive conference with David and us. These sessions basically served in planning programs for David's development and outlining possible future needs of treatment or surgery. Each session was always productive and helped us stay focused on David's growth and needs.

Dr. Decker, like Dr. Crosby, became a close friend. Six times a year he and one of his interns traveled to Salisbury to conduct a two-day orthopedic clinic for our health department. Several times during those overnight stays we would invite them to our house for dinner. Dr. Decker (we called him Scot when he was in our home or when we were out socially) was like an old shoe. Soon after a visit or two to our home he accepted it as his home away from home. Even though we didn't drink beer we always made sure we had an ample supply of his favorite in the refrigerator. On nights he visited we always invited his intern. Eventually, Scot just knew the invitation was always open to both of them. Soon after their arrival they would help themselves to the beer. Then they would find a place in the kitchen to sit and talk with us as we put the last touches on the meal.

There was one time Scot came by himself and immediately took his shoes off and stretched out on the couch in the family room. As he closed his eyes for a quick rest his words to Sara Belle were, "Sara Belle, it's been a long day. Call me when dinner is ready." It was wonderful getting to know Scot as a very down to earth, caring person. However, we always treated him with professional courtesy and respect calling him Dr. Decker in the hospital or in the clinic.

The bond between us grew over time. For two summers in a row Scot, with his wife and two sons, parked their camping trailer in our driveway. They used our home as a base while they vacationed at the beach during the day and visited areas in and around Wicomico County at night. One of the highlights for Scot and us was a time when Jimmie Rae Silvia, David's physical therapist, joined us for dinner and brought with her some of Scot's favorite seafood already cooked and ready to eat. This was one of the great nights to remember. Scot and Jimmie Rae had lots in common since they worked together in the clinics.

As David entered eighth grade, we began to realize he was leaning more and more to the right and, at times, seemed to be having a little difficulty breathing. In the last three years or so one of the major concerns that always surfaced in discussions

SHELDON LARMORE

during the clinic was the possibility of scoliosis surgery. Was the time nearing? During our next scheduled visit to the clinic we asked if the scoliosis surgery was in the near future.

"Yes. We need to make plans for this soon. In fact, I think we need to make a date for the operation at our next clinic," Dr. Decker said.

In the next couple of months, we had a relaxed, uneventful midwinter vacation from worry and serious medical concerns. However, in the back of our minds loomed the pending surgery. Every time the topic surfaced we fought to push back our memories and fears experienced during David's last major surgery in Mercy. John Wayne was heard to say one time, "Courage is being scared to death—and saddling up and moving on anyway." This was what we had always done over the years, so why stop now! At times like these it also helped me to think about what one of my college friends, Jim Brummell, used to shout with laughter in our carefree days on campus, "Bravery never goes out of fashion!" He often would use this phrase to ease tension or stress of those around him facing unusual or unpleasant situations. We all loved that young man so much. He had numerous physical handicaps but was always positive and on top of the world.

Watching David gradually lean further and further to the right as he sat in his Amigo we decided it was time to face the scoliosis operation. Our next clinic visit was a month away, which gave us time to prepare David. We did some research on our own so we could be prepared to ask the questions we felt we needed answered as we proceeded with plans for the surgery. Shortly, after our decision was finalized in our minds, the phone rang. It was Dr. Crosby's secretary.

"Hello, Mrs. Larmore, Dr. Crosby asked me to call you to let you know that Dr. Decker passed away last week," she said in a solemn voice. "He knew you were friends with Dr. Decker, and he didn't want you to be surprised when you came to the clinic next month."

What a shock! Later in the month we received a short note from the Decker family stating Scot had passed away and thanking us for our love and the good times we had together. It was not until we saw Dr. Crosby in the clinic that we learned Scot had died from complications of a melanoma on his back. It was too late by the time it was discovered. His death was sudden and obviously a shock to many who loved him. He was another wonderful, skilled, and knowledgeable physician who was approachable and interested in the welfare of his patients. Unfortunately, there are some doctors, like some Christians, that give the idea they were baptized in vinegar. If only we could understand that happiness is not having and getting. It consists of giving and serving. Scott Decker was a true example of this.

With Dr. Decker's death taking its toll on so many, our plans for surgery lay pending. It was at Dr. Crosby's suggestion he would contact an orthopedic surgeon he knew and would recommend at A. I. DuPont's Children hospital in Wilmington, Delaware. In less than a week Dr. Crosby's office called with an appointment for us to meet with Dr. Jay at A. I. DuPont hospital. During our initial meeting with Dr. Jay, he explained to us David had what's referred to as congenital scoliosis. Children with this condition are at high risk (two words we really did not want to hear) of neurological or nerve injury while having this surgery. The older the child, the greater are the chances for complications. He also shared with us children suffering with neuromuscular problems such as spina bifida, cerebral palsy or muscular dystrophy have a high risk of developing serious lung problems after surgery. We knew we had no choice but to accept the advice of the professionals and proceed with the surgery. As parents, we needed time to prepare ourselves for the unexpected.

The date for the surgery was set for late March. David, as usual, was a trooper about the whole ordeal. So why should we as his parents worry? Could it be our faith needed another bolt of energy? We were constantly learning from these wonderful (...

that's a laugh) experiences we were having. We have discovered there are two ways to meet any difficulty. We can alter the difficulty, in this case that was not possible. Or we can alter ourselves to meet it. David's acceptance of whatever comes and his trust in the Lord helped us put our anxieties at rest. The question always was: Why is it that we, as adults, allow ups and downs in our faith when we know the good Lord is always with us and will always love us? We must continue strengthening our Christian lives and beliefs. David taught us that life is like a mirror, we get the best results when we smile at it.

The day of surgery arrived. Fortunately for us, we have good friends who live in New Castle, Delaware, Bunny and Pete DeAscanis. Bunny and Sara Belle, both teachers, shared an apartment in Salisbury for three years before Sara Belle and I married. They graciously invited us to spend whatever time we needed with them while David was in the hospital.

When we entered David's room at eight, he was sitting up in bed ready to greet us with a cheerful, "Good morning, Mom and Dad." The operation was scheduled for 10:00 a.m. This gave us time to visit and play a couple games of checkers before his nurse arrived to prepare him for his journey down the hall to the surgical area. Being in David's presence anytime gave us a lift. He was always the one who gave others strength and the reassurance that everything would be okay. He was at peace in difficult times while others went to pieces. I can't help but think with great humility that David was touched by the hands of God. He went through life with such grace and ease it was amazing to see him shrug off so many adversities in his life. I often think far back to the time I picked up that magazine in the doctor's office while waiting for Sara Belle to be examined. The one with the title, "What If Your Child Is Born With a Birth Defect?" I knew then, and I definitely know now, God had His hand on David. He got his cues about life and living from somewhere, and it wasn't necessarily always his parents.

While we waited in David's room for the completion of the surgery, a nurse appeared to tell us there were two gentlemen in the waiting room who would like to see us. We each looked at the other with a puzzled expression. Who in Wilmington, Delaware, would want to see us? As we turned the corner and walked into the waiting room, we were pleasantly taken by surprise.

Our visitors were two dear friends from Salisbury. Harold Fulton, superintendent of schools, and Fred Livingood, assistant superintendent in charge of finance. They took the day off from their duties in the office to travel to Wilmington to be with us. They were as concerned as we were about this operation, knowing what anguish we and our extended family in the central office had experienced from previous surgeries. We were ecstatic to have them with us. While we waited they took us to the cafeteria and treated us to a leisurely lunch. They will never, never know how very much this meant to us. It helped pass time and provided us with the comfort zone we needed while waiting on the results of surgery.

Shortly after one, Dr. Jay walked into the waiting room. He joined us at a table where we were sitting. After we introduced him to Harold and Fred, Dr. Jay stated, "The surgery is over. Everything went well. David is in the recovery room and should be back in his room in a couple of hours." After making sure we were okay, Harold and Fred bid us good-bye. They both had meetings at home that evening. As he left Harold told us to keep them informed of David's progress because everyone in the office would want to know. He also stated that we needed to stay with David as long as he needed us and not to worry about the office. Jokingly, he added, "We might even find out we can do things just as well without you."

"Thanks, a lot!" I responded with ample sarcasm.

David progressed extremely well from the operation and was ready to return home within a week. It would be pure torture to have him sit up or even recline in the car seat with a full body cast (from under his arm pits to the bottom of his hips). The trick was getting him home safely with as little discomfort as possible. Each little bump in the road would be multiplied ten fold during the two-and-a-half-hour ride. Lucky for us we had a station wagon with back seats that folded down. We bought a small air mattress and placed it in the back of the station wagon. This served our purpose well in providing a safe way to bring David home. The whole journey home he laid on his back not being able to move, not even his head. As he focused on the inside roof of the car Sara Belle entertained him by catching him up with things that happened while he was in the hospital. She sang him funny camp songs she learned as a counselor at Camp Arrowhead, an Episcopal camp on Rehoboth Bay. She also exposed us to many of her corny jokes that even made me laugh.

Driving down the state of Delaware that day, we could see in the fields and feel in the air the transition of winter into spring. It was as if Mother Nature was slipping off her heavy, gray winter coat and putting on a brightly colored, airy spring jacket. Leaves were beginning to bud on barren trees while the gentle rains and warm days were beginning to unlock the wild flowers from their winter beds to paint the fields with the beauty of fresh growth. It was as if nature was saying shed your worries and start noticing the beauty around you.

UNEXPECTED GIFTS

*Our friends are like angels who brighten our days in all
kinds of wonderful magical ways.*

—Emily Matthews

Once we were safely home with our precious cargo we
settled into learning how to manipulate the *cast boy*.
Obviously adjustments in the house had to be made to best meet
David's needs. Moving David about from bed to chair, chair to
wheelchair, or from wheelchair to the shower or tub was always
a chore. With the added *decoration* of the cumbersome, heavy
body cast wrapped around his mid-section it was going to be
even more fun.

For the next month David received home teaching while
he mended and adapted to his new shell. A close friend, Jack
Hastings, belonged to one of the community's civic clubs, and he
volunteered to borrow an oversized wheelchair for David's use as
long as he needed one. He stated if they could not borrow one
his family would go together and rent one for David. As would
happen, the two chairs belonging to the club were in use for the
next couple of weeks. So Jack and his brothers rented one. They
brought it to our house for David's use until a free one was available through the club. We accepted the rented wheelchair with
much humility. The Hastings family probably could not afford
the rental of the wheelchair any more than we could.

Their families were growing, and we knew money had to be
tight. We knew the one thing that kept them together was their
devotion to each other and their church. They were living and

active Christians. They lived their lives in such a sharing, caring way. As people got to know them they couldn't help but feel that their own lives had been touched by Christ. These kind of generous, unselfish acts are never forgotten. It has been said a Christian shows what he is by what he does with what he has. The Hastings family was living proof of this kind of generosity. Eventually Jack's family relocated across the bay. Over time we lost contact. However, we will never forget their love and their generosity.

David never really complained much about the bulkiness of his body cast. However, he did complain when he itched under the cast. We learned how to eliminate some of the discomfort by using a long, soft cloth soaked with rubbing alcohol. We would insert it between his cast and skin moving it back and forth and up and down to give him some relief. As late spring became hot and miserable, we were glad for window air conditioners in David's bedroom and our family room. Both were well over ten years old and not performing at their peak. However, they were a blessing on those hot days and humid nights.

One of our frequent visitors was a neighbor and close friend, Ray Scheck. Ray and his wife, Rose, were two of David's fans and supporters. We would get together two or three times a month either at our house or theirs for dinner. After dinner we would play cards or table games with David. Most of the time the card game David and Rose enjoyed most was *Old Maids*. When Rose lost a game she would exaggerate her disappointment to the point where she had David doing belly laughs. David loved being with his Uncle Ray and Aunt Rose. Less than a year before David's operation, Rose was diagnosed with incurable cancer and passed away shortly afterward. After Rose's death Ray came to our house for dinner at least once a week.

One day in early May, I heard a rap on our back door. It was Ray. We invited him in and reminded him it was not necessary for him to knock, just open the door and say, "I'm here. Anybody home?" Even though we didn't expect him to do this we always wanted our friends and visitors to feel welcome and comfortable in our house anytime. We kiddingly said if we are scrubbing floors, washing clothes, power washing the house, etc., don't let that stop you from visiting. You can just join in with whatever is going on while we talk and enjoy each other's company.

He hardly sat down before he said, "Before Rose died she and I talked about David and how we could make life easier for you and him. What I want you to do is have central air conditioning installed in the house."

"What?" We couldn't believe what we heard him say.

"I'm serious," he continued. "I know Rose would approve. She told me before she died to make sure we did something nice for David. Knowing how uncomfortable David must be in that cast and watching him move in and out of air conditioned rooms I decided this is the least we could do." We were speechless. Sara Belle began to cry with joy. As Ray prepared to leave he told us to contact companies for estimates.

"Once you find a company you feel can do the job then contract with them and get the unit installed. Have them send me the bill," he said.

To this day we both feel we never thanked Ray and Rose enough for such a generous gift.

Ray, one of our many angels on earth, could not have been happier with the completed work. It truly was an unbelievable gift given by a compassionate, caring man who always enjoyed sharing with others. I don't feel I'm at liberty to share stories of other gifts and acts of kindness he and Rose shared with others but there were many. There is a saying that goes something like this, "A selfish heart loves for what it can get; a Christian heart loves for what it can give." Ray and Rose were certainly examples of Christians who enjoyed extending their lives and love to others in need.

Out of Cast, into New Adventure

Life is either a great adventure or nothing.

—Helen Keller

Don't be afraid to expand yourself, to step out of your comfort zones. That's where the joy and the adventure lie.

—Herbie Hancock

David's recovery from surgery progressed well. He mastered the skill of sitting up in his Amigo without too much difficulty from his body cast. With determination on his part he was able to return to school for the last month and a half before the summer vacation. David, as usual, launched himself totally into life again with only minimal drawbacks from his cast. He attended church regularly, had friends over to play games, watched baseball or other kinds of sports on the television, and visited the mall on a regular basis meeting friends, having lunch, or playing games in the arcade. David truly was a people person.

In mid-July we made our fourth visit to A.I. DuPont for an appointment with Dr. Jay. We felt if the X-rays and Dr. Jay's examination of the surgical area were good, David's body cast might be removed.

David's face beamed brightly when he heard Dr. Jay say, "Well David, I think we can get you out of that armor today." What a joyful time for the three of us. As we prepared to leave, Dr. Jay complimented David on his positive attitude and his ability to endure life in a cast always with a smile on his face. He reminded David and us to be careful for a time because falls, sudden twists, or things such as a hit or a bang on the back could cause fractures or dislocations.

From mid-July until school opened in September the three of us tried to squeeze as much fun into our times together as possible. I usually took a week at a time for vacation. However, this summer I took two weeks together. We played, traveled, and did all we could to enjoy our time before the reality of work and school brought us back to the real world in September.

During the last year, Sara Belle's home business through the Faye Swafford Pocket Book Company was really beginning to flourish. She was booking more home parties than any previous year. I knew if David and I could keep her out every night selling pocket books we were destined to become millionaires. So as a result of Sara Belle's success, we decided to travel to Nashville, Tennessee, at the end of July to attend a Faye Swafford convention. A tour of the company's new multi-million dollar plant in Cleveland, Tennessee, was going to be one of the highlights of the trip. We planned to spend three days traveling the seven hundred plus miles to Nashville and stay two nights in motels. We wanted to take it easy with David as well as enjoy every moment together as possible.

When we registered in our motel the first night of our trip the desk clerk noticed David was handicapped. She asked us if we would like a handicapped room. Since we had not traveled much we never thought of asking for any special provisions or accommodations. After making sure it did not cost extra we said yes.

As we entered the room we expected to have symphonic music, soft, caressing lighting, and gentle breezes drifting across our faces with the sounds of a soothing flowing waterfall in the background, just like a television commercial! Golly! How naïve of us! Instead, as we surveyed the room we saw nothing different from any other room we had stayed in except it was a little older and drabber than most motel rooms. The only obvious difference in the room was it did not have a tub or a shower curtain. The bathroom was totally open space. Sara Belle and I just looked at each other and with playful sarcasm said almost in unison, "This is a *handicapped* room! Oh well! Another adventure for the Larmores. Who cares! We're just sleeping here over night."

With that, we left to find a place to eat and explore the town. When we returned to the room I planned to give David a bath and help Sara Belle get him ready for bed. This was a bigger chore than first met our eyes! The thirty-two-inch doorframe was still in tact—only the door had been removed thus giving no privacy to those using the bathroom. We could not maneuver David's Amigo around the corner and into the bathroom. I had to carry him in and sit him on the commode. My next task was how to wash him. No bathtub, no shower curtain, only one hand-rail on the back wall of the stall and a son who had a fragile back from being in a cast for six months.

The only solution I saw was to strip both of us buck-naked and get into the shower together. I amused Sara Belle with my display of clumsiness as I tried to hold David while juggling the soap and the washcloth from hand to hand. My next obstacle was to learn to bend and move in a manner to make sure the water streaming down from above hit all the right places. A second or two after the shower was turned on, the water began to mix with the soap. I frightened Sara Belle out of her skin as I called for her.

"Sara Belle! Help! Hurry!" Fearing the worst she appeared as fast as a strike of lightning. "I'm slipping! Help! I can't drop David."

Sara Belle stood helpless for a second or two in sheer panic.

"Come over and push me against the wall," I shouted over the commotion of slipping around and soapy water pouring every-where. Fully clothed she walked through the water and literally pushed me against the wall with David in my arms. Sara Belle drenched from the top of her head to the bottom of her shoes began to slip down the wall as she held on to me, bringing all three of us, sliding in slow motion, to the floor of the shower. I held David tight as if he was a keg of dynamite ready to explode. My chief and only goal was to make sure he was protected and had a soft landing. With our butts planted firmly on the shower floor we looked at each other and broke out in laughter.

"The only thing I know to do is to wash David on the floor," I said. I proceeded in placing him between my legs. Sara Belle, already wet, just sat there in the puddles of water enjoying the warm stream of water falling over her head.

"Well, I was going to wash my hair tonight anyway," she said.

After washing, the three of us were presented with another *fun* obstacle. We had to find a way to get out of the bathroom. We couldn't stand. The floor was covered with soapsuds floating in an inch or two of water. I needed to get David to the safety of dry land—the bed. We needed to take care of his medical needs since it was way past time for his medications. Surveying the situation, there was no way I was going to attempt to stand up and carry David to the bedroom area. That was a disaster waiting to happen. My only recourse was to hold him tightly and slowly walk out on my knees. After two or three steps on my knees I realized that wasn't going to work. My knees, like my feet, began to zigzag on the soapy floor.

My last resort was to lie on my back, roll David over on my stomach, and kind of back stroke in an inch of water out of the bathroom until I reached the carpet in the bedroom. That would give me enough traction to stand up and carry him to the bed. Wrong! Just as I prepared my Olympic-style swim out of the room Sara Belle informed me we had another problem. The water from the shower had not only covered the bathroom floor but it had continued its meandering flow into the carpeted hallway, drifting slowly toward the bedroom area. I had no choice but to forge ahead. We finally made it out of the war zone with

David's giggling breaking out into a full-fledged belly laugh. After an hour or so we all settled down to a good summer's nap.

Our trips to Nashville and Cleveland, Tennessee, were enjoyable. We had countless fun adventures. We visited lots of landmarks and met many wonderful people we will keep in our memory banks forever. On our way home from Tennessee we stopped at a large, three-story Holiday Inn. After registering we began our trek across the lobby floor toward the bank of elevators. Sara Belle was carrying a small carry-on bag and a small suitcase we always used for David's supplies, medicines, and other necessary items we needed when traveling with him. I had two large pieces of luggage strapped over my shoulders with another piece in my hand. About half way to our destination I turned to see if David was following. I noticed he was stopped in the middle of the lobby. I said, "Come on, David."

"I can't," he replied. "I think my batteries are dead." I walked over, checked, and sure enough they were dead! When this Amigo dies it is like trying to move a 170 lbs. locked piece of equipment. This was like being stuck out in the Sahara Desert. There was no one in the lobby except us nomads, a dead camel (the Amigo), and an elderly semi-awake gentleman behind the desk. Again I was challenged. By now I realized it did not take much to overload my thinking capacity. We had no choice but to transport our luggage, David, and his Amigo, one piece at a time, to our third floor room. Sara Belle stayed with David while I took all of the luggage and her bags to the room. A Charles Atlas *I'm not*! By the time I got off the elevator on the third floor and looked down the long, long, long hallway to our room I was ready for a serious coronary. With great determination and perseverance I eventually made it back to the lobby.

The next goal was to get David and Sara Belle safely to our third floor room. With this accomplished, my third and final mission was to get the Amigo to the room. Knowing it wouldn't move I prayed to the good Lord to send Superman. Well, I tried!

Knowing that was a stupid prayer, I just apologized to God and accepted the problem as my own. I once heard that ulcers are a direct result of mountain climbing over molehills so I decided to deal with this situation head on. The only way to move this Amigo upstairs was piece by piece. So I disassembled it in the center of the deserted lobby while the desk clerk turned his back and commenced to tinker with something on the table. I guess he was afraid I would ask him directions to the elevator or something else as difficult to answer. Poor man! He looked to be all of fifty but obviously very much ready for retirement.

Moving this 170 pounds of metal machinery was definitely a task I extremely enjoyed. The Amigo can be dismantled into five separate parts. I proceeded to move each of these parts across the lobby to the elevator door. When the elevator door opened I put both of the twenty-five pound batteries on the floor, turned around to get another part, and whirled around again just in time to see the elevator door closing with the two batteries on board. Have you ever witnessed the body language of victims on *Candid Camera* as they are being subjected to an unbelievable happening? Well, I must have given a similar appearance as I stood and unbelievingly threw my hands up in the air. When the elevator returned three ladies stepped out as I thanked them for returning my batteries unharmed. The manner in which they hurriedly passed by me without comment gave me a clue they didn't quite appreciate my humor.

What I experienced next is not even conceivable in most people's lives. With the elevator doors open and the rescued batteries waiting to be transported once again, I propped the elevator door open with a small stool from the lobby. This time I reached down using both hands and began to lift the base of the Amigo into the elevator. Yes! *It happened again!* The elevator received a call from the second floor and went. Understandably, the small stool was not heavy enough. The doors closed, pushing the stool inside *with the batteries*. Finally, much to my relief, we all ended up on the third floor—baggage, David, Sara Belle, me, and the Amigo. That evening, since the Amigo's batteries had to be recharged, we had to order out and eat in while we relaxed and enjoyed being together. I guess the long and short of this is: Enjoy what you can, and endure what you must.

Shortly after returning home from our vacation, we were noticing David's batteries were not holding their charges as they should. Eventually, we had to order new ones. Delivery of the batteries took from two to three days. The batteries were still charging enough for David to use his Amigo around the house. While waiting for the batteries to arrive we used his wheelchair if we went grocery shopping or went walking through the mall. With his left hand semi-paralyzed it was difficult for him to maneuver about, so Sara Belle or I would push him around in the wheelchair. One evening while he was without his Amigo we decided to go shopping for his school clothes.

He was going to be a freshman in high school in September. By all means he wanted to look his best and be in style. He loved clothes and always wanted to look nice. He reminded me numerous times if he was going to wear a tie, then I had to wear a tie. As we went from store to store we took turns pushing David's wheelchair. On more than one occasion, he had to remind us he needed a push as we left one area and moved to another. I always took every opportunity I could to tease him. We stopped in the ladies' department so Sara Belle could look at a nightgown on display. Afterward, we began to walk toward the men's department. With concern, he reminded us in a voice loud enough for others around to hear, "Dad, have you forgotten something?"

I turned around knowing exactly what he meant and said, "No, I don't think so. What do you mean?"

He looked at me with a grin on his face saying, "Dad. You know what I mean. You know I can't move my chair."

"So what?" I replied. "We thought you would be happy waiting for us in the lingerie department while we shopped. We'll be back to get you." Because I loved him so, I just couldn't continue to tease him. I got behind him and looked carefully down the aisle of the store. Seeing it was clear I pushed him fast through the aisles.

"Dad, wait a minute, Dad, wait a minute," was all he could say in the few seconds of his joyride. I know I was bad, but David and I, much to his mother's disapproval, would find some way to taunt each other most days. After shopping for David we started walking down the mall enjoying being out. We were well down the corridor when it occurred to me I should turn around to see how far David was behind us. When I turned I didn't see him anywhere. I touched Sara Belle's arm and said, "We've done it again."

"What?" she asked.

"Left David somewhere," I responded. We both laughed realizing our mistake. We were so darn used to the independence his Amigo gave him we forgot he was in the wheelchair and could not move it without help. We were not overly concerned since it seemed most everybody in the mall knew David. We started our journey back to Hecht's Department Store. As we entered the store, sure enough we spotted David and guess what? He had found someone he knew and was busy talking. As we approached, he and his friend were finishing their conversation. She moved on without realizing we were nearby. As soon as David saw us he gave us his usual happy, but mischievous grin as he pointed a finger at me, "Dad. Good old Dad, you've done it again."

"Done what?" I said kiddingly. The rest of the evening I pushed David in front of me. Unfortunately, this was not the first, nor the last time this happened to David. We share this for a purpose. Just a word of advice to our many young friends and couples: you'd better think twice if or when you have babies and we become their adopted grandparents. You may want to be somewhat hesitant or cautious in asking us to baby sit after our confessions of leaving David behind so many times. To the many young couples who have so lovingly and generously accepted us as part of their family we are only kidding. We'll baby sit for you anytime you need us between midnight and six while everyone, especially the children, are asleep.

PHOTOS

This was David's first Christmas 1970. I insisted
he have his first electric train.

Sara Belle begins teaching David about Jesus - Christmas evening 1970.

Sara Belle teaches David how to talk with
Jesus through his nightly prayers.

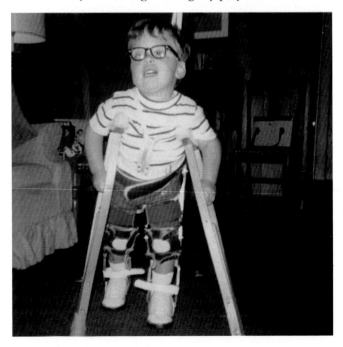

At age 3, David learned to walk with heavy
duty long legged braces and crutches.

David is waiting for the school bus to take him to his first day in the third grade. Notice he has graduated from long legged to short legged braces.

David is a happy first grade student.

This family portrait was taken on Easter in 1978 by Uncle
Walt. This shows David and me dressed as "twins." Notice, all
my teeth are in - thanks to several sticks of chewing gum.

This portrait of David and Sara Belle glows with the
immense love they shared for each other.

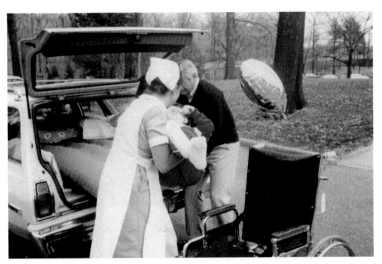

We are placing David on an air mattress preparing to bring him home from A. I. DuPont following his first scoliosis operation.

Danny Harris is teaching David to swim. Danny was like a brother to David and a second son to us.

Our Children! Danny, David, and Michele following David's confirmation at St. Peter's Church.

David and his pony, Jelly Bean, at the completion of a day long horse
show. Notice the first place ribbon he is proudly displaying on his coat.

David is cheered on by his Aunt Doris as he and his hospital team prepare to walk for the March of Dimes.

David with Miss Teen Maryland 1985 and the four runner-ups.

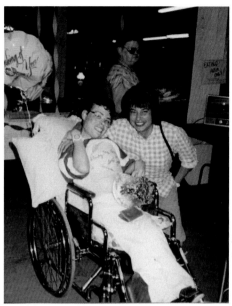

David, in a body cast, celebrates his 17th birthday with his Salisbury
Flea Market "family" and teacher and special friend Joan Devancy.

David is in his glory each day he spends in his growing flea market business, *David's Venture.*

Our proud son, David, on graduation night with his poodle, Nicholas. Notice Nicholas is wearing a graduation cap also.

This is a genuine picture of father and son love. I'm sure David was teasing me about something.

David traveled to Annapolis, Maryland three times in three years to accept awards from Governor Schaefer. This picture was taken when he was recognized as Wicomico County's Most Beautiful Person in 1994.

In 1994, Mr. Dan Akin, President of PRMC and Mr. Alan Newberry, Vice President of PRMC (later to become president of the hospital) honored David during an open house reception following his recognition as *Maryland's Most Beautiful Person.*

David's nurse friend, Marsha Hopkins, arranged for David
to meet one of the Washington Redskins Hogs.

David enjoys time with John Sharpe, a true friend and brother
in Christ. John is one of our angels sent from heaven.

Rocky Burnett and David share a photo time while David recovers
in the hospital from a serious shunt operation. David always enjoyed
Rocky and his constant joking. They truly were soul brothers.

Bob Caldwell, pictured here with David, was always present or close by
whenever David or we needed extra support or a shoulder to lean on.

Many hospital employees traveled to Annapolis to honor David as he accepted the *Maryland You Are Beautiful* award. From left to right are: Betty White, Marsha Hopkins, A.J. Forget, and Barbara Sturgis.

David is celebrating his 32nd birthday at Tokyo restaurant with his two favorite "girlfriends," Holly Evans, and Kathy Montelone just one week before his death.

Salisbury Mayor Tilghman is presenting David with an award during an evening City Council Meeting just three hours before he passed away.

This is an unbelievable picture of David's dog, Kayla, mourning the loss of her master. The day they came to remove the rented hospital bed from David's room we had to literally pick Kayla up from the bed. She immediately laid on the floor and did not move from that spot. The gentleman removing the bed had to work around her.

A team of over 125 hospital employees and friends of David marched in the 2003 March of the Dimes Walkathon raising over $25,000 in his memory. The back of each shirt has David's face imprinted with the slogan "Walking for our hero, David Larmore."

We are very humbled and honored that PRMC created a garden on the hospital grounds and dedicated it in memory of David.

Peter's Voice presented us with the first CD of "David's Song" during
church services at St. Peter's Church on the Sunday of the first
anniversary of David's death.

Members of Peter's Voice clockwise are: Sue Burnett, Shannon Donoway,
Dick Van Gelder, Sean Fahey, Art Johnstone, Steve Rumney and
Rick Fahey.

THE FAMILY
ENTREPRENEUR
EMERGES

*One of the greatest pleasures in life is doing what people
say you can't.*

—Walter Bagehot

The summer before David entered his junior year
in high school was a pleasant and busy one. David
received an invitation to return to Camp Fairlee Manor for two
weeks in July. After considering all the fun and new friends he
enjoyed during his first stay at the camp he decided he wanted
to return. He also in his very unselfish way told us it would be a
good time for us to go somewhere for a few day as long as we told
him and the camp where we were! He qualified that by suggest-
ing strongly that when he returned from camp maybe the three
of us could take a short vacation. As a result of David's decisions,
he went to camp, we went for an overnight stay in Williamsburg,
Virginia, and in late August, just before school opened, we took
David to New York City for a weekend to visit his Aunt Ellie and
Uncle Bob.

The weekend following David's return from camp we had
a two-day yard sale. David helped us set up the table displays
by spreading out the items and arranging them in some kind
of presentable order. The days of the sale he was our sales representative as he circled about the tables and customers. Not to

our surprise, many of the customers knew David. All joking aside this probably helped our sales. Our question was and always has been, "How in the world do so many people seem to know and love David so much?" I guess we should have attached a sign on his Amigo that read, "Politician in Training."

As we began to organize the miscellaneous junk left from the yard sale David said, "Dad, I would like to make some money. Do you think I can have a yard sale?"

"Sure. I don't know why not," I responded. "Tell you what we'll do. Let's box up the best of the stuff that's left over. Next weekend we'll set you up in the front yard and see how you make out." I was as excited about David having his own yard sale as he was. I've heard it said many times, "When opportunity knocks, about all some people do is complain about the noise." Well with David's attitude it was, "When opportunities knock, you have to get up and answer the door." It was exciting watching him reach out and move beyond his comfort zone.

The following Saturday we all were up early, ready to launch David into his new role as business man for a day. By seven, I had set up a card table under an umbrella in the front yard with a big sign reading, "David's Yard Sale." David's inventory of mer-chandise consisted of the finest (using the term loosely) once treasured items left over from our previous yard sale. What an amazing morning! This unadvertised adventure netted David a cool $23.50. He was ecstatic. It's been said, "Eighty percent of success is just showing up." David proved this. Wallowing in his success and newfound wealth, he asked if he could have another yard sale next week. Of course, the answer was yes. Why not? As parents, we were thrilled with David's new interest. Amusingly, we concluded that if he continued and became an overnight suc-cess as a junk dealer and salesman, perhaps we would be able to retire and live off his wealth.

Little did we know how much David's initial journey into the world of business was going to change our lives. I guess part of life is getting used to the things we hadn't expected. David's developing philosophy seemed to be life is either what you make of it, or what it makes of you, so let's roll. David's one card table full of yard sale items grew and grew into a weekly mini flea market in our front yard.

Have you ever ventured outside facing a smoldering eighty-seven degrees at 6:00 a.m. in the middle of the summer? The humidity must have been one hundred plus and the heat index felt as if it was 120 degrees. These were the kind of working conditions my boss, and son, David, subjected me to during the second Saturday of his junk business. With sweat running briskly down my face and drenching my shirt, I hauled his precious items to the front yard setting him up for his second weekend of business. At the close of business this day he netted $36.00. Wow! We were on our way to becoming financially secure! But something was going astray. In packing up the merchandise there seemed to be more stuff than I carried out at 6:00 a.m.

"David, where did you get all this stuff?" I inquired. He explained that our neighbor, Judy, across the street gave him things to sell. David further stated Judy did not want any of it back. She told David he could keep whatever money he got from selling the items. After spending another triumphant day helping my son in his business, I noticed how the boxes of his stored stuff were engulfing my tool shed. *Oh well*, I thought, *it will be over soon*. Wrong! Almost every day the rest of the summer, friends, family, neighbors, and a few enemies took great pleasure in helping David restock his inventory of what we, out of their earshot, commonly called overrated junk.

By the end of the summer, David's stock room, previously known as my shed, had expanded in three additional rent-free locations, namely: a corner of his bedroom closet, our attic, and the trunk of one of our cars. I guess those individuals who contributed to David's inventory were living the adage that states, "Whatever we possess becomes of double value when we share it with others." Another saying is, "Give till it hurts." Jokingly, I must remind the givers it means till it hurts *you*, not me. I lost count of the number of times stored boxes of stuff fell on my foot, or the numerous times I banged my head on some old "Donate to David's cause" lamp, iron pot, etc., hanging from the rafters in the shed or attic.

Once September arrived David enthusiastically entered the eleventh grade. We were happy and much relieved, not just because David was enjoying school with his friends once again, but we were unemployed. David's Flea Market was shut down. We hoped forever. That boy had worked his mom and dad to nubs. They needed a much-deserved vacation.

David's many experiences in high school opened a whole new and rewarding avenue of discoveries. His social life began to blossom as his involvement in school and church related activity increased. David liked all of his teachers. He never had a harsh word about any of them from pre-kindergarten through twelfth grade. However, there were two teachers he met in his tenth grade experience that had an impact in developing his confidence. Both were very supportive and encouraged him to reach for the stars.

Mr. Pat Briscoe, head football coach for Parkside High School, took David under his wings. He and members of the football squad named David the team's manager. This was a tremendous lift to his self-esteem. Almost from the time David could sit up and watch TV he loved any kind of sport. As he grew older he loved to sit in his wheelchair and watch the boys and girls in the neighborhood play softball, baseball, football, or do wheelies on their bikes. If he could have physically participated there is no question in our minds he would have developed into a "super jock." Rarely did he miss a televised Oriole baseball or a Red Skins game. If one was on the radio and one was on television he was involved in both. Mr. Briscoe made sure David was on the sidelines of every home game. If he wasn't there, he would find out why.

Mrs. Joan Devaney, David's resource teacher, had the patience of Job, the teaching skills of Jesus, and the compassion and love found in a "Mother of the Year." David loved school, but she made it even more enjoyable and meaningful for him. With her encouragement and her intervention in his academic progress he was able to successfully complete his high school career with honors.

One of Mrs. Devaney's many interests was buying and restoring antiques. As her inventory of restored furniture and other antique items grew she decided to rent a booth at the Salisbury Flea Market. This gave her a diversion from teaching and also a way to profit from her hobby. In an attempt to find new treasures, she would spend most Friday nights and Saturday mornings attending auctions and estate sales in the area. At times she would have to trust other vendors to oversee her booth as well as their own. There were times she would not open her booth until she returned from a sale. Obviously, this did not seem to be very profitable. She realized she was losing a lot of business by not having someone in the booth on days the flea market was open.

For whatever reason, in the fall of his junior year in high school she asked David if he would like to watch her booth on Saturday mornings while she was taking in the auctions and yard sales. His job was to take names of people who had questions or showed interest in any of her items. This gave her an opportunity to contact them when she returned. She also stated if someone wanted to buy an item as priced he could sell it. When David shared this with us we were flabbergasted. We loved Joan *to death* as an old saying on the Eastern Shore of Maryland goes. But why in the world would she ask him? He had no experience handling money except his own. He absolutely had no experience dealing with the public in a setting such as this. Sara Belle talked with Joan about what she expected from David.

Having great confidence in Joan we agreed to give this opportunity a chance. We thought we knew Joan fairly well at this point in David's schooling. However, there was much more to learn about this very caring and extremely optimistic individual. Not only did she teach David in school, she was anxious to help him expand his world outside of school. She certainly gave new meaning to the old saying, "Believers eventually become achievers." Her goal was to make David a believer in himself. She wanted him to realize he had much to offer by setting an example for others to follow.

On Saturday morning at nine on November 7, 1987, David proudly and excitedly entered the doors of the Salisbury Flea Market ready to conquer the business world. Of course, in tow he had his mother and father as his cheering section. Joan was waiting for us, passing time by working on a piece of furniture she had bought at an auction the night before. After a brief tour of the flea market and quick introductions to several of the vendors, Joan wished us luck and departed for an auction. When David was having difficulties at various times in his life Sara Belle would remind him of what Kermit the Frog on *Sesame Street* would say, "It isn't easy being green." Well, you know, we found out that day it *really* isn't easy being green! After the first two or three customers wandered over to the booth and started questioning us about a particular piece of antique furniture or item, we realized what little we knew. It wasn't long before we started praying that each new customer who entered the flea market would keep on walking as they neared the booth. Joan shouldn't know this, but we even found small, out of way places to sit or hide so as customers passed by, they wouldn't see us.

This arrangement with Joan continued well into the winter months. David and Sara Belle or I would substitute for Joan on Saturday mornings. We would be with her in the booth on Sunday afternoons to learn the ropes of the flea market business. It didn't take long for us to feel comfortable dealing with customers. The vendors were like family. They all helped each other and worked together in assisting customers. It wasn't long before the three of us really looked forward to the weekends in the flea market as a break from the week's routine duties and stresses.

In late February or early March, Joan approached David with the idea of taking over her space in the flea market. She assured him she would help him get started with his own little business. To help him get started she would leave some of her items in the booth for him to sell. Initially, we were hesitant about this idea. It would mean a commitment on our part to man the booth each Friday, Saturday, and Sunday. It would involve a constant search for items to build and expand his inventory. And, the scariest part of all was making enough profit to pay the fifty dollars a week rental fee for the flea market space. Since David enjoyed his time at the flea market so much we decided we would take on the responsibility on a trial basis. Sara Belle was still involved with her home party business selling Faye Swafford pocket books, and I was working more than full time as Director of Elementary Education with the Wicomico County Board of Education. Once we adjusted our work and family schedules, we settled into the lives of flea market vendors.

As a family we accepted this new responsibility for David's sake and really made it a fun activity for the three of us. Most Fridays we looked forward to being together at the flea market with the other vendors. They could not do enough to make us feel part of the family. With the help of David's Aunt Chotts and Uncle Sonny Hayman he chose the name for his business, *David's Venture*. At David's request, Sara Belle ordered sweaters for each of us to wear while on duty at the flea market. The sweaters were Parkside High School's colors of green and white with *David's Venture* monogrammed on them. We still have them today in our museum of clothes we can't wear anymore.

Within months David's inventory exploded from the numerous gifts of treasures given to him by neighbors, friends, relatives, and even some of his regular customers. Some of his regulars donated really nice stuff for him to sell that they no longer wanted. Many times after donating an item they would find something they could use and purchased it from him. Over time he gathered quite a collection of novels, magazines, and puzzles that attracted many of his customers. One day as we were rearranging his displays, David gave us a reason for true joy. He had accumulated several used Bibles from yard sales and the packs of books some of his customers had given him to sell.

Out of the blue David said, "I don't want to sell these Bibles. Let's put them out on a table where people can see them. Dad, will you make me a sign that says, 'Free. Please take one'?"

We, like all parents, knew our son had special qualities, but this request from him totally blew us away. From that day on we had to keep replenishing his inventory of Bibles. People really did take advantage of his offer. Learning to obey God, as David was beginning to understand, certainly served to strengthen his spiritual health. Thanks be to God!

One of the pleasures of being in the flea market business was attending auctions and traveling around the countryside finding yard sales. After a short time the auctioneers in the area became aware of David and his flea market business. To this day we feel they watched over him. They made sure, the best they could, he didn't overbid. By the same token it was obvious to us that they made sure he got some items fairly cheap by quickly bringing the bidding to an end with David being the last bidder. Quickly, they moved on to the next item. On one occasion, we arrived at an auction late. All of the items outside had been sold with the exception of an old, genuine, well-used steamboat trunk. For some reason it was sitting to the side, not sold. As the auctioneer began to move inside he spotted David and said, "David, will you give me a dollar for the trunk?"

David, without consulting with his business partners (Mom and Dad) immediately answered, "Yes!"

Sold was the response from the auctioneer.

Since I was the in-house furniture mover and truck driver I thought, *How in the heck am I going to get that thing to the flea market?* While I was contemplating how I was going to handle this delivery, Sara Belle and David followed the crowd inside. They proceeded to bid and buy several other items in the auction. We had a station wagon with just enough room from David's Amigo. No room for a six-foot long stream trunk! Puzzled, I had to use my limited powers of thinking. The solution was to take David and Sara Belle back to the flea market, then return for the trunk and the other priceless junk they had purchased. Loading up the station wagon using every space possible under the seats, on the seats and with things hanging out the windows, I headed back to the flea market.

Being a flea market vendor many times is like being a roaming gypsy. Once the trunk was placed on the floor in David's booth I went in search for Henrietta Moore, a friend and one of the vendors. I asked her what she thought would be a fair price for the trunk. She said she would try one hundred dollars.

"What?" I said in shock. "You've got to be kidding." She assured me she wasn't. She told me it was rare to find this kind of trunk in such good shape even though it looked like it had been through the war (Civil War!). We relied on Henrietta's knowledge. Within minutes the trunk was becoming more and more beautiful as we placed a price tag of one hundred dollars on it. In the afternoon of the same day we witnessed once again that miracles do really, really happen. A young, pleasant lady who looked like one of the flower children out of the sixties entered David's booth. She immediately was drawn to the trunk. After examining it, measuring it, and talking to David about just the right place she could use it in her house, she offered him ninety dollars. I was standing behind the lady straightening up David's booth. As soon as I heard her say ninety I caught David's attention and began to shake my head up and down so vigorously it's a wonder I didn't dislocate parts of my neck. Through mental telepathy I kept repeating, *Yes, yes, yes, yes*, until he finally got the message. Once the sale was completed, I got another vendor to help me transport the kind lady's purchase to her van. We walked carefully and handled the trunk with great care. My sole objective was to get that thing in her van safely and watch her drive off with it into the horizon. Mission completed. We learned again to be quiet and listen, to listen to our dear friend Henrietta whenever she quoted a price for any of our precious merchandise.

We continued to have many wonderful adventures at auctions. On one Saturday evening we were unfamiliar with the auctioneer but the auction was a large one with many potential flea market items on display. As the auction proceeded, the crowd of people surrounded David, separating us from him for a while. We could see him but could not get close to him without pushing people aside. David was holding court as the saying goes, talking with that person and another. They all knew David and kept him distracted from the auction as they talked. Meanwhile, we watched the auctioneer as he worked diligently acknowledging one bid after another on an old, broken wooden antique chair. As I listened to the bidding, $40.00, $42.50, $43.00, so on and on, I could not help but think, *What fool in his or her right mind would pay that much for that piece of antique trash needing so much repair?* Bids kept going, $69.00, $71.00, etc., etc., until it got to $80.00. Going once, going twice, sold to the gentleman in the wheelchair.

Who? I thought, as I looked around the room. Much to my chagrin I found out it was David who placed the winning bid. I thought, *How could he have done that?* He wasn't even bidding. I knew because I was keeping my eyes on him. Well, holy smoke, upon investigating, I soon found out what happened.

While David was socializing with his friends, he held the card with his auction number on it close to his chest *with the number facing outward.* To the auctioneer this meant David was still bidding against every other bid placed. We all learned another lesson in business that day. However, it's given us many laughs over the years. When we returned to the flea market with our extraordinary purchase, we asked several of the vendors what price we should place on it. The highest price any would quote was between $25.00 and $30.00.

"What do you mean?" I said jokingly, knowing the mistake we had made. "The auctioneer said we stole it for eighty dollars." To this day that chair remains in the Larmores' possession. Now for sentimental reasons alone it is worth well over a thousand dollars.

David was successful in out bidding two old men for a box lot. After the dust cleared we examined the content of the box. To our wonderful surprise we found utter enjoyment in sorting through what seemed like ten thousand old, rusty screws and bolts, washers, pieces of wire, rolls of rotten twine, and other such riches. They obviously had been hidden from mankind in the dark shadows of a barn for decades. What happened to this wooden box of jewels is anyone's guess. Perhaps it was shoplifted.

Even though he was not making much profit, he was learning how to manage money, the importance of establishing good credit, and most importantly how to deal with the public and relate to many sorts of personalities that entered his business. It truly was a joy and a blessing to us as we witnessed how many of his regular customers would pitch in and help David in the booth. They helped him by waiting on people, wrapping or bagging a purchase, giving change, or simply stopping by and chatting with him. Several times we would leave David while we ran errands. When we returned it was not unusual to find a friend or a customer straightening his booth or rearranging the items for better display.

Two of David's closest adult friends were Bob Caldwell and David Rogers. They were always by his side giving him much encouragement and support. Bob frequently told David he wanted him to be rich and famous someday. He would always correct that statement by saying, "You're already famous. Now we've got to make you rich." With Bob's help David incorporated his business, David's Venture. Ideally, in the future after my retirement, we did court the notion of eventually moving from the flea market and opening a small gift shop. Bob was a special friend to us as well as David. Both he and his wife, Penny, are two of our heroes.

Dave Rogers was a great friend and without question a true saint. He loved to tease David but always was there for him in his time of need. While David was in the flea market business Dave felt he needed to assist David in establishing credit for future needs. He had David borrow three hundred dollars from him. He set up a monthly payment of twenty dollars for David to pay down his debt. Both he and Bob visited David frequently during his hospital stays. Their goal was to keep his spirits high. They also participated in several of his high school senior year activities and his graduation parties.

WHY DOES THIS NOT SURPRISE US?

All God's angels come to us disguised.

—James Russell Howell

The magnitude of life is overwhelming. Angels are here to help us make it peace by peace.

—Levende Waters

We always felt God near us in our time of need. However, we tried not to overwork Him in the Larmore household. We did realize there were other individuals, families, and world crisis that also needed His attention. So with our blessings, we sent Him on His way knowing He was only a prayer away.

My position as Director of Elementary Education was most enjoyable and very rewarding 97 percent of the time. The other 3 percent challenged my self-control, twisted my personality, and taught me too much about human behavior I really could have survived without knowing. Fortunately, I was trained to teach, encourage, and guide children not to deal with all the insecurities, distrust, and childish jealousies of adults. Thank the Lord I did know I could clear my thoughts of anger and disbelief by moving away from the situation to a place where I could be quiet and listen.

After a Monday morning directors' meeting with our new superintendent, I needed an escape. I could not believe what

I was hearing coming out of the mouths of some of the more trusted and respected members of our school system. In this one meeting there was so much jealousy, gossiping, and backstabbing that I began to realize why the overall morale of the central office, and the school system as well, was beginning to deteriorate. One member was trying to out do the other to gain favor with the superintendent. My chief concern was to do my job the best I could without being influenced by the politics of the system. This was no easy task.

Shortly, after the meeting I found reason to leave the building to regain a sense of worth and direction for the rest of the day. I traveled to Bennett Middle School to observe the teaching of adults in our Continuing Education Program. This was always a rewarding and relaxing experience. The teachers were superb and the students were eager to learn. Following my visit, I walked across the campus to the student parking lot. It was a beautiful, balmy day; a day that encourages one to walk slowly taking in the beauty of the moment while being thankful for all the serenity God provides in nature. There was no one in sight, just a bird or two flying aimlessly above in the gentle breeze. Opening the car door, I slid into the seat, looked down to adjust the safety belt, and up to place the key in the ignition. Much to my surprise, standing in front of the car was a man. He looked to be in his late fifties or early sixties with a short white beard and wearing work clothing. He just stood there as if he wanted to talk. I felt somewhat puzzled as to where he came from so quickly and why he was on school property. I got out of the car to investigate.

"Hello, I'm Sheldon Larmore. Can I help you?" I said in a cautious manner.

"Yes, I know who you are. You're Toby's son. He is a mighty fine man."

Toby was the nickname for Talbot, my dad's name. He passed away in 1955.

"How do you know my dad?" I asked.

"He's okay. Your family is okay. Are you having a good day?"

"Not really. It could be better. But you know how it is. Some days are good, some days we can do without." I was feeling oddly comfortable conversing with this gentleman.

"Your days will be better. See you later," he said. "Have a good day."

Quickly settling into the car, I looked around and could not find any sign of the man I had just spoken to. There wasn't another soul in the parking lot. Where did he get to so fast? Again, focusing on the school full of students and a stranger in the parking lot, I got out of the car and looked in all directions. There was no sign of anyone. There was no noise of an automobile starting up. There was not one car moving anywhere on the lot. Slowly I drove off the parking lot, still looking in all directions. Nothing! By the time I got half way back to the office I received a shock wave to my brain cells. I thought, *What just happened!?* All I could think was there are a lot of unanswered questions that have surfaced in the last twenty to thirty minutes. I pulled off the side of the road and simply wrote down as much of the conversation I had had with the man. Something told me I needed to share this with Sara Belle.

After hearing about the strange incident and verbal exchange I had with the man, Sara Belle was as perplexed, yet as interested in the *whys* and *hows* of this happening as I was. Pausing in silence for a short time she shared, "Do you suppose he might have been an angel?"

"Get real, Sara Belle. Why would an angel be talking to me?" I said jokingly and then followed my response by saying, "Well, I guess I'm important enough for an angel to want to talk with me. Maybe he wanted some advice." We laughed this event off and commenced our evening chores. However, the more I tried to forget about the man the more I thought, *What if he really was an angel?*

Wednesday evening David left with friends to attend an event at school. Sara Belle and I left to attend a Bible study at St. Peters. It was a damp, chilly, and dark evening. As we pulled into the city parking lot we noticed there were only three or four other cars. No one was on the street or in the parking lot. As we opened our doors to get out of the car we both immediately noticed a gentleman standing beside it. Initially I was inwardly frightened and surely shocked. Obviously, my first thought was, *I've got to protect Sara Belle.* Then, my fear vanished, realizing it was the same man I met in the school parking lot on Monday. The man spoke softly, "Have your days been better since we had our talk?"

"Yes. Thank you." I turned to take a couple of steps toward the church as Sara Belle said, "That was your angel. Wasn't it?"

For the first time, I believed it truly could be. I excitedly responded with a resounding, "Yes. It is."

As we both turned around to say more to this "angel," there was nothing. Nothing anywhere is sight. No person anywhere on the street. No person in the parking lot. There were just four cars on the lot none of which were blocking the view of the area. Within seconds, five at the very most, the man had evaporated! Once in church neither of us could focus on the lesson at hand.

On Friday of the same week I left the office and started walking toward my car to visit one of the schools. I stopped dead in my tracks. Looking across the lot toward a clump of trees there stood the same man. He watched me as I took a few steps toward him and then somewhere, somehow he disappeared. I had a feeling, a feeling of calmness, a definite feeling of tranquility that just seemed to flow throughout my body. At that moment I knew I had been touched by powers greater then any I had experienced. I never questioned again. I never shared this experience with anyone except Sara Belle until recently.

Sunday morning we were on the highway returning home from church. As we stopped at a stoplight, a car pulled up beside us and started honking its horn. Sara Belle looked over and said,

SHELDON LARMORE

"You won't believe this but it's our angel." I looked and sure enough it was the same man. This time he simply rolled down his window and said, "See you later. Bye." Then he drove off, disappearing from sight. You may believe what you would like, but we know because we both lived this experience.

Another angel incident happened when Charlotte Hayman's mother was spending some time in Ocean City one summer. Since she and David were true buddies she wanted us to bring David over to have lunch with her. When we arrived at the restaurant where we were to meet, the crowd waiting to get in was packing the sidewalk. David attempted to move around them with his Amigo. As he did one of his wheels ran off the curb, causing his Amigo to turn over onto the highway. He fell from his Amigo onto the roadway with heavy traffic moving in both directions on a six-lane highway. Immediately across from the restaurant was a fire station. In seconds I reached David. He was surrounded by four firemen with an ambulance parked by the curb waiting in case it was needed. I had no idea how, in split seconds, four firemen and a large, easy-to-see noisy ambulance could arrive in an instant without me noticing the commotion. I asked one of the fireman how they got to us so quickly.

He replied, "We saw the situation developing and something told us to run to help."

David escaped with one small bruise and his Amigo suffered no damage. Angels? We think so. An act of God? We know so!

David truly believed in angels. Every time we drove through the city park there was a spot on the island where David always asked his mom if she could see the angels playing and dancing.

Sara Belle would always answer, "Yes." Then she might add, "David, do you see those two angels flying up into the trees?"

"Yes," David would say.

This conversation between them would continue until we passed the *spot of the angels*. The first couple of times I was with them I would strain my eyes to the point where they suffered blood-shot. *I didn't see any angels.* I thought, *You two are crazy. You are hallucinating!* Then as time went by I began to play their game. I pretended to see angels. On one rainy day I took David to volunteer at PRMC. As we passed by the spot in the park, I said, "David, I don't see any angels playing in the park today."

David replied, "I do. Rain doesn't bother angels. They can go or play anywhere in the rain or snow."

I had to wonder, *Does David really, actually see angels in the park? Could it be?*

With numerous experiences under our belts one would think we would understand that angels surround all of us. They are awesome beings who deserve our respect. We just have to be quiet and listen as they move about us. Angels give us many unexpected blessings. We don't have to be special to be helped by an angel. We just need a little bit of faith. John 20:29 says, "Blessed are they that have not seen, and yet have believed."

TIME TO REFRESH OUR FAITH

Faith is the person stepping out into the unknown, obeying God's commands.

—The Complete Book of Zingers

In January of David's junior year in high school, during one of David's periodic check-ups at A.I. DuPont, Dr. Jay discovered that the first scoliosis operation had not been successful. For some unknown reason the metal rod implants had become disconnected. His upper body was beginning to lean to the right. The fear was if we delayed a second operation or chose not to have it, one of the rods could puncture the lungs. Without hesitation, we urged Dr. Jay to schedule another scoliosis operation. Fortunately the surgery was scheduled within a month and everything went smoothly. David was back home and recovering well by the first of March.

It had been six months since our last visit with Dr. Crosby. At that time David's health had leveled out, and he seemed to be progressing fairly well. Dr. Crosby felt we should be okay to wait for six months before our next visit with him. Realizing this Sara Belle felt it was time for us to schedule another appointment with David's "godfather." She called Dr. Crosby's office and scheduled a visit for the end of March. Less than a week later, Sara Belle received a call from Dr. Crosby's office.

When she answered, the voice on the other end of the phone said, "Mrs. Larmore, I'm sorry to have to tell you Dr. Crosby passed away on Tuesday."

What a shock to hear this unexpected news. We were deeply saddened. It was as if we had suddenly lost a family member. We felt we had nowhere to turn. First it was Dr. Decker, and now Dr. Crosby. Up to this point David had not been seen by any local doctor except his pediatrician. Since his birth defects required the skills and knowledge of doctors specifically trained in a given area of expertise, we had to travel to the metropolitan areas. However, God had a plan, and He had already put it into effect. We just had to be quiet, listen and understand what He had arranged for us.

As a result of Dr. Decker's death, Dr. Crosby transferred us to A. I. DuPont Hospital for David's hip surgery. While there, Dr. Jay introduced us to a neurosurgeon and a urologist. Even though not a Dr. Crosby, the neurosurgeon did meet with us on our next visit with Dr. Jay. He was pleasant and assured us he would be glad to accept David as one of his patients. This did provide us with security, but fortunately, we never had a need to use his services.

The spring of this same year Sara Belle and I were invited by our church to be candidates on a weekend retreat to be held in Clayton, Delaware. We had absolutely no idea about the retreat, what to expect, who was going to be there, or if we were going to be the only ones from St. Peter's Episcopal Church congregation attending. What we gained from members of the church who had attended previously was sketchy to say the least. We did find out the weekend was called *Cursillo*. Whenever we asked for an agenda of the weekend, we were told it was not easy to explain *Cursillo* because behind the mystery was God. We were told no one could fully explain how God touched each person in His special and unique way through the various elements of the *Cursillo* movement. All those we asked about the weekend described it in the same vague mysterious way. Their united advice was, "Go! Have Faith! It will be the best dose of heavenly medicine you will ever have prescribed."

I must admit Sara Belle's faith and trust, like David's, has always been stronger than mine. I never have been keen on unknown challenges. My weekends were precious to me. I couldn't see spending them sitting in all-day meetings, listening to what I thought would be lectures on the Bible, salvation, or the wages of sin. Sara Belle really wanted to go on the retreat. I most definitely did not want to go! However, I didn't want to ruin the enthusiasm she was developing every time she talked about or heard someone else talk about the excitement of this planned weekend. She made plans for our "other children," Dan and Michele Harris, to spend the weekend with David. We felt comfortable with this arrangement since David always enjoyed being around them and accepted them as his brother and sister. I kept thinking of all kinds of excuses for not attending. Short of me jumping off the Brooklyn Bridge, I could not come up with a viable reason. I knew when the day arrived for us to go I would have to dig my heels in the dirt and throw a temper tantrum.

On Monday, three days before we were to leave for what I expected would be that dreadful weekend, David came home from school with a fever of 102 degrees. I really felt sorry for him but I felt an excuse surfacing for not going to Cursillo.

Sara Belle placed a call to David's pediatrician. She was told he would be out of the office until Thursday. With David's medical history and knowing of his recent Scoliosis operation they suggested we contact Dr. Jay at A.I. DuPont. As a result Dr. Jay wanted to see him the next morning. After a thorough examination including X-rays of his back and urine and blood tests, it was determined David was suffering from a severe bladder infection. Dr. Jay admitted him in the hospital stating it would take several days for the antibiotics to kick in.

Outwardly, as usual, David seemed to be okay and was accepting the fact he would have to stay in the hospital for a few days. It sure was a relief for us knowing it was not anything more serious. All I could think of was, *Praise the Lord! He has provided me with a legitimate reason for not going on that weekend retreat.*

As I was silently rejoicing in this turn of events I heard David speak some discouraging words, "I still want both of you to go this weekend."

Hardly letting him finish his statement I said, "David, how about I stay with you and we'll let Mom go."

"No, I want both of you to go. I'll be okay," he replied.

"We'll get Dan and Michele to visit you this weekend," Sara Belle said.

Trying to curb these new plans as quickly as they seemed to be developing I said, "Since they don't have to stay with David this weekend they probably have made other plans." Besides that means they will have to travel two hours from home to Wilmington and two hours back."

"Well, we'll see," Sara Belle said.

The long and short of it I was doomed to spend the weekend in total desolation. Poor me! When we left David at the hospital that evening he was smiling. I was selfishly sad. When Sara Belle talked with David by phone four or five times before we departed for the weekend, she was happy and relieved he was in good spirits and improving nicely. I was very happy about David's improvement but distressing over the coming weekend. Up to the very moment Father Harry Johnson and his wife, Hope, arrived at our house to drive us to Clayton, I was still hoping for a reprieve. It didn't happen! We were off! When we reached Clayton, we stopped for dinner. Before leaving the restaurant Sara Belle called the hospital to talk with David.

He was fine and said, "Don't worry about me. I want you guys to have a great weekend. I'm okay. I just talked with Dan and

Michele. They're coming up on Saturday to spend the day with me. Have fun. See you when I get home."

Just hearing his voice made us realize just how mature and loving he was. We learned once again to just, be quiet, relax, and listen—listen to our son who seemed to have more wisdom then we did about the weekend.

God does work in mysterious ways. After fifteen minutes at Clayton for the start of our Cursillo weekend, we were totally involved. The Holy Spirit was present all over, in the hallways, in the meeting rooms, outside, and most importantly in the hearts of all present. After thirty minutes, unbelievably, a team of wild horses could not drag us away. The events of the past week all came into focus. We were destined to be candidates on this Cursillo weekend. Yet again it was not a coincidence but a God-incidence that David developed a fever *before* we left for the weekend instead of during the weekend. It was also a God-incident that Dr. Jay admitted David into the hospital for treatment and safe keeping while we were parted from him. God did not help me by changing the circumstances of the week, but, by golly, He sure had plans to change me. And He did!

Every moment of the weekend was like being in heaven. Peace surrounded our very being with new Christian friendships constantly evolving. There was nothing dull about this weekend. It was a joyous workshop in the fundamentals of our faith where everyone learned by experiencing a living community. It truly was an encounter with Jesus Christ. What a gift to us from our church community! Cursillo and other weekend retreats such as Walk to Emmaus help Christians link together in a spiritually-satisfying program that guides them in supporting others in their attempts to remain Christ-centered. It certainly helped us to renew and deepen our Christian commitment.

On Sunday morning we were involved in our group session activities when someone entered the room asking for Sheldon or Sara Belle Larmore. There was a phone call for us in the main building. This alarmed us since outside calls were not permitted during the weekend except in cases of emergency. Secondly, to our knowledge the only ones having the number of the mission facility was A. I. DuPont hospital. We hurriedly followed the gentleman across the field to the main building. Taking a deep breath while saying a silent prayer, Sara Belle answered the phone.

She heard on the other end, "David is ready to be released today. Mr. and Mrs. Harris are here and will take David home. We just have to have your permission to release him to them."

"That's fine. Thanks for calling. Tell David we will meet him home," Sara Belle said with great excitement in her voice. Was this another God-incidence? We know so! This proves again God has no problems; He has only solutions if we believe in Him.

After our weekend we served as members of the team on two other Cursillo weekends. David became almost as involved in the weekends as we were. He was pleased to be a candidate on the last Cursillo weekend sponsored by the Diocese of Easton, our church's ruling body. He was excited as his mother was about attending the weekend even though, through association with us and by attending several of the meeting, he knew basically what to expect. Even though he knew what was going to happen each day of the retreat he never gave it away to the other participants. As I watched his reactions I thought, *You little actor. You act as surprised as everyone else.*

SENIOR HIGH SCHOOL LIFE IS MAGICAL

When I use the faith I have, God not only answers but goes an extra step and gives things I could only imagine.

—Unknown

"God will take care of what you go through; you need to take care of how you go through it." This statement so much describes how David approached his senior high school experiences. He loved all parts of his school life. The more involved he was the happier he was. Out of a class of over 250 students, the senior class selected two of their members as Sensational Seniors. They were Amy Jen, a friend of David's, and David. David, Sara Belle, and I were most humbled again by this wonderful and meaningful honor given to David and his friend Amy Jen by their classmates.

The following descriptions of Amy and David are taken from the pages of their 1989 senior yearbook:

> Amy Jen: "In addition to having Junior and Senior Class President, Valedictorian, Honor Society Treasurer, and co-editor of the school newspaper under her belt, Amy Jen is also known as 'Miss Teen of Maryland.' On August 15, at the Annapolis Ramada Inn, Amy was crowned among twelve semifinalists based on an interview, scholastic

achievement, general awareness, and poise and appearance. She received a $1000 scholarship to the college of her choice. Amy will be attending Stanford University in the fall."

David Jefferson Larmore: "When David Larmore won 'Most Spirited' for the Senior Superlatives, no one was surprised. David has been a sensational senior and an outstanding young man in the community. Inspired by a grandfather who had owned an antique business, and encouraged by Joan Devaney, one of his teachers, David opened up a space in a local flea market. His business, 'David's Venture,' flourished, and when David went to the National DECA competition in Orlando, Florida, he placed in the top fourteen in General Merchandising nationwide. David has also won other awards, but the one that means most to him is the Lana K. Reinhart Memorial Award given to a senior who has triumphed over hardships."

We feel so blessed God shined his light on David. Our family has struggled over the years due to the ever present financial needs we had to address in providing the very best for David. God saw to it we always got by and never really suffered because of not being able to do many things other families did. Over the years we became masters at robbing Peter to pay Paul. However, if it had not been for my family and several close friends we may have taken on water and sunk a little deeper in debt. In retrospect, we realize that knowing God as we do simply makes us more humble. By the same token knowing ourselves and our limitations without God keeps us humble. Thanks be to God!

I can't begin to discuss all the exciting and wonderful happenings David experienced during his senior high school years. We were truly amazed when, with the help of Joan Devaney and his other teachers, David made the honor roll each marking period except one during his junior and senior years in school.

David was an enthusiastic member of DECA, Distributive Education Clubs of America. Under the guidance and leadership of one of his teachers, Mr. Bob Koontz, he participated in the state level competitions during his junior and senior years in school. Both years he won first place in his area of competition and traveled to the national convention to compete with other students representing all fifty states. During his junior year, the national convention was held in Salt Lake City, Utah. To our pleasant surprise, much of this expense was financed by the Maryland State Police Association, which was initiated by his Uncle Sonny Hayman. At the time he was second in command in the State of Maryland. One evening Richard Tyler, a member of the local state police barracks, delivered David a check for a very tidy sum. As the result of this visit, Richard and his wife, Karyl, became close friends of ours. David thought Richard was the tops. On occasion, Richard would pick David up and take him to meetings at the Tri-County Lodge of the Maryland State Troopers for a night out with the men!

The National Convention of DECA was held in Orlando, Florida, the spring of David's senior year. He placed fourteenth nationally in his division. He thoroughly enjoyed his time at the convention with over eight thousand other students from across the country. The secretaries and staff from my office in the Wicomico County Board of Education provided for a large portion of these expenses. For this wonderful act of kindness we were most appreciative and very humbled.

Overall, David did not miss out on many of his class's activities. He attended all the bonfire pep rallies, most all of the home football games, many of the home basketball games, and several of the school's dances. When it was time for his senior prom we were afraid he would not be able to find someone to attend with him. Even though he had many, many friends, finding a girl who would go to the expense of buying a gown and attending a prom with a partner in a three-wheeled Amigo who could not dance seemed unlikely. Without him knowing, we fretted and prayed about this many times. We did not broadcast our concerns with others, but we really wanted his senior year to be all it could be.

Many nights after David went to bed we would sit and reflect on the day and thank God for all of the goodness and love He had showered on our family over the years. One night we really spent thinking about how we could approach David about his up and coming senior prom, especially if he was unable to find a date. I will always remember that night as another one of those special evenings we felt particularly close to God. Sara Belle had attended a Bible study earlier in the day. She reminded me of a proverb we both had heard many times, "Give your troubles to God for He is going to be up all night anyway."

As we prayed that night before going to bed, we did just that! We gave Him our concerns about David and the prom. The following week Sherri Koontz, Bob and Barb Koontz's daughter, called David. She offered to go to the prom with him. Another prayer answered! They did the whole bit: dinner before the prom, dancing at the prom with Sherri and others moving David in his Amigo around the room to the rhythm of the music. Afterward, they attended the after prom party for breakfast.

David's graduation was a *major, major* event in our household! We can't help but remember those fateful first days after David's birth. We can still hear precisely the words spoken by one of the physicians at the nurses' station, "Expect nothing and appreciate anything. If it was me I would institutionalize him. My advice is don't bond with him." Many, many times since that day we have thanked God for loaning David to us to nurture and raise into a very caring, loving, and responsible Christian.

The Sunday afternoon before David's Tuesday evening graduation ceremony we gave him (and us) an open house graduation party. We were blessed to have several of our friends offer to help with the decorations, prepare the food, and clean up afterward. When one friend asked about how many were invited, so she could estimate how much food to prepare, Sara Belle cheerfully replied with a big smile on her face, "A little over four hundred."

"A little…a little *over* four hundred! Honey, where are you going to put all of them?"

Sara Belle said without skipping a beat, "Oh, we'll find a place. Remember it's an open house. Hopefully they all won't come at the same time."

At the peak hours of the open house, 2:00 p.m. to 4:00 p.m., our house and backyard were wall to wall full of people. The streets immediately around our house were one big traffic jam. While David was with us, we always enjoyed having anniversary and birthday parties as well as wedding rehearsals and reception parties for our friends and relatives. But this…this was the party of all parties. David's last guests, mostly friends from his flea market, left just before eleven. Afterward, we were exuberantly and gratifyingly exhausted.

The night of David's graduation was most definitely another milestone in his life. He led the other 250 graduates through the aisles of the Wicomico County Youth and Civic Center to their seats in front of the auditorium. The moment they called David's name to receive his diploma was the moment Sara Belle and I could not hold back the flow of tears any longer. Words will never be enough to describe our overwhelming joy. David never gave up. He always accepted a challenge and worked diligently to complete it successfully. For a graduation gift, Bob Caldwell gave David a caricature of David sitting on the engine of a little train climbing the mountainside. Written on the caricature was, "The little train that could…and did!" That says it all.

THE QUIET TIME
BEFORE THE RAGING
FLOOD OF LIFE
BEGINS AGAIN

It's a beautiful life when family happiness is homemade.

hortly after graduation, David purchased a computer with profits from his flea market business. The week of my retirement in 1990, David, at his request, returned to Camp Fairlee Manor for a week's computer training course. With David at camp, Sara Belle and I decided to spend three days at the beach, to relax and celebrate my retirement. The first evening we strolled down the boardwalk. All of the sudden something went *splash,* all over the front of my nice clean blue shirt. Just about the time I started to look down to investigate something else went, *Splash! Splash!* on the top of my head. On my first night out as a free AARP member I had been knighted by a creature of Mother Nature. A flock of one hundred or so (a mild exaggeration) sea gulls had enthusiastically welcomed me to Rehoboth Beach.

Four days after our mini vacation we arrived home. That afternoon I went to the attic to survey what thirty-three years of neglect had caused. In my excitement of seeing all the treasures we had stockpiled, I took one step too many backward. Within moments, my right leg to the hip was hanging from the ceiling in our newly painted and wallpapered bedroom. This venture resulted in a contusion of the knee. We left the emergency room that evening with my leg in a removal cast. When we got to the car, I just stood and looked.

"What's wrong?" Sara Belle asked.

"What do you think? Look at me. How am I going to get in the car? I can't bend my leg."

After ten minutes or so we finally figured a way to get home. I opened the back door of the car, worked my way onto the seat, legs first. Then I raised my right leg high above the front seat on the riders' side. Boy, I was finally in. But there was still a problem. The back door would not shut because my head was in the way. So I maneuvered myself so my head hung down toward the floor with my right leg high above the front seat headrest. In other words, I traveled home upside down. Welcome to retirement! I pondered if it might be safer to go back to work.

After a month or so, things began to settle in around the Larmore household. Sara Belle and I thoroughly enjoyed our time together. There was no need to worry. Sara Belle's home pocketbook business was showing potential of developing into a profitable family enterprise. David was happy knowing his business was becoming a little more profitable. What the heck! I was becoming the *kept man*.

About this time the building that housed the Salisbury Flea Market was sold and transformed into the Country House. As a result David accompanied two other vendors, Henrietta Moore and Bernice Smith, to a building in Delmar. After the unexpected death of Bernice Smith, Henrietta moved her business back to Salisbury. She was kind enough to ask David if he wanted to join her, but David decided to take a break from his flea market venture. He wanted to explore other avenues of the business world that would provide him with benefits. His major concern was what to do with his inventory that had grown to the size of a small retail store. Fortunately, his Aunt Faye and Uncle Lee owned a storage warehouse. They had two open storage areas they insisted David use to store his items without cost until he made a decision about what he wanted to do. The storage bins rented for thirty dollars each per month in 1990. His inventory is still stored in the bins some twenty-two years later. That means his aunt and uncle have donated well over $16,000 just for the storage of David's inventory. This remains a true act of kindness and love.

With this turn of events I thought, *Oh well! There goes a chance for the family to rise out of major financial poverty*. Still, we can easily supplement my retirement with Sara Belle's business, I told myself. No problem! Just relax! Well, a week after Christmas Sara Belle got a notice that the Faye Swafford Pocketbook company was stopping production of their pocketbook line of business immediately. The letter to its seven hundred or so distributors explicitly (without reason) stated, "As of this date we will not accept party orders for any merchandise."

My well-planned retirement was going so well! Both of the family business conglomerates went bankrupt so to speak. Through all of this we were still having fun. We often said in a joking manner, "If worse comes to worse we could always apply to be a family of greeters at Walmart." Most of the greeters we'd met were retired, happy, and very nice people to know.

In the spring we decided it was time to take a long, long, long overdue family vacation.

Late April of 1991, we started our trip northward. Our goal was to reach the New England states. From there we would take inventory of our diminishing bankroll. Based on those findings we would either start back home, travel farther north, or find a job for a few days to finance our safe return to the eastern shore. We wanted to take the Cape May ferry across to New Jersey then travel north. However, the cost of the ferry ride was not in our travel budget. We were careful with our money, eating breakfast and lunch at fast food restaurants. Dinners were at upscale restaurants such as Denny's, IHOP, or Bob Evans. Our nights were spent off the tourist route in mom-and-pop motels or other places that looked cheap and clean. We had no idea about where we were going. We just decided to go. We employed God as our co-pilot.

He guided us one evening into Mystic Seaport, Massachusetts. To us, this was just another overnight stay. Our first goal was to find a motel. From one street to another from one avenue to another we looked and looked. All of the motels, hotels, and even a few shacks had posted, "No Vacancies." Finally, I spotted a vacancy sign. The entrance was beautifully landscaped. The lawn looked like it had been manicured by the hands of heavenly angels. Standing by the desk I asked the clerk if he had a room available. He stated he had two rooms left, each with two queen size beds for $115.00—which was significantly more than even the best rooms in those days.

"Sir, would that be cash or credit card?"

I thought, *You've got to be kidding. Our whole trip thus far for two days of travel, motels and eating had cost us a little over a whopping $150.00.*

Weak and tired from travel, and knowing we had seriously searched for a room over an hour, I pulled out my credit card. I handed it to the gentleman behind the desk nonchalantly; I wanted to play the role. My male ego insisted I live in the moment of the wealthy. Afterward, I knew Sara Belle was going to crown me when she found out how much I paid for the privilege of letting David and her sleep in this castle for one night.

Surprisingly her comment was, "Oh well, we have to stay somewhere tonight."

From that point on it went downhill. Pulling out and laying down our credit card was done with caution at first. However, the frequency in using credit cards increased gradually. We were having the time of our lives. It's amazing what plastic money can buy. Our first plastic purchase after the motel was a couple of overnights in Hyannis Port, Massachusetts, where we met one of Robert Kennedy's sons on the street.

One of the highlights of our trip was a two-day stay in Bar Harbor, Maine. We were encouraged by the hotel desk clerk to go to Cadillac Mountain in the Acadia National Park to see the sunset. What a breathtaking experience that was! Standing on top of the tallest mountain on the east coast of North America watching a brilliant sun sinking into the horizon was beyond human expression. Hundreds of tourists and locals stood watching the sun as it descended slowly, picking up speed the closer it got to the horizon. In moments it disappeared into total darkness. Immediately, there was a spontaneous outburst of applause from the hundreds of people around us. This demonstration of the power of God still brings chills to our souls and tears of joy to our hearts. In retrospect, it was well worth the money we had to squeeze out of our monthly budget to repay Wilmington Trust Bank.

TOUCHED BY THE CARE AND LOVE OF OTHERS

Give oneself to other people, one way or another, is one of the greatest joys of living. Nothing we get or take equals the joy of giving. How unfortunate so many people never discover it. We each must do our part, and give as long as we are able—while we have something to give.

—*Albert Loden*

By the middle of August 1991, it was time for the Larmores to settle down and plan for their future. David was missing the flea market business, I was missing the daily routine of work, and Sara Belle, bless her heart, would miss both of us if we abruptly returned full time to work. We pondered our options for sometime. Even though we were surviving okay we could see some of our meager savings were beginning to dribble off into the sunset. An urgent problem was beginning to surface as we realized our old station wagon was in need of serious work to keep it running. We had already replaced the transmission six months earlier. We just couldn't see sinking more money into a ten-year-old car.

God and our guardian angels were watching after us. Four amazing things happened within two weeks without any kind of initiation from us. A very dear friend of the family for many years dropped by the house one day and gave us a sizable check to purchase a van capable of handling a heavy automatic lift. We were, to say the least, knocked off our feet. She said she just wanted to do whatever she could to make our lives and David's as pleasant and comfortable as possible. How could anyone see this any differently than having an angel directed from heaven visit with us? Next, the board of education called me unexpectedly. They asked if I would be interested in a full-time substitute job for an assistant principal who would be out on an extended medical leave.

Knowing I was going to be working with my friend Barbara Stephens, principal at East Salisbury, I immediately said yes. The money was good. The pleasure of working with Barbara and her faculty was beyond words. I finished the second half of the year filling in for an assistant principal at Pinehurst. This also was a pleasant experience since I was working with my friend Joana Donovan and her very capable staff and faculty. The third surprise came when the Gospel Shop in Salisbury contacted Sara Belle asking her if she would be interested in a part-time job in their store. She gave it a try one weekend and stayed for several years afterward. In fact, David and I felt so much a part of the "gang" we were in and out of the store almost as much as she was. The fourth amazing thing to happen changed our lives forever. We were encouraged to contact Peninsula Regional Medical Center, our local hospital, to ask about the possibility of David volunteering at some level.

The local hospital had a growing and active volunteer program but had never had a handicapped volunteer in its services. Sara Belle knew David wanted to go back into the flea market business or find a paying job. She also knew she was not going to be happy with him sitting around home waiting for a job to pop up. After talking to David about checking on opportunities the volunteer services department might offer him, David very reluctantly agreed to go for an interview. The day of the interview David and Sara Belle met with Barbara Sturgis, manager of volunteer services. She went out of her way to make Sara Belle and David feel comfortable.

Shortly into the interview Mrs. Sturgis asked David, "Honey, why do you want to volunteer here at the hospital?"

David answered as truthfully as he could without hesitation, "I don't. My mom wants me to."

Surprised, but with a chuckle, Mrs. Sturgis replied, "David, I think we can use you. Why don't you give us a try?"

As the interview continued, Mrs. Sturgis explained the program. She shared that the hospital had never used a handicapped individual, but she was willing to give David a chance if he was willing. She placed David in the Materials Management department under the supervision of Claudia Hayward and assigned one of the seasoned volunteers, A. J. Forget, to train him. He was a wonderful and special person who cared and watched over David as if he was one of his own.

Before the interview was over Mrs. Sturgis insisted she be called Barb. She and her husband, Paul, became part of our family and have remained close ever since that initial meeting. David's acceptance as a volunteer is history. He fell in love with the hospital and everyone in it. What he gained from his association with the employees and the administrative personnel of PRMC, he treasured for the rest of his life. We, as parents, will always remember the many kindnesses and friendships that were showered upon him. We will never forget Barb and her willingness to take time out from her lunch break each noontime to catheterize David. Her care and love for David will never be forgotten.

One of the rewards David received from his association with the hospital came from the many wonderful people he met. He had a great desire to help them in times of their need. Many times he would stop by a patient's room to check on how they were doing or to see if they needed anything. A. J. Forget encouraged him to carry pieces of candy in his pockets to share with the nurses and staff. Before long we had to rig up a bucket to his Amigo to carry around his candy. Our family food budget increased by 10 percent. This increase was just to keep him in supply of candy to share with staff, patients, and visitors to the hospital. He became known affectionately as the candy man. It was obvious to many his real love was helping someone for Jesus's sake who could not, because of their illness or situation, return the favor. David was fortunate to be touched by so many. Each touch nurtured his compassion for others.

Nine months after he began to volunteer he spent the weekend at an antique show at the Civic Center with his idol, Joan Devaney. Sunday evening during dinner Sara Belle noticed David was having a difficult time breathing. She asked him if he was okay and, of course, he said he was fine. The more we watched him the more labored his breathing became.

Sara Belle left the dinner table, went to David's room, got his coat and hat and said,

"We are going to the emergency room."

She reacted so quickly, yet so calmly, I didn't even have time to chew my mouthful of food I had started to eat before she got up from the table and returned. Sara Belle *always* took good care of me. However, when it came to David, it was like we had a full-time physician living in the house.

After David was examined, he was promptly admitted in the hospital with bacterial pneumonia. This was a new illness for David. His condition was described as serious, but this form of pneumonia could be treated with antibiotics. Once David was settled in a private room he encouraged us to go home and get some rest. He would be okay. Early the next morning we called the hospital to check on his condition.

His nurse's response was, "He rested over night but still is having difficulty breathing. The doctor has ordered a low level of oxygen to ease the stress."

I went to work, and Sara Belle went to the hospital. I talked with Sara Belle and David a couple of times by phone that morning. I was relieved that things seemed to remain stable. Early that afternoon Sara Belle called my office in tears. It was really difficult to understand what she was saying but I knew it was not good. She finally was able to tell me the doctor did not think David was going to make it. They had rushed him to intensive care. I raced to the hospital. Sara Belle was in the ICU waiting room with Doris Hammond and four or five other hospital employees. They had come to the waiting room to comfort Sara Belle after hearing about David. We had to wait for the doctor and a team of nurses to stabilize David before we could see him. In the meantime, the waiting room filled with friends and other staff members as the word circulated about the hospital. We were overwhelmed and blessed to see so many of the teachers and other staff members from Pinehurst and East Salisbury Schools join us in the waiting room. What a wonderful tribute to David to have so many praying for his recovery.

Once we were able to see David lying in bed so weak and helpless we couldn't help but relive our many past experiences with him on life support. We were told he was stable. That's all the information the staff felt they could share with us at the time. Many of our friends stayed with us through the early evening. We did not leave until after the 10:30 p.m. visiting hour with intensive care patients.

The next morning we arrived in the intensive care waiting room just before the scheduled 6:00 a.m. visiting hour. As we turned the hall leading to the waiting room we saw Dr. Cockey standing at the door waiting for our arrival. Not wanting to hear what we knew we were about to hear, we asked how David was.

"I've been waiting for you. We are doing all we can. We are at a loss as to what to do next," Dr. Cockey said.

"Should we call family?" Sara Belle asked.

"Yes."

"Can we see him?" I asked.

"Give us time to prepare him for the day. Someone will come out to get you."

Once again we fell into the depths of fear and desperation. We felt a great wave of loneliness wash over us. As we sat with arms around each other, we sensed the spirit of the one we loved more than life slipping away from us. Throughout our married life, Sara Belle has always been my strength, my rock of Gibraltor. She was the one who said we needed to pray. She was the one who took hold of my hand and softly whispered a prayer for David's healing. A peace seemed to surround us. It was as if someone or something was reminding us we are never alone when we are alone with Jesus.

Soon the waiting room was filled with family members and friends, each in his or her own way giving us support, love, and comfort. Father David Tontonoz, our Episcopal priest, gathered those present and raised David up in prayer. A nurse entered the waiting room and led Sara Belle, Father David, and me through the intensive care unit to David's bed. Shock! The reality of death struck hard. David lay in his bed swollen two and a half times his size. His eyes were wide open covered by a glassy film. Tubes and machines of all types and sizes were once again connected to his body. Father David prayed over our David and then prayed with us as we stood helpless at his bedside. When we left his room we were sure death was imminent. Those gathered in the waiting room stood in silence as we entered. There was little or no exchange of words, just tight, lingering hugs dampened by tears. Father David left to attend to other businesses of the church.

During this time of waiting, Dr. Kel Nagel, David's pulmonary physician, entered the room with Dan Akin, President of the Hospital. Mr. Akin made a special point to have Dr. Nagel introduce him to us. He stated he had been so impressed by David and his dedication to the hospital he wanted to meet his parents. In our conversation he shared, "The hospital switchboard had been inundated with calls from people in the community asking about

David. One of the ladies who has been on the switchboard for some time said she can't remember of anybody who has gotten more phone calls regarding their condition."

Moments later, one of the Catholic priests, hearing about David during one of his patient visits, entered the room. After receiving a report on David's condition he asked if he could offer a prayer. His prayer was so comforting and reassuring. There was no doubt God was in our midst. Several of our friends had to return to work by midday. However, shortly after noon Beverly Porteus, assistant priest at St. Peters, arrived. She instantly gave both of us a hug. She, too, prayed with us and for others in the room. Soon after, one of the respiratory therapists and close friend of David's, Kathy Monteleone, stopped by to check on us. She generously offered her help in anyway we could use her.

The 2:00 p.m. visiting hour for ICU finally arrived. When we entered David's room we were emotionally overcome by what greeted us. David was conscious, his swelling was beginning to subside, and he seemed to acknowledge our presence. *Praise God to the highest.* Prayers answered. A miracle created by His grace. We stayed in the hospital waiting room all day and through the evening hours. We did not feel comfortable leaving until we visited with David during the last scheduled visiting time from 10:30 to 11:00 p.m. Without exception, Bob Caldwell, a close friend of ours and one of David's mentors, met us in the ICU waiting room each night about nine, and remained with us until after the ten thirty visit. Bob was always there when we needed him!

During the next three to four days David's health steadily improved. Since he was still having some residual difficulties breathing it was decided David needed a temporary tracheotomy as one of the first steps toward releasing him from the hospital. With this procedure successfully in place, David was transferred out of ICU within a week to a regular room on the fifth floor. We had planned to spend nights with him until his release. However, our friends, Doris Hammond and Virginia Layfield were adamant that we needed our rest in preparation for David's return home. Before we realized what was happening they both shared the cost of a sitter for two nights or longer if we needed it. This true act of kindness and love gave us a chance to catch up on our rest without worrying about David's well being. After two days out of ICU, David's doctors decided he had progressed well enough to be discharged. We brought David home with a trac, another new experience. It was imperative we clean it several times daily and keep it as sterile as possible.

The first night home David finally settled down for bed late in the evening. Since birth David could only void his urine by manual pressure we placed on his bladder or by the use of a catheter. Back then our insurance company would only pay for four catheters a month. This necessitated boiling them after each use. Late that night we placed the four catheters on the stove to boil. We immediately fell across the bed and accidently fell asleep. We woke in a start with smoke burning our nostrils. Realizing what we had done we rushed to the kitchen. We were greeted with an overwhelming smell of burnt rubber and a black sooty haze seeping throughout the house. Immediately, quick-thinking Sara Belle ran to David's room. Finding him sleeping peacefully, she shut his door and put a towel on the floor to cover the crack between it and the bottom of the door.

Until the wee hours of the morning we removed shelf after shelf of dishes, canned goods, pots and pans, and washed them and placed them outside on our screened porch. There was no clean place in the kitchen area. Early in the morning Sara Belle called Faye, my sister, and asked if she could come down from Laurel, Delaware to help us get things back in order. Without hesitation, she was at our house within the hour. Working well into the evening hours we finally completed the task. David enjoyed the attention he was getting from his Aunt Faye. She made sure he was served his meals in his room always with some added treats. Ever so often she would go to his room to chat with him or watch whatever cartoon show he had on.

To help David's (aging and forgetful) parents through the next three or four nights, Kathy, the respiratory therapist and friend of David's, volunteered to watch over him at nights. We jumped quickly at this offer. After work each night she slept on the floor next to David's bed. Whenever, he had to be suctioned, take medicine, be turned over in bed, or had some other need, he would wake her up by throwing or dropping a soft, stuffed teddy bear on her head. At least this provided employment for an otherwise useless stuffed piece of cloth.

ACCEPTING LIFE AS A RAY OF SUNSHINE

Those who bring sunshine to the lives of others cannot keep it from themselves.

—*James M. Barrie*

*L*ife is good! Life is even better when we stay focused on our dreams and the blessings showered upon us from above. I'm sure there are many times all of us feel as if we are constantly living in the thunderstorms of life. But remember what this book title tells us: *Be Quiet.* Be still, rest in silence and reflect on the good things that have been placed in your life. *Listen.* After David recovered from his serious bout with pneumonia he was once again ready to face the challenges of the world. His volunteer career at PRMC continued to be the center of his existence. He felt totally responsible to be on duty at the hospital eight hours a day, five days a week. As he told us once when we felt he needed to take some time for himself, "I have committed myself to volunteer and they expect me there." On three occasions he asked to volunteer on the four to midnight shift. Even though this meant we had to stay awake to pick him up from work, we gladly did this because we respected his sense of responsibility at the hospital. If the real truth be known, we think the reason for this desire to work the four o'clock shift resulted from one of his nurse *girlfriends* being assigned to these nights.

One thing David used to relax at home with was his computer. It served as a source of information about his sports teams and an outlet for playing games. He and his mother took three or four mini evening courses together to learn basic computer skills. One time he asked me if I would take a course with him.

The first boys' night out with my son in the computer class went relatively well. The second lesson began to slip into the mud. The female instructor was a thirty-something, six-foot cement statue with the personality of a steel goal post. She talked and walked like an automated machine. The first time I didn't understand what she was saying I asked if she could explain it further. She explained! She explicitly read exactly each word for word *again* from her notes. The explanation I received was the same information I didn't understand in the first place. The class continued. *She continued.* She continued to read from her notes without stopping or looking up until she finished each segment of her manuscript.

Another class member asked a question. She *again* responded the same way. She explicitly read word for word from her notes. Believe me, each time a class member asked her for clarification she would literally reread from her notes. What an amazing teacher!

Well the worst insult of the class was still to come. The third night the instructor gave directions on how to obtain a given screen. Everyone in the class including David had the same image projected on the screen, except *me*. I would lean over and ask David for help. He willingly showed me what to do. The next time directions were given everyone had the same screen projected their computer but *me!* I would lean over begging David to help me again. The third time the same thing happened. David helped.

The fourth time it happened David just looked at me and said in his fatherly voice, "Dad, just sit and listen. I can't follow the teacher for helping you. I'll teach you when we get home, okay?"

Well! I considered myself told. I sat, I kept my mouth shut, and I listened during the rest of class. The truth of the matter was

David learned very quickly many skills in using his computer. He was a godsend to me many times when I had to use the computer daily while I taught at the university.

Most of us have one or more hobbies we enjoy as an outlet for our energy and/or talents. David had one major hobby that he thoroughly enjoyed. He was totally absorbed in watching, listening to, or reading about any kind of sports. David had the opportunity to attend four or five Redskins home games. One of the most memorable times was a PRMC sponsored bus trip with a nurse friend, Marsha Hopkins. She made sure David did not miss a thing the whole evening. She even made it possible for him to meet the Hogs!

On one occasion in mid July Sara Belle and I took David on another PRMC sponsored bus trip to see an afternoon Orioles game in the new Camden Yards stadium. What an adventure! We left Salisbury at nine with the temperature registering a little over eighty-five degrees. By the time we arrived at the stadium there already appeared to be a massive crowd of what seemed like three million people. Being unfamiliar with the layout of the stadium it was no easy task finding our way to our assigned seats. Once we were on the first level of our section we asked an usher for help in pointing us in the right direction to our seats. Seeing that David was in his Amigo he instructed us to go back out where the elevators were located. By this time we had been on the premises of the stadium a good thirty to forty minutes and still had not found our seats.

Picture this: Have you ever tried to go out an entrance way with three million people trying to go in at the same time? Well, without breaking an arm or leg or losing our sense of respect for others, we finally reached the third level. By this time a good hour had transpired since we stepped our first foot on the sacred grounds of Camden Yards. Approaching an usher I showed him our tickets and asked him if he would point us to our seats. As he pointed to the very, very, very top of the outfield bleachers I caught a glimpse of the thermometer. A cool ninety-nine degrees in the sun in Baltimore City! The usher informed me I could leave David's Amigo with him. With that I bent over, picked up all 102 pounds of David, looked skyward to our seats in the clouds and started.

We journeyed for what seemed like another half hour to the peaks of Camden Yards. We were ecstatic! Instead of having to go beyond the clouds to the top row of seats we were lucky to have seats two rows below. However, our seats were six seats in from the end of the row. Surprisingly, all of these seats looked the same. They were all shaped the same way. They were all the same color. They were all the same height from the cement floor. The only difference we could tell was a little numbered silver plate on the left arms of each seat. Wouldn't you think the group of five fans on the end would graciously move down so David's old, sweaty, gray-haired dad and mom could have the three end seats? Well! They didn't! By the time I got everyone and everything settled I realized I had had just too much coffee in the morning. The short of a long, long story is that I suffered! I figured sitting still would be much better than being pushed, shoved, pulled and knocked sideways going through the millions of nomads below I experienced on my journey upward. Fortunately for David the game was very exciting going into two extra innings. Fortunately for me, it was so hot that dehydration had taken care of my excess coffee problem. David was mesmerized. Sara Belle and I were hot and melted to our seats. We could see nothing more but what appeared to be tiny, tiny little ants playing something on the field.

David was also a loyal fan of our local baseball team, the Shorebirds. On one occasion Dr. Kel Nagel offered David his box seats at Perdue Stadium. David was elated to say the least! It was mid to late April. The temperature was a pleasant seventy-five degrees when we entered the stadium. This being a special night we decided to eat expensively. By the time we purchased three hot dogs, French fries, drinks, and later an ice cream treat

SHELDON LARMORE

and popcorn, we felt we had spent enough to eat three hardy meals at the Atlantic Hotel in Berlin. Once settled in our seats we relaxed and enjoyed the game.

As the evening stretched into night the temperature began to drop. A gentle, cool breeze began to sweep through the stadium. By the fourth inning, the thermometer was reading a little below sixty degrees. The gentle breeze, to me, was beginning to feel like a category 1 hurricane. Needless to say when we left home in seventy-five degree weather we had no reason to consider taking a sweater or jacket. Again, David was engrossed in the game and could care less. All I could think was, *Just get this thing over before we turn to blocks of ice*. Once again, fortunately for David, the Shorebirds played exceptionally well. The game went into an extra inning. But the real bonus was yet to come! It was fireworks night after the game at Perdue Stadium.

Even though David loved sports and everything connected with sporting activities, his first love was for his church and his salvation. Religion has always been an important and personal part of Sara Belle's and my life. However, I don't think anyone would describe us as religious fanatics. Even though I know the year, month, day, and the hour I accepted Jesus as my savior, Sara Belle knew Him far longer than me. Through her kindness, strong faith, and compassion for others she was able to instill in David and me an unwavering faith. David's love for his Father simply grew stronger and stronger with each phase of life he experienced and through each new friend he gained.

David talked freely with us about heaven. One of his primary goals was to prepare for his last day. Toward the end of his life David would express with great joy how he looked forward to the time when he would feel the loving arms of God wrapped around him. Ironically, one of the first sympathy cards we received was a very simplistic card of the famous painting, *Welcome Home* by Danny Hahlbohn. The painting is one of Jesus hugging a young man as they stand amidst the clouds in heaven. We immediately took this card to Michaels to have it framed professionally.

David was a lay reader in our church. Even though his speech was not always clear he would practice, practice, and practice until he felt comfortable reading before the congregation. For several years every other Wednesday evening we hosted in our home a Bible study. At its peak membership we had as many as twenty members who gathered for a Bible lesson taught by our very capable leader, John Sharpe. On alternate Wednesday evenings and most every Sunday evening, David would attend the church services at Abundant Life with Kathy Monteleone and other friends. Through this association with his Christian friends and studies conducted at Abundant Life, David learned the Bible. Without hesitation he could turn to any of the books of the Bible and would begin to memorize several scriptures. Whenever David went on family vacations or spent recuperation time in hospitals he always made sure he had his Bible, praise music, and a cassette player with him.

As discussed earlier, David could not empty his bladder without the use of a catheter and could not have a bowel movement without an enema each night. This process took an hour to an hour and a half each evening. David, sitting with a card table in front of him, would put this time to good use reading his Bible and copying Scripture as a means of learning the Word. If David was not in the congregation at Abundant Life on Sunday evenings, he usually was visiting another church with other friends. There were Sundays when Sara Belle and I would go to the communion rail at St. Peters to receive the sacraments without David. Father David Tontono would usually ask if he needed to go across the street to give Holy Communion to David. He was well aware David would go to Trinity United Methodist Church with his friend, Holly Evans, whenever he had a chance.

In essence, David had a great fondness for all sports, a genuine love and compassion for others, and most importantly a strong faith and a tremendous need for the Holy Spirit. Many times we found ourselves being quiet and listening to our son who taught us many lessons on how to live with adversities. He believed! He believed in others and in the simplicity of God.

To him, God was not complicated. He was his heavenly Father who taught him he could do all things through Christ who gave him strength (Philippians 4:13). From his readings he was pleased one evening to share with us that prayer is simple. Prayer should not be just a lot of unusual words said to make us seem as if we are smart and religious. It is just a two-way conversation between a person and God. David was not afraid to face life. He worked to discover his world; then with all his heart gave himself to it.

Dark Clouds Do
Have Silver Linings

Getting well is not the only goal. Even more important is learning to live without fear, to be at peace with life and ultimately death.

—Bernie Siegel, M.D.

It takes both rain and sunshine to make a rainbow. In our family we have always felt fortunate because we witnessed so many rainbows of warmth and love in our times together. When troubles began to surface, we learned by keeping our faces toward the sunshine, the shadows of life would always fall behind us.

Late in the spring of 1995, David's health started on a mini-roller coaster ride once again. He was experiencing numerous attacks of kidney stones and periods when he seemed to be having difficulty breathing. Frequent trips to doctors and the emergency room gave little or no indication of any medical difficulties. Without a clear diagnosis his breathing dilemma was thought to be caused by the numerous allergies in the spring air. We kept a close eye on David and his behavior each day. We knew from our experiences and reminders from his doctors that we were living with a human time bomb. David's health in the past had been so iffy with many unexpected ups and downs; we had to be on our toes.

This same spring, Sara Belle had her semi-annual physical examination. During the examination her gynecologist, Dr. Floyd Gray, detected a lump in her right breast he labeled suspicious. He immediately ordered a mammogram and breast ultrasound. The tests showed a calcification in the breast and indicated cancer was present. Shocked, Sara Belle asked Dr. Gray where he could send her for a second opinion. He suggested Georgetown University Hospital outside of Washington, D.C. Our visit with the cancer team at Georgetown confirmed the malignancy. However, the more she learned about her condition from the people at Georgetown, the more comfortable she became in facing another bout with cancer.

She had two choices to make. She could either receive her treatment at Georgetown or return to Salisbury and be treated by a local oncologist. Not wanting to face time away from David or me, she decided to get treatment at home. She felt fortunate to be accepted as a new patient by Dr. James Martin. After speaking with him she felt very comfortable with her decision. She trusted his knowledge and years of experience. This was a marriage made in heaven between doctor and patient. Dr. Martin made her feel very comfortable with his pleasant manner and the compassion she witnessed him showering on other patients as well as herself. The summer months leisurely rolled into the fall as Sara Belle gradually recovered her strength. To witness her renewed lease on life was an answer to many prayers and a pure joy for David and me.

By October, Sara Belle was able to return to her part-time job at the Gospel Shop. Things went well until shortly before the Christmas holidays. With the Christmas rush in the store, preparation for Christmas, holiday dinners, and visits to her mother's home in Milton, Delaware, Sara Belle was really beginning to show signs of fatigue as well as depression. At the same time Sara Belle and I began to notice her mother, who lived by herself, was becoming more and more forgetful and unsteady on

SHELDON LARMORE

her feet. Numerous times in the past year Sara Belle visited with her mother once, sometimes twice a week. Without success, she tried to convince her mother to get help doing chores around the house. She also encouraged her to consider moving into an assisted living facility. David's constant daily needs coupled with Sara Belle's lack of energy and wavering health made the possibility of her mother living with us a last resort.

During the Christmas holidays we had Sara Belle's mother, her sister Eleanor, and our brother-in-law Bob as our houseguests. In all the holiday excitement and through two large family dinners prepared by Sara Belle on Christmas Eve and Christmas day, no one seemed to notice how lethargic David was or how anxious Sara Belle was becoming as each day passed. Our family salvation came in the times we spent in church during the holidays and the quiet, reflective times Sara Belle and I spent together after everyone was safely nestled in bed.

After the holidays, everyone resumed their daily lives except the Larmores. Our calendar the first week of January was hectic with work schedules, meetings, doctors' appointments, and general family responsibilities. Therefore, we encouraged Sara Belle's mother to stay with us until the weekend. That week winter arrived with vengeance. The temperature hovered around freezing nightly with snow showers falling intermittingly most days. There was no way we were going to let Sara Belle's mother stay in her home in Milton, Delaware, by herself. We didn't ask, we told her she *was* moving in with us for the winter, at least.

We knew this unexpected addition to our family was going to add a new dimension to our already overtaxed life. However, we did not know to what degree. Sara Belle's mother had been suffering from forgetfulness for some time. Once we began to observe her on a daily basis we discovered her forgetfulness was worse than we thought. Sara Belle made an appointment for her to have a thorough physical examination. The results indicated for someone ninety-two years of age she was in reasonably good health. However, she did have dementia.

Sara Belle loved her mother dearly. She did everything she could to make her comfortable. However, her mother was going through a stage when it was not always easy to relate to her. It was increasingly difficult to provide the kind of care we knew she needed. Some days she was less than cooperative. At the time, I was teaching a full schedule at the university, Sara Belle was working at the Gospel Shop two to three days a week, and David was volunteering at the hospital eight hours a day.

Initially, it took quite an effort in arranging schedules, caring for David's needs, and making sure there was consistency and order in our daily lives. This was so necessary since patients with dementia function much better if daily routines are pretty firm. Either Sara Belle or I had to be home with her mother during the day. If Sara Belle was working, I would have to leave the office to be with her mother. Many times I had to return to the office in the evening or during the weekend to finish my work. Needing an hour and a half or more in the morning to get David ready to leave the house, and the same amount of time or more at night to prepare him for bed was wearing on Sara Belle.

Most nights, unless I had a meeting or a night class to teach, we worked together. On nights I was not at home, it was very difficult for Sara Belle to address David's needs while at the same time making sure her mother was not wandering outside, turning the stove on or simply rearranging items in the house that, when needed, Sara Belle could not find. The caring of Sara Belle's mother continued until early June. At that time the physical well-beings of Sara Belle and David became major issues again.

There was no doubt in our minds that changes had to be made in our household if we, as a family, were to survive. Sara Belle discussed her mother's rapid mental deterioration with her brother and sister. Since they had not lived with her on a daily basis and had no clue of the drain it had on Sara Belle, they were somewhat surprised. However, it was agreed we should search for an assisted living home where Sara Belle's mother would be taken care of and feel comfortable in her surroundings. After several visits and phone calls we found there was a vacancy at the John B. Parsons Home. Sara Belle took her mother for a tour and immediately she rebelled. She stated she was not ready to leave her home. She already had forgotten she had not been in her home in the last six months. She was determined not to give the move another thought. As a result, Sara Belle's brother asked if she would consider keeping their mother with us. It was difficult for Sara Belle to think about placing her mother in a home but our answer was a resounding *no!* Obviously, no one was quite aware of the burden she would have taking care of both her mother and David. No one had lived it but us!

A Return to the Darkness of Illness

We cannot truly face life until we face the fact that it will be taken away from us.

—Billy Graham

he day after Sara Belle's mother moved to John B. Parsons Home, Sara Belle began to have strange feelings in her head and numbness in her right arm. Even though I pleaded for her to go to the emergency room, she insisted she was feeling better. If the condition continued she would go. I mostly stayed awake through the night periodically checking on her. The next day she was up early, feeling great, and ready to tackle the chores of running the house. We just assumed her feelings the evening before were due to stress and just plain exhaustion.

In the early afternoon David called from the hospital and asked us to pick him up early. He stated he was not feeling well and wanted to come home to rest. When I brought him home, Sara Belle took his temperature. It was 103 degrees. He was chilled to the bones, so he said.

"We're going to the hospital, David," she said.

"Good." David responded without any resistance. After the doctor examined David she told us, "David has a hefty case of pneumonia. I'm afraid he is going to be one very sick little puppy."

David was admitted. In less than twenty-four hours he was in the intensive care unit. It was heart breaking for us *again* to see David lying so helpless in a semi-conscious state.

Early the second morning of David's admittance to ICU the hospital called.

"Mrs. Larmore," the voice on the other end of the phone said, "David's condition has worsened during the night. His breathing is much labored, and he is not responding to treatment. We will have to put him on a ventilator."

"We'll be right over," Sara Belle replied.

Looking puzzled I asked, "What's happening?"

For a moment she could not answer and then, "David's in trouble again. They have to put him on a ventilator." With that she broke down in an uncontainable cry as I held her close. As quickly as she started crying, she stopped. It was as if she was telling her body to stop! Straighten up! Be brave!

"Oh, God, please be with David! Please! Help us through this," she said.

"Are you ready? Let's go." I headed to the door.

As we walked into the ICU area we could see several nurses and a doctor's physician moving about in David's room at the end of the hall. The worst of the worst thoughts began to enter our minds. Were they trying to revive him? As we watched the nurses remove a couple of the machines out of his room we feared he had already passed. We stood by the door to his room, totally devastated, waiting for some word or words from those intensely working around his bed. Finally, his assigned nurse for the day saw us anxiously waiting by the door, and came out of the room to speak with us. She explained,

"When I arrived at work this morning I was told David's condition had deteriorated. It was going to be necessary to put him on life support. His body has taken quite a beating, and it needs time to rest."

"Can we see him?" we asked almost emotionless, as our insides seem to be crumbling.

"Let's let the team finish their work and then you can go in," she answered.

Standing by David's bedside brought back all those difficult life-threatening times of the past. Our first glimpse of David as we entered the room was upsetting. His face and body were swollen from the retention of fluid making his skin taut. Seeing David so ashen white and motionless gave us the frightening feeling that death was near. We had been through this so many times over the years we just knew we had to put our trust in the Lord again. We had to be quiet and listen. We were *quiet* with the exception of muted sobs as we held back our tears. There was the constant murmuring, clicking, beeping, and ringing of the machines attached to David to keep him alive. We did *listen* as we stood helplessly by him holding hands and hugging each other as we talked to God. We felt His presence as an uneasy stillness gently flowed through the room. We had to rely on God's will just as David would tell us we had to do. David told us many times he was ready to go home to be with Jesus when that time came. We knew he was ready. God knew we were not. However, we had to trust in God's divine intervention and stop trying to adjust His plans.

With our many, many stays in the hospital with David, there were times when minutes seemed to pass like hours. This daytime had no meaning. Hours passed by unnoticed as we watched David lay in a state of unconsciousness; not moving a single muscle, not making even the slightest sound. Throughout the day nurses would come into the room to check the machines, to adjust this or that, or to restart a piece of equipment after an alarm sounded. There was little conversation between the nurses and us mostly because there was little or nothing to be said. There was no change in his condition. In our grieving we couldn't help but think, *Is this going to be our last day with David?* Ever so often we could not control our emotions. We would break down in muffled cries as we moved away from David's bedside.

Our conversations with God were frequent as we prayed for his recovery. Day turned into night. As we looked out the window onto Salisbury Boulevard we could see life moving on as people traveled to and fro. They were carrying out their responsibilities and enjoying their adventures of the moment. It seemed they realized that this was prime time. Life was in season, and there would be no reruns. We had been and probably would still be part of that "culture" when or if our lives ever got back to normal. However, in the small, dimly lighted hospital room with precious David we were reminded that the most important things in life are not things. We treasured the love God continued to shower on us and the deep love the three of us shared together as a family. We knew and still know how wonderfully blessed we are. It is such a tragedy for the people who have plenty to live on, but really nothing to live for.

We reluctantly left David's room late in the evening to go home for some rest and a change of clothes. Waking up early in the morning and feeling relieved we had not heard from the ICU staff during the night, we went to the hospital praying for improvement. As we started down the hall we noticed a young man sitting just outside David's door plugging information into a computer. As we approached him he stood up from his portable desk. He shook our hands and introduced himself as Chris Clifford, David's nurse for the day.

"David is a mighty fine young man," he shared with a pleasant, caring smile. "He is well loved by all of us in the hospital." He led us into David's room and stated David had rested comfortably during the night and remained stable.

"David. David, honey," Sara Belle whispered. She leaned over the bed standing on her tiptoes to gives him a kiss on his forehead. There was no outward response. I stood by his bedside not able to voice a word for fear I would break down in tears. I leaned over, kissed him, and rubbed his upper arm as Chris moved close, putting his hand on my shoulder. I could see that Sara Belle had moved to the window with her back to us. I could feel the same emptiness I knew she was feeling. Her silence was deafening only broken at times by a soft sniffle.

Before Chris left the room to complete his morning reports on David, he asked, "How about a cup of coffee? We have a freshly brewed pot." Our immediate response was *yes*.

Through the years we had been privileged to have so many excellent nurses and doctors watching over David. However, there are those few, like in any profession, that carry out their duties like little robots with little or no feeling for the patient or the patient's family members. Chris cared! Chris will always be extremely special to us. Chris was patient and displayed sincere compassion for each of those in his care. It was as if God had gifted us again with another of his angels.

By noon we felt the need to take a break. After spending an hour or so having lunch with friends we returned to David's room.

As we entered, Chris was standing by David's side and said to our utter disbelief, "David, your Mom and Dad are here."

We walked over to David's bed, lost total control, and broke down in tears of joy and relief. David had his eyes open. What a beautiful, marvelous sight! Chris was as elated as we were. David did not move and could not communicate because of the ventilator, but he was conscious or, at least, in a semiconscious state. Very soon his eyes closed again. He fell back into a sound, motionless sleep. He opened his eyes for short periods perhaps a half dozen times during the day. However, his stats were beginning to show gradual improvement, his color was slowly returning, and his swelling was lessening. Thanks be to God! He never leaves our side.

This was the end of another long day at the hospital and the beginning of another sleepless but more restful night at home. On the third day when we arrived at the hospital David's nurse was Linda Tuthill, a former student in the Westside Primary School where I served as principal. David was fortunate again to be blessed with a very compassionate, caring, and knowledgeable care giver. Linda's professional skills were excellent. Like Chris, she really knew how to comfort parents just by her presence and kind words as she entered and left the room. Even though there was a ray of hope yesterday, David's condition remained unchanged.

Our emotions had taken so many turns and had made so many crashes with reality they were basically dead. We had maintained an outward appearance of coping so well it hid our true state of sanity. We were simply a pair of walking, hardly existing shells of human life. As the saying goes, "It is better to know some of the questions than all of the answers." The good Lord knows we had a lot of questions. We asked them but each time we were afraid of the answers we were going to hear. David had been on the ventilator for almost seventy-two hours with little or no change. We never gave up hope. Our faith remained strong because we knew how much God had done for us over our lifetime. We remained strong because David was strong—strong in his faith and Herculean in his love for God.

Another morning was spent sitting by David's side remembering the wonderful times we had together. David experienced great things mostly because of his determination and his desire to help others. We conversed with God in prayer throughout the morning. It never entered our minds that He was not listening. We knew God was doing more than just hearing our words. He was reading our hearts and knew we believed. We also took great comfort in knowing our friends, family, and many churches in the area were lifting David up in prayer.

After telling Linda, David's nurse, we went for lunch in the Junior Board Shop in the hospital. After lunch we returned to David's room. As we entered, Dr. Rod Layton, one of pulmonary and respiratory doctors at PRMC and Linda were by David's bedside. Linda looked up and then back to David, saying to our total surprise, "David, your Mom and Dad are here."

I had to think. This was twice we left his room for lunch and twice we returned to find him awake and his eyes open. If that's what it takes, I jokingly told myself, then I will go and come from lunch eight or nine times a day. We walked over to David's bed and saw the most beautiful angel imaginable. Even though David had his eyes open you could tell he was having difficulty focusing. It was impossible for us to get close enough to David to give him a kiss or hug since his bed was surrounded by many machines and pieces of equipment. As we watched, he began to slowly, very slowly move his eyes with some jerkiness as he attempted to focus on things in the room.

When Dr. Layton completed his assessment of David's condition he cautioned us to not be overly optimistic as he shared, "David is still gravely ill. He is far from being out of the woods. Don't think this is going to be an easy road from here on out. It won't be."

After he left with Linda, we moved as close to the bed as we could so we both could at least put our hands on him. Again, a familiar quietness fell upon the room as David fell in and out of sleep. When he was awake he couldn't do much but just look at us. The ventilator blocked his smile or any attempt of making facial expressions. We were so thankful his eye movements seemed to be more regular instead of being erratic as we had noticed earlier. In the early evening John Sharpe, a wonderful friend of ours and David's, came for a visit and to see if we needed anything. David was unable to demonstrate how pleased he was to see John. However, his eyes opened wider, and we could tell just by the faint way he was able to move his hand he was very happy. John witnessed the difficulties we were having communicating with each other since David could not utter a sound because of the tubing stretching from his mouth down through his throat. His arms and hand usage were hampered by being connected to the various pieces of equipment in the room.

The next day John returned with a homemade language board. Almost anything David could wish for was pictured or coded on the board. It also had an alphabet chart. If David wanted the nurse, we would hold the board near him so he could touch the word *nurse*. He could answer questions with a *yes* or *no* by pointing to one or the other printed on the board. If he wanted to move up or down in bed or have his pillow fluffed he could point to up, down, or a picture of a pillow. If he wanted to communicate in words he could spell them by pointing to each letter. As David got feeling better we *really* had fun with the board. He did not mind being teased, and we took advantage of his good nature. As he started to spell a word we would try to out guess him. Many times we knew the word he was trying to spell, but we would pretend he was spelling something else. He would just roll his eyes and/or wrinkle his nose as to say, "No, that's not right!" or, "Don't fool with me." Each day we took to heart the little miracles that occurred during his recovery. They served us well, especially on the bad days we had to endure when he seemed to be regressing.

David's progress moved at a snail's pace over the next ten days or so. However, he did reach the point where he was weaned off of the ventilator. Oh, what a happy day for all of us. A couple of days later we were jubilantly rejoicing in David's slow but sure recovery. Midmorning Dr. Layton entered the room to check on David.

"We are so glad to see how well David is doing. What do you think?" Sara Belle asked.

"You can wipe that smile off of your face! He is a very sick young man. Things could change in minutes." With that he turned leaving the room with, "I'll see you later after I see the results of his morning X-rays."

For moments we just stood looking at each other. Seems our life had taken another turn, putting us in a place of confused limbo.

We did realize what Dr. Layton was trying to convey to us was for our own good. He was trying to safeguard us from the unexpected. We had and will always have great respect for Dr. Rod Layton and Dr. Kel Nagel. They have stood by us through thick and thin and have always come to our assistance when we needed them. Even though we were shocked by Dr. Layton's comment, we loved him for being honest and forthright with us. What he said to us was true, and we knew it.

David continued to be a resident of the intensive care unit for the next couple weeks. We became permanent fixtures in ICU leaving only to get a quick bite to eat or to go home to sleep and prepare to return to PRMC the next morning. Obviously, our normal life and routines were suspended during this time. We were blessed to have neighbors and friends who kept our lawn mowed and our shrubbery and trees trimmed. Occasionally, we would come home late at night and find freshly baked brownies, a cake, or some cookies on the kitchen counter. All of our friends knew Miss Lillian, our ninety-something spry next-door neighbor. She had a key to our house and was the Santa who would enter during the day and deliver these goodies brought to her from our friends. Several times over the long summer, friends would either invite us to their home for a quick dinner or take us out to one of the restaurants in town. Along with John Sharpe, David's other constant visitor was not surprisingly Bob Caldwell. They seemed to be with David almost as much as we were, and we truly loved them for their care, support, and encouragement.

Just as the doctors were about to set a date to move David out of ICU into a regular patient room we were faced with another traumatic experience. While recovering from his illness David's diet consisted mainly of Jell-O and liquids. A couple of evenings before his scheduled move, David enjoyed a dish of cherry Jell-O.

Early that next morning his nurse found wet red spots on his sheet and pillowcase. She was really concerned that he might be bleeding from somewhere. When he woke up he seemed to be lethargic. He was coughing up a greenish mucus which was a sure sign of infection. His temperature was over 102 degrees.

After a quick examination by Dr. Nagel it was evident he had aspirated the Jell-O. His pneumonia was returning with vengeance. After a day of close monitoring, antibiotics, numerous intravenous fluids, and a series of X-rays, David's condition seemed to be weakening rapidly. His temperature fluctuated between 102 to 104 degrees. There was a noticeable blue tint under his fingernails and around his lips. We were totally devastated. How much more was his fragile body going to have to endure? Through all of this, we never asked God why. He knows and we will know in time. In heaven, God will reveal what on earth He chose to conceal. We had to trust in our faith and the goodness of our Lord. We prayed. We prayed. And we prayed.

By early evening David was back on the ventilator. Our emotions were at a breaking point. We stood over David whispering loving words into his ears, kissing him, touching him, dropping fallen tears on his body. If only we could hug him. If only I could pick him up and hold him close to my heart. If only...if only... There were times we were like children crying, hugging each other, and grieving from the possibility of losing a lifetime of happiness and love.

Walking into David's room the day after the ventilator had been inserted for the second time was like visiting a tomb. The curtains were pulled shut, the room was a shadow of darkness, and the air was cool, too cool for comfort. In the background the disconcerting sounds of the machines added a heavy eeriness to the atmosphere we felt closing around us. We thought, *Even though he was in a deep sleep he was alive. Now, let's bring some light and life to this room.*

Our first act of parents' love was to pull the curtains aside, open the blinds wide, have the air conditioner turned up, and turn his praise music on soft volume. Immediately, hope arrived! Hope in our household has always won over despair. We have learned from the past when one reaches for the stars, one never gets a handful of mud. We have to think that our reaction upon entering David's room was orchestrated by the powers in heaven. This had to be a way our guardian angels used to take our minds off the soberness of the day.

The morning was spent quietly. We passed the time by sitting at David's bedside, being uplifted by listening to his praise music and attempting to read. Our emotions were being nurtured by the seeds of faith and hope. However, in moments of reality, human doubts would run rampant through the hallways of our minds: *Just how long can David's body fight off the evils of these illnesses? Again we had to think will this be the day the good Lord will call for David to come home?* Feeling an increased level of anxiety we just had to stop thinking about all of the *what ifs*. Stretching back in our chairs we joined hands, closed our eyes, and realized we needed to be quiet, rest our minds, erase the negative thoughts (the best we could), and listen—listen to what the Lord was trying to say to us. One message we constantly got in these situations was, *Despair, if you must! But how is it going to pull you through? Burden Me with whatever burdens you.*

Early in the afternoon, Dr. Nagel visited with us. He was like our security blanket. He checked David's X-rays and general condition. He was not pleased with the progress David was making. In fact, he felt he had regressed. This was becoming a puzzling situation. David was not responding at all to the various antibiotics or the respiratory therapy being administered to him.

"Has David ever had a blood transfusion?" he asked.

"Yes. Twice. Once when he had his hip surgery and once during one of Dr. Crosby's operations," Sara Belle answered.

"Has he been tested for AIDS?"

"No."

"Some of his symptoms give me cause to question if this might be the problem. Maybe we should have him tested."

The test came back negative. His condition remained critical.

"Where do we go from here?" Sara Belle asked.

"I don't know. I will get back with you later," Dr. Nagel said. Within the hour Dr. Nagel returned to explain a procedure he wanted to put in place.

"We know David's condition has worsened. We have to help him get over this hill. We are going to use a drug-induced paralysis [muscle relaxant] therapy. I'm prescribing this procedure primarily as a means to control his breathing and secondarily it can favorably affect any underlying pulmonary disease or associated complications. It will help by giving his body a chance to rest."

We had always felt confident in having Dr. Nagel, Dr. Layton, and their team administering treatments for David. This time was no exception.

That evening we stayed with David until neither of us could hardly stay awake. When we prepared to leave, we both stood by his bed with salty tears dripping from our eyes. We knew better but the weakness of our bodies more than our minds began to direct our thoughts again to the remote areas of despair. *Stop it! Stop it!* were the words ringing in my ears. It was like something was saying to me, "Get a grip! Haven't you felt God nudging you all day? Didn't He promise He would be with you? Boy! Where is your faith?"

With that little bit of spiritual shock from heaven, we snapped back. Sara Belle, my personal pillar of strength, was outwardly in control as she stood by David, rubbing his arm, and conversing with God.

The next couple of days brought no noticeable change in David's condition. Our daily routines remained the same. We arrived at the hospital early. We stayed by David's side with the exception of going to the Junior Board Shop for a sandwich or soup at lunch and dinner. We usually stayed well past visiting hours traveling home as if we were on automatic pilot. One of our comforts during David's stay in the hospital was knowing he was being provided the best of care. During this period in ICU, Mey-Lie Salimian—a friend and an extremely compassionate, caring, and skilled nurse—was frequently assigned to David. Her presence at David's bedside always gave us peace and comfort knowing he was getting the best of care. The rapport she and David developed between them was a true blessing to us.

One afternoon, shortly after David's second ventilator was in place, Bill Sadler, a retire surgeon and great friend of ours checked in on us. While we were talking, Beverly Porteus, our assistant priest at St. Peters Episcopal Church in Salisbury, arrived for a visit and joined in the conversation. After a period Bill stood up and went over to David's bedside. He talked to David in whispers and gave a beautiful prayer. We all noticed that there was no reaction from David. All the readings on his monitors remained the same, and his breathing machine was constant. When Bill left David's side, Beverly moved close to David. Putting her hand on his she conversed with him in a soft voice. Immediately, David's temperature spiked, and his blood pressure began to fluctuate. Beverly stepped back from the bed, threw her hands up in the air, lightly stomped her foot on the floor and with a big smile announced, "Yes! I've still got it!" She made David's blood pressure rise and Bill didn't.

Around the fourth day a subtle improvement in David's condition was noted. As the day continued, improvement in his general appearance and in his vital statistics continued. We were overjoyed with his progress. However, remembering the words of Dr. Layton, we tried to remain cautiously optimistic.

Day by day David improved. We still couldn't talk with him because of the ventilator, but thanks to John wc had the language board. It was still a long time before we could take off our artificial smiles and replace them with genuine, bright smiles.

However, it didn't take long for David's eyes to light up the room as we talked to him.

In less than ten days the ventilator was removed, and David was free *again*. What a relief to all of us including Dr. Nagel, Dr. Layton, and the many nurses who poured pounds and pounds of love and compassion on David and us. David's overall physical condition seemed to be better than when he was taken off of the ventilator the first time. Once the excitement of having David removed from the machines died down, it was time again to totally focus on him. Between periods of rest we played cards, watched the Orioles, listened to praise music, played board games, and enjoyed comedy shows on television.

David loved coffee. Each morning on our way to visit we would stop at a donut shop and get three coffees and three donuts. This was our morning family time. Everything went well for a while until one morning with coffee in hand I tripped over one of the cords attached to David's IV pole. I caught my fall but succeed in spilling my coffee all over the room. After David saw I was okay, he broke out in uncontrollable laughter. Imagine, he was laughing so hard his bed was almost moving. After a period he calmed down and said, "Sorry, Dad."

"Right! You loved every minute of it," I said.

To think, not more than a few days before we had doubts we would ever hear laughter from him again. For another three weeks, David remained in the intensive care unit. His temperature would spike periodically as he fought off his lingering pneumonia. The ups and downs of his blood pressure and oxygen level frequently fought for first place on everyone's concern list.

By the end of the first week in August, after spending nearly two months in the intensive care unit, David was transferred to HealthSouth Chesapeake Rehabilitation Hospital in Salisbury. Upon arrival at HealthSouth David was extremely weak from such a long duration of bed rest. The physical stress on his body from erratic changes in heart rate, blood pressure, breathing, and general lack of normal physical exercise had taken its toll. Through a program of intensive, persistent occupational and physical therapy coupled with his relentless determination, he was able to recover most of his strength before he was discharged in late August.

GIVING FREELY AND GAINING MORE

It is more blessed to give than receive.

Acts 20:35

There is no greater happiness than that which comes from sharing…no greater joy than that which comes from loving, giving and caring.

—Sharing Quotes

As fall approached David was chewing at the bits to get his life in full swing again. He returned to volunteering full time and restarted his active social life. Friends visited often or took him out to movies, shopping and socializing in the mall, or visiting other friends in their homes. Attendance in church was at least three times a week including Sunday morning at St. Peters and Sunday evening and Wednesday evening at Abundant Life. David loved church and enjoyed the Christian fellowship it offered. He may have been small in stature, physically handicapped, and living in a body the doctors referred to as a "living time bomb," but he treasured life. He was never ready to give into his pains and disabilities.

In late fall David was asked by Barbara Webster if he would be interested in joining a team from Holly Center designed to increase awareness of the life of handicapped individuals. The program was called Developmental Disabilities Awareness. Without hesitation, our little "joiner" joined the team. The team traveled to all the elementary schools in Wicomico, Somerset, and Worcester Counties each year to meet with third grade classes. The purpose was to provide children an opportunity to meet and talk with a handicapped individual first hand. David and the team emphasized disabled people can do many things despite their limitations. It was his wish the students would see, through his example, that handicapped people are people the same as everyone else. They have the same needs, desires, and dreams. He would always try to guide them in realizing all of us are handicapped in some way. We just have to believe and live life by being everything we can be with the talents God has given each of us. His relationship with Barbara Webster and the team was one of mutual love, respect, and admiration. Barbara was his rock and his mentor. We will always love her for the increased self-confidence she instilled in him.

David always saw the best in everyone or anything. From an early age, David gained an understanding of the need to help, support, and encourage others who passed through his life. Helping others seemed to bring his life meaning and a greater fulfillment. He had a good teacher who taught him many of life's little secrets of success. Sara Belle lived what she modeled for David. She proved to him many times that when we share our good fortune, our happiness, our talents, and our faith with others it makes the world a better place to live. By doing this, we find true meaning and satisfaction in our own lives.

Three other individuals who gave freely of their time and talents to David were Dr. Alex Azar, Dr. Harold Genvert, and Dr. James Gaul. Each time he was in their company he would light up like Fourth of July fireworks. They are three of many individuals in David's life that radiated warmth, compassion, and a sincere interest in the welfare of others. Dr. Azar would always unmercifully tease David about all the girlfriends he had and about being stuck in the hospital elevators with pretty, young nurses. David loved it and loved Dr. Azar. He always appreciated the time Dr. Azar took to talk with him and listen to him with interest.

Dr. Genvert had a knack of putting David at ease whenever he had to treat him for kidney stones or resolve one of the many problems we had with his catheter. His friendliness and positive manner were always a welcome relief and good medicine for us in time of crisis. It was obvious he genuinely liked David and cared for the welfare of our family. We will always hold him in the highest regard.

Dr. Gaul was truly a genuine friend to both David and us. Even though his medical care of David with limited, he was always there when David or we needed a word of encouragement or a hand of comfort. David and Dr. Gaul constantly bet each other as to which team would win in football, baseball, basketball, etc. The trophy was a two-liter of Pepsi to the winner. There were occasions we had to hand deliver the winnings to Dr. Gaul's office, especially when David lost three bets in one week and could not carry three or four two liters in his Amigo basket.

Dr. Gaul has continued to be a part of our lives. We see him during office visits as well as in social gatherings. He always takes some time to reminisce about the fun times with David. Some people come into our lives and quickly go. Some stay for a while and leave footprints on our hearts, and we are never, ever the same. Dr. Gaul is one of people we have adopted into our family and will never let go.

These three wonderful people modeled the saying, "We grow in joy as we grow in love for others" (Matthew 22:37-39; Mark 12:30-31; Luke 10:27). How lucky we are when we have friends who are so hard to say good-bye to at the end of the day.

TROUBLES SHARED ARE TROUBLES DIVIDED

Eventually you come to understand that love heals everything and love is all there is.

—Gary Zukov

Living with David brought us pure joy! He was constantly teaching us the importance of being active and involved in life if we intended to live it to its fullest. He was determined not to allow his parents to drift through life aimlessly. During his grace at the dinner table it was not unusual for him to thank God for the good life the three of us were living. He would ask his Father for forgiveness at times when we seemed not to love it enough.

A year after David's near-death experience in the summer of 1996, he began to develop new symptoms of respiratory problems. In spite of numerous doctor visits, additional medications, and adjustments in his daily life, he was admitted to the hospital *again* with pneumonia. Fortunately, it was caught in time. He recovered well enough to be released within a week. This became almost a monthly event. He was in the hospital for a week and out four or five weeks. Then the cycle would begin again. Through prayer and the excellent care provided by the doctors and nurses, he was able to fight back and conquer at least eight of these minor pneumonia attacks. We called them minor as compared to the times he was put on life support.

Shortly after these pneumonia episodes became a pattern, Dr. Silvia, David's internist for whom we have tremendous respect, gave David a series of swallowing tests. It was determined David was a silent aspirator. Normal healthy people usually turn red and start to cough when they have swallowed poorly in an attempt to prevent the food from going into their lungs. Due to David's weakened condition and his poor swallowing techniques, aspiration happened silently. This created an extremely dangerous situation because food and liquids glided easily into his lungs causing pneumonia. This type of pneumonia is difficult to treat and doesn't respond well to a multitude of antibiotics. Following this discovery Dr. Silvia had us thicken all his liquids. Every glass of water, bowl of soup, cup of coffee, soda, etc., he drank at home or in restaurants had to be almost the consistency of wallpaper paste. David, as usual, adjusted well in handling this new way of drinking. Actually his coffee, water, etc., were so thick he had to eat them with a spoon instead of drinking them normally.

David's approach to life had to be directed from something greater than everyday energy and earthly determination. It's clear David truly survived by his simple faith in an awesome God, and his belief in the power of hope.

During this period in time, Sara Belle began to have reoccurring health problems. One evening while I was teaching at the university, Sara Belle was in charge of an activity at church. At the completion of the program she stood and immediately dropped to the floor unconscious. Fortunately our friend, Dr. Bill Sadler, was in attendance. He checked Sara Belle's pulse and heart rate and decided she needed to be transported to PRMC. After several days of observation and numerous tests it was determined she was suffering from Mitral Valve Prolapse. The cause for this condition is unknown. It basically results when the flaps and chords that control the opening and closing of the heart valve thicken, enlarge, and lengthen due to an abnormal formation. Within a week she was released from the hospital with little restrictions in her daily activities. However, she had to be aware of symptoms such as fatigue, lightheadedness, or palpitation of the heart that may signal another attack.

Things continued as normal as could be expected in the Larmore household until one evening we decided it was time to entertain old friends we had not seen for sometime. Sara Belle has always enjoyed entertaining, so we invited Bill and Kit Zak and Jim and Sarah Bounds over for a relaxed Saturday evening dinner. Roast beef, three or four vegetable dishes, homemade rolls, and homemade apple pie were all readied for a night of fun and lots of laughter. As the afternoon advanced, David began to develop a fever and chills. Our friends were to arrive at six. At a quarter of five, Sara Belle called Sarah Bounds to tell her dinner was ready. She gave her instructions about last minute things that needed to be done and told her we were on our way to the hospital. She insisted they come to dinner, enjoy the food, and visit with each other in our absence. They did. They also cleaned up the kitchen; washed the dishes, pots, and pans; and fixed a large plate of food for both of us to heat in the microwave when we returned home. They stayed until almost ten waiting for us to return. The emergency room was filled when we arrived. Therefore it was almost one in the morning before David was admitted and we left for home. The pneumonia was quickly controlled again and luckily David was home in a week.

Following this latest pneumonia, Dr. Silva explained to us it was time to place him on a permanent feeding tube. We couldn't risk another pneumonia attack. The next one could be fatal. The feeding tube would bypass the normal eating and swallowing process thus eliminating the possibility of aspirating.

With prayers from his friends and total trust in his faith, David was fine with this decision. However, our hearts were aching. Selfishly, we realized we could not enjoy dinners together again as a family. We would not be able to go out to restaurants again with David. There were just so many changes in our lives we would have to adjust to as we concerned ourselves with David's wellbeing. Millions of commercials flash on the television screen daily advertising the delicious taste of foods, desserts, and drink. People on feeding tubes have to endure this knowing they can't partake. The one and only time David reacted to the idea of having a feeding tube came the night before he was to be admitted to the hospital for the insertion of the tube.

He loved pizza almost as much as he loved life. There was a Pizza Hut commercial that seemed to last at least forty-five minutes advertising a new pizza. After watching this, David sat quietly for sometime. Then he tried to speak between sobbing and wiping away a flow of endless tears. "That means I will never be able to have a pizza again."

Our hearts crumbled as we fought back tears. We both went over to him and had a huge family hug.

After I gained some composure I hugged him more and said, "David, your mom might be able to fix this. Do you suppose she will be able to mash and mash and mash a pizza so much it will turn into a liquid? Then she will be able to run it through your feeding tube." This was a corny attempt to bring us back to reality. We always joked with David and this time, thanks be to God, it worked! It wasn't long before he was smiling again.

The night before David was going to have the procedure to insert the feeding tube he decided he wanted food better than that served by the hospital. He wanted seafood. So I traveled to Fratelli's Restaurant and got him the biggest seafood dinner on their menus. Darn it! He ate the whole platter. I was hoping to get a taste. When we left the hospital that night David was content and ready to face the next day.

For our anniversary on April 7, David, without us knowing, bought three tickets for us to join members of the hospital staff on a dinner cruise up the Choptank River. The cruise was the

SHELDON LARMORE

week after he received his feeding tube. When he presented us with the tickets we were surprised and expressed our pleasure for the gift. We talked to him about how much we appreciated his thoughtfulness but told him maybe we could find another activity we could all enjoy that would not involve food.

"No. I want us to go on the cruise. I will be okay. I will enjoy the boat ride," he said.

Reluctantly, we agreed to go. We did not know how we were ever going to be able to eat in front of him, but we knew this was his wish. Our saving grace was in the thought, *He's not making a big deal about this so why should we?*

Throughout his life David had always made the best of whatever life dealt him. David made the cruise bearable by the positive way he accepted not being able to eat. He enjoyed the boat ride, the fellowship and the many laughs shared among the group. He made everyone feel comfortable about eating in front of him.

He joked with those around him by saying things like, "Is that squash? Ugh! I'm glad I can't eat. I hate squash!" When dessert was served he asked, "Is that pound cake? Where is the ice cream?"

"I don't think we will get ice cream. You are supposed to put a cherry topping on it," Sara Belle said.

"Pound cake isn't good without ice cream. Glad I don't have to eat those cherries," he said.

In late May David asked if we could take a trip to Philadelphia. He talked to his Aunt Faye and Uncle Lee about the trip and asked them if they would go with us. They readily agreed. In David's absence we did remind them that eating in front of David may be a problem.

His Aunt Faye said, "That's not a problem. We all need to lose weight anyway. This is David's trip, and we will do just fine."

That weekend was one of the most enjoyable we had experienced in some time. Faye and Lee were always very flexible and full of fun. We laughed from the time we left Salisbury until we returned home. There was no gloom and despair on this outing. When it came time to eat we would take turns disappearing for a while to catch a quick sandwich at McDonald's or another fast food place. Eating was never an issue. The focus was on David having a good time seeing the sights of Philadelphia.

FAITH STRENGTHENS HEALING

A sense of humor can help you overlook the unattractive, tolerate the unpleasant, cope with the unexpected, and smile through the unbearable

—Moslie Waldoks

*E*ven after David had the feeding tube inserted he continued to develop pneumonia. Each time he was admitted to the hospital for treatment. As his health began to deteriorate his spirit did not! He always found time for his friends, volunteering, and participating in any church activities in any church in the community. He simply loved God and enjoyed praising Him anytime and wherever he could.

In early September 1999, David's energy level and his zest for life began to slide from on high where it always seemed to dwell. He was ready to wake up at six, but his body was not as eager to get up. His spirit was ready to go out with friends, but his mind was trying to tell him to rest. One thing remained the same. He read his Bible daily and prayed for those in need. He found peace in listening to his favorite hymns and praise music. Appointments with doctors confirmed what they and we already knew but did not want to face. David's body was fighting to survive, perhaps too hard. His overall condition was weakening.

One early evening the last week of September, David's breathing, without warning, became very labored. His temperature spiked over 103 degrees. Sara Belle immediately had us in

PRMC's emergency room within minutes. On this particular trip, the emergency room was not busy and it seemed everyone in the examining area knew David. Since there were no real emergencies that evening David was treated as a king. He loved it. Almost immediately the diagnosis was bacterial pneumonia. He condition was listed as very serious. He was *again*, without hesitation, transported from the emergency area to ICU.

The first couple of days David's condition remained stable. His body was able to function on its own without assistance from elaborate machines. The antibiotics seemed to have leveled the progression of the pneumonia. We remained cautiously optimistic as we visited with David each day. On the third day our world went spinning out of control. As we arrived in the early morning we noticed two nurses working over David as we approached the room.

After a few moments of observing we asked, "Is he okay?"

"We've noticed he is moving from consciousness to semi-consciousness. His oxygen saturation is dropping, and his heart rate is increasing," one of the nurses replied.

"What does this mean?" I asked.

"His condition has worsened overnight. We have a call in to the doctor." These nurses, unfamiliar to us, increased his oxygen and adjusted his bed to make him more comfortable and left.

We moved close to the bed so we could give David a hug and observe his behavior first hand. He was conscious but weak.

As usual, no surprise to us, he said, "Hi, Mom. Hi, Dad. How are you?"

"The question is, how are you, Bunky?" I asked.

"I'm okay," he said.

Not long afterward, Dr. Nagel entered the room. Following a brief examination he said, "The latest X-rays show David's lungs are becoming more congested. This is causing increased stress on his heart since it has to work extra hard to pump blood through his body. This could easily lead to congestive heart failure. We don't need that. He's fighting enough problems now."

"What's the next step?" Sara Belle asked.

"We will try to treat it with medication. We'll see."

Much to the disappointment of Dr. Nagel and us David did not respond to the aggressive treatment. The following day he had to be placed once again on a ventilator. For the next two or three days we did not leave David's side except to go home for a quick nap and a change of clothes. Foremost in our minds was just how much more was his body going to be able to tolerate.

Word spread through the community about David's grave condition. We were overwhelmed with the many phone calls of concern we had on our answering machine each night and the cards of encouragement we received from friends. It was humbling to hear of the number of churches in the area that had David on their prayer list and the number of ministers who stopped us in the hallways of the hospital to express their love by letting us know we were in their prayers. This in itself did not surprise us since David at one time or another had visited their congregation within the last year.

Praise the Lord! Prayers are answered. David's condition gradually improved under the skilled care of Dr. Nagel and his partner Dr. Layton, obviously guided by powers much greater than theirs. David's whole appearance seemed to change. He looked and acted stronger, he was alert, and his presence glowed as if touched by the glory of God, and it truly was!

The next day Dr. Nagel told David he was on his way to Virginia Beach for a week of golf. His orders for him were very simple. "When I return, I want to visit you on the floor" (meaning in a regular hospital room). Two days later David was transferred out of ICU into a room on the third floor of the hospital. Things went well for the first few days. However, on the fourth or fifth day David developed a severe fever. His temperature shot to over 104 degrees. Even with several blankets covering him he shook so violently from chills he was experiencing the railings of the bed actually rattled. Needless to say he was back in ICU by evening. By early morning of the next day he was placed on a ventilator. A renewed feeling of absolute disbelief washed over our weary souls. The uncertainty of tomorrow emerged in the shadows of our despair.

Out in the waiting room family and friends once again gathered to offer their love, support, and prayers. The day dragged endlessly as if it was suffering from the same feeling of lifelessness we were experiencing. Surprisingly, a sense of serenity gently flowed through the room providing us with a welcomed calmness. David's fragile body appeared to be resting more peacefully. His breathing was less labored. His heart rate, blood oxygen, and temperature were all gradually moving toward normal. We looked at each other with eyes dampened by shedding tears. We knew we were living in our own regenerated spiritual awareness. For the many times we felt hopelessness we never suffered from a loss of faith. David had often and unrelentingly taught us to believe—believe in God's will, believe in His love. In less than a week David was released from ICU and returned to the third floor.

David always enjoyed having people stop by his room to give him encouragement, pray with him, or just pass the time of day. One of his frequent visitors was his Uncle Rocky Burnett. Rocky was a true friend of David's. When the two of them were together we knew time would pass quickly. We also knew with the loud laughter, crazy antics, and the teasing of the nurses by both of them we were all subject, at any time, to being transported out of the hospital. Rocky's presence in the room was always a welcomed relief. Whenever he arrived the nurses should have placed a sign on David's door, "Beware! The sounds of roaring laughter coming from this room are far more contagious than any cough, sniffle, or sneeze." We've learned as you're recovering from one critical illness after another not knowing what tomorrow will bring, you make adjustments. You can either fold up your tent and feel sorry for yourself or you galvanize yourself and live for today. As a family it was our intent to try to live so the shadows of yesterday did not spoil our sunshine of tomorrow. We hope we were examples of that to our family and friends.

Soon David's general condition began to improve each day. His gradual recovery certainly gave credibility to the age-old adage, "A priceless medication of laughter is fun, free, and easy to use in bringing about healing." Whenever we entered his room he always greeted us with a smile. In truth, smiling was David's favorite exercise! Even though David was seriously ill, we knew things were taking a turn for the better.

Reflecting on the many miracles we had witnessed over time, Sara Belle and I had to step back from the day and be quiet. We needed to quietly talk with God and thank Him for being with our family daily. We had to listen. We could hear the words written in 1 Corinthians 2:9 echoing in our minds. It was as if He was speaking to us: "No eye has seen, no ear has heard, and no mind has imagined what I have prepared for those who love Me." We live with the thought of expecting God to do something amazing each day. Our faith has taught us to live by believing and not by seeing as stated in 2 Corinthians 5:7.

It had been over two months since we arrived in the emergency room with David. It was Thanksgiving. Sara Belle, exhausted, was home cooking Thanksgiving dinner for her family. David was well on his way toward being discharged from the hospital in a few days and she needed to be busy. I was elected by Sara Belle to visit David midday with the message she and I would visit later in the evening. As I entered the room, who did I see? No one other than David's Uncle Rocky. As usual they were laughing about something.

"Good Lordy, Miss Molly! David, who washed your face with 'ugly soap' this morning?" I said.

David, being used to his dad's teasing, simply rolled his eyes and said, "Dad, be nice." As I glanced at Rocky, his mouth was open and his eyes conveyed shock and surprise. Moments later we were all laughing and joking with David what a poor job the "ugly soap" had done on his face. David just grinned and offered to share the soap with me the next time. Just about that time we heard loud talking and giggling in the hall by what seemed like a herd of young kids.

An assistant we all knew entered David's room and in a quiet laugh said, "The lady next door is a really sweet lady. She has three teenage children but no other abnormalities."

It took a minute for that statement to sink in but we all enjoyed another good laugh.

SHELDON LARMORE

A SHOCKING
SETBACK

Give your burdens to the Lord, and He will take care of you.
He will not permit the godly to slip and fall.

Psalm 55:22

The first week of December entered our radar screen so quickly we could not believe most of our fall had been spent traveling to and from home to PRMC. This being mostly behind us, we were anticipating, with great joy, David's return home in the next couple of days.

The first weekend of the month we stayed up into the wee hours of the mornings turning our home into a festive winter wonderland. We wanted David's arrival home to be a huge celebration colored with all the joys, wonderment, and rituals of a truly meaningful, blessed holiday. On Sunday, immediately following church, we went to visit with David. Part of our time was spent watching the Salisbury Christmas Parade from the fifth floor windows overlooking the parade route down Eastern Shore Drive. Following the parade we returned to David's room. We talked about him coming home, our Christmas plans, and a short trip we always wanted to take to Cape Charles, Virginia.

After a time Sara Belle noticed David's hair had not been washed for days. His bedclothes needed to be changed, and his general appearance needed his mother's overhauling. She asked if we could give David a shower and make him into his original handsome self. As Sara Belle washed David's hair she noticed a huge lump on the side of his head. I felt it, and we both agreed it was not normal. Our immediate concern was it was on the same site where his shunt was located. After the shower Sara Belle told the nurse in charge of our concern and requested a doctor look at it as soon as possible. Later in the day, we left David to rest while we went home to change clothes and get a bite to eat. Returning, Sara Belle asked the nurse if a doctor had looked at David's lump.

"Yes," she said. "However, he didn't see a problem. There was some swelling, but he thought you were overreacting." The nurse looked at David's files and returned. "Well, I guess he thought it was so insignificant he did not enter any comments on David's chart."

Sara Belle, our home-trained physician with many real and vicarious experiences, was not pleased. She called Dr. Silvia and explained the situation. He immediately contacted Dr. Zant, a neurosurgeon, and asked him if he would examine David.

In less than an hour, Dr. Zant—a pleasant, gentle man—was in David's room. As he examined David we sensed a growing fear about the seriousness of the lump. He finished the examination, straightened himself up and stood for moments looking at David. "We are going to have to operate as soon as possible."

"When?" we asked.

"Tonight. We have to work fast since his shunt could erupt at any time. If this happens it would be fatal."

We agreed to the operation. We signed the necessary papers and waited for an available operating room. David, our steadfast believer that God was always in complete control of his life, heard all of this conversation. As I watched him it was obvious he understood every word. His appearance was one of trust and quiet calmness. His manner in dealing with this latest setback was one we had witnessed from him in similar circumstances in the past.

"If it has to be done, let's do it. Let's get it over with and move on with life," he said.

SHELDON LARMORE

In the meantime our friends contacted friends who contacted friends. In less than an hour we were surrounded and supported by twenty-five or so friends and relatives. Most of those were members of my Wednesday morning men's prayer group and Sara Belle's Friday morning women's Bible study. They were our angels. They lived with us through so many illnesses and operations. We will never be able to fully express our appreciation to them even if we started now and continued through eternity.

Before long we received word the operation was scheduled for ten o'clock. At 9:50 p.m. nurses came into the room to transport David to the surgical area. After many hugs, kisses, and ample tears we released David to them for his awaited trip. Just as David was being rolled out of the room a nurse from the other end of the hall frantically yelled, "Stop! Stop!"

We stood frozen, stunned by this demand.

"The operation has been canceled," she stated.

For moments we were speechless, devastated, and in disbelief. However, the nurse came to the room and shared Dr. Zant had been operating all day and had just finished an emergency surgery. He felt he needed to rest before he tackled David's surgery.

After this explanation we fully understood and appreciated the reason for the delay. However, in silence, we worried and wondered about how much time we had before the operation came a real crisis. We put our trust in God and our complete confidence in Dr. Zant. To have a skilled doctor in the operating room with our son was a blessing. To have Dr. Zant, a very skilled neurosurgeon and a true Christian who was a devout servant of our Lord with David, was a real gift from our Father above.

Knowing it was going to be a long, long night I told Sara Belle I was going home to shower and change clothes. When I returned I sent her home to get a good night's rest while I stayed with David. After Sara Belle left for home I settled down in a chair next to David's bed. I watched him sleep as if he didn't have a worry in the world. It was hard for me to comprehend that

David, our thirty-year-old son, had just heard and understood his condition could be fatal, but his strong faith and commitment to God allowed him to rest in peace.

As I sat by his side I began to relive the many, many happy and meaningful times the three of us had shared. I prayed a simple prayer, *Oh God, bring David safely through this.* Later, *Oh God, please. Please…*

I couldn't help but think this might be the last night David would be with us. His condition was critical. My mind kept generating all the *what ifs…what ifs…what ifs…*

I prayed again, *God, don't let anything happen to David. He's not through teaching his mom and dad yet. We can't go on without him.*

Then I dissolved into an uncontrollable cry sobbing loudly. Realizing this might wake David I tried to muffle my sounds, which caused me to experience painful contractions and convulsions.

All I could pray was, *Oh, God, Oh, God.* I knew from the past just a word, even a simple cry, is enough for God who sees in our hearts even before our words are expressed. I tried to control my outward cries of distress. I prayed silently. I watched David sleep so quietly as if the hand of God was touching him tenderly while He whispered words of peace and promise in his ears. I stood and walked to the window. There was stillness throughout the town below. I felt an ever-so-gentle breeze flow around me. A sense of serenity entered my body, my soul. It truly was like someone standing quietly by my side.

I remember saying, "Thank you, God."

I leaned down and gave David a kiss, then moved back to the chair. I knew I had to be quiet to take in the presence of the Lord and enjoy a taste of heaven on earth. I knew I had to listen to hear the words of comfort and feel the love God wanted to share with me. My tears were gone. My body was relaxed. My thoughts were of hope. I drifted off into the twilight.

SHELDON LARMORE

When day broke I woke up to David saying, "Good morning, Dad. Where's Mom?"

"Good morning, Bunk. I sent her home to get some rest so she can keep us straight today."

It wasn't long before Sara Belle arrived with her cheerful smile and enthusiastic, "Good morning, guys."

By midmorning our friends and family gathered again to wish David well and to be with us through the operation. David's friend and our angel, Kathy Monteleone, was busily running about the hospital helping patients. However, she frequently checked on us and kept us posted about David's whereabouts and progress. After more than three hours, Dr. Zant entered the waiting room with the good news the operation was over and successful. David made out fine.

It wasn't long before Kathy came to the waiting room to tell us she'd been with David in the recovery room. "He is doing just fine. He is wide awake, and all his signs are good. I asked him how he felt. He said, 'Great! It was a piece of cake.'"

David arrived home late on December 23, 1999. Christmas was always a meaningful holiday at the Larmores. We always attended the midnight services at St. Peters Episcopal Church and listened to Christmas music throughout Christmas day. With David around, our home was filled with friends and relatives from early Christmas morning until late Christmas night. This time was no exception. However, Christmas had even a deeper meaning this year. We had so many things to be thankful for and so many blessings we had to sincerely give thanks for to our Lord. We were prepared to resume our lives and move forward. We tried to never dwell on unpleasant happenings of yesterday because we learned it uses up too much of today.

FAITH CONQUERORS ALL

Getting well is not the goal. Ever more important is learning to live without fear, to be at peace with life, and ultimately death.

—Bernie Siegel

By mid-January, David was ready to jump back into life with great enthusiasm. Sara Belle's kitchen once again became *David's Cookie Shop*. For four straight days our stove oven stayed hot while Sara Belle and her two elves namely, David and Sheldon, baked chocolate chip cookies, counted chocolate chip cookies, and boxed chocolate chip cookies for delivery to all the areas of the hospital. This was the third marathon type of chocolate chip cookie baking Sara Belle and her staff had done to show appreciation to the hospital employees for all their efforts in giving us comfort and for caring for David over the years. This home production was first initiated in December 1994 as our gift to PRMC employees at Christmastime. The second time was in late fall of 1996 following David's lengthy stay in the hospital during the summer of that year. As a family we thoroughly enjoyed this time together.

The unfortunate part of these endeavors was each time the cookie shop was put into production, I ate at least five pounds of oven warm, deliciously melted fresh chocolate chip cookies and drank at least two gallons of ice-cold milk. I jokingly said to David one time, "David, I can't make up my mind. I'm not sure if

I want you to have another long stay in the hospital so I can enjoy more homemade delicious chocolate chip cookies or if I want you to stay out of the hospital so I won't get so darn fat. I'm going to have to think on it."

"Dad, get a grip! I'm not going back into the hospital so you are just going to have to stay away from Mom's cookies," he said.

Reflecting back on our many happy days together one of the things I surely miss is being able to tease him. Don't worry about "poor little David." He could give back as much as he received.

In January of 2001, I was scheduled for a total knee replacement. Obviously this meant I would be unable to lift David or take care of several of his other daily routines for a period of time. Conscious of the energy and time it took, David was most concerned about how his mom was going to be able to provide for his care by herself. He proceeded to work this out on his own without our knowledge.

David belonged to a prayer group at the hospital that met each Wednesday at noon in the chapel. At one of the meetings David asked for prayer for me and especially for his mom. He prayed the Lord would give her the energy and strength to handle him, the house, *and me* during this period of my recovery. The members of the prayer group saw his need and gave answers to his prayer. Following the meeting, a group circulated through the hospital a request for individuals to join in helping the Larmores through this time. As a result, a team of fifteen to twenty employees signed up to assist us nightly. Each evening around nine for the next two months two hospital employees showed up to help get David ready for the evening and lifted him from his wheelchair to his bed. We knew several of them through our association with the hospital. However, our circle of friends increased as we all became a family. I still become emotional just thinking about how supportive and loving these individuals were. Each of them unselfishly left their warm homes at eight thirty at night to travel in the cold of January and February to assist Sara Belle.

Many of us have committed the Golden Rule to memory. These individuals wholeheartedly and faithfully committed it to life.

Among the several new friends my knee surgery brought to us, there is one who has remained with us and has become a part of our extended family. This angel from heaven is Jane Graves. How we survived without her over the years we will never know. She has become one of our lights in the dark and surely is one of our family's strongest cheerleaders. She was one of David's greatest advocates. She not only provided David with opportunities to travel about but she also provided us with mini respite times when we could quietly go out to dinner or a movie by ourselves knowing David was in good hands.

Two other special people that helped us through this period were John Sharpe and Dan Harris. Over the years we have grown close to John. He, like Rocky Burnett, Bob Caldwell and many others has rushed to our side in times of need. They are like brothers. Dan and his wife, Michele, are treasured members of our family. They are like our son and daughter, David's brother and sister. As mentioned earlier David from birth was never able to naturally void his body waste.

The last four years of his life he wore a permanent catheter. Each night he had to be given an enema. This process took a minimum of an hour. It involved lifting him up from his Amigo or wheelchair, placing him on the floor, inserting the enema and then picking him up and putting him on toilet. Afterward, came the physical task of giving him a shower and preparing him for bed. Following my knee operation I was advised to not lift David for at least three months. Dan and John came to our rescue. On a rotating schedule they shared the responsibility of giving David his enema from mid January through August. I kept telling them I could resume my "duty" in May but they kept coming. After Sara Belle and I had handled this task well over thirty years we just gave in and told them, "Hope you are having fun. Knock yourself out!"

Out of the blue one evening David looked at me and said, "You know, Dad, I think we are ready to go to Cape Charles."

"Now! It's almost midnight," I said.

"No dummy. I mean soon."

We made that trip to Cape Charles with his Aunt Ellie and Uncle Bob traveling with us. As the year continued we made many day and overnight trips. David wanted to go to Norfolk, Williamsburg, Philadelphia, Lancaster, Harper's ferry, and to the beach as often as possible. We attempted to take him to all those places. Looking back, we're glad we did. David's enthusiasm for life never weaned. It truly was a gift to him from God. It was as if he realized God created each day and invited him to live in it to his fullest. As Joel Osteen wrote, "Enthusiasm is our way to tell God, 'Thank you.'" We know without any doubt David thanked God each day for his blessing and his life.

Two other people who entered our lives during this time were Holly Evans and Dean DeFino. David's life "sparked" whenever he was with them. They cared for David in such a way he had to feel their healing ripples of friendship and love. David always came home refreshed after an outing with them. Evenings spent at home with Dean and Holly sharing funny stories of life and Dean playing his guitar as we sang along filled our home with joy and much laughter that lingered in the air long after our "party."

One Wednesday evening Holly stopped by to take David with her to a Bible study Dean was conducting at his church, Crossroads Church of God, in Fruitland. Holly felt comfortable driving our handicapped van and was familiar with how the lift operated. When they arrived at the church, Holly drove up to the door so David could exit the van from the lift onto the cement pad. By some quirk the lift malfunctioned dropping David from the lift some four feet onto the cement pad with his two-hundred-plus-pound electric wheelchair falling on top of him.

While David was with Holly and Dean, we took a mini vacation to Zia's restaurant for a night out. Shortly after our dinner arrived, Sara Belle received a call on her cell phone from a member of the church saying, "David is on his way to the hospital by ambulance. He fell off of his lift. Holly is with him. She asked me to call you."

We paid our bill and rushed to the emergency room. As we walked in we saw Holly entering one of the cubicles. As soon as she saw us she hurried over and broke down in tears. Sara Belle hugged her and helped calm her. Not far from us we saw David sitting up in bed. He appeared okay.

As we approached him he greeted us with his normal cheerful, "Hi, Mom and Dad."

"Are you okay?" Sara Belle asked.

"Yes, I fell from the lift, but I'm okay," he replied.

After being examined David was released from the hospital, and we all went home. Holly was still shaken. There was no way we were going to let her leave our sight until she was calm and realized this situation could have happened to any of us. We fixed hot chocolate and talked. After all was said and done, we realized fully what had happened. We knew who was present with Holly and David. Without a doubt it was Holly, David, and one or more angels present. We know! In our minds we reenacted this whole situation. Just think, David was strapped into the seat of his electric wheelchair, fell some four feet off the lift onto a cement pad head first with a two-hundred-plus pound wheelchair landing on top of him.

David had one very small scratch on his nose, no broken bones, no concussion, no cuts, and no bleeding. His eyeglasses were intact, but his wheelchair was in serious disrepair. It had to stay in the wheelchair hospital for a week while parts were ordered and repairs were made.

Another wonder came when we examined the new Redskins jacket he was given as a Christmas gift by our friends Bill and Judy Wyatt. There was absolutely no tear, scrape, or any other damage to the jacket. We are totally confident in our belief angels are around us, angels are beside us, and angels watch over us. Just be quiet, and feel their wings wrap gently around you. Listen to hear them whispering in your ears, "We love you. You are blessed. We're here to protect you."

PREPARING FOR HEAVEN

Time is short. When I do leave you to go to my Father's place, grieve not, nor speak of me in tears. I will want you to laugh and talk of me as if I was beside you. If not, my life was in vain.

—Unknown author

Live for today. You steal if you try to touch tomorrow for it belongs to God.

—Unknown author

We all want to go to heaven when we leave this material world. Our Christian dream is to reside in the house of our Lord and meet our Creator one day. We look forward to the joys of everlasting life, united with all our loved ones in happiness and harmony.

David's endless battle with pneumonia, infections, and setbacks from his shunt malfunctions continued to lessen his strength and weaken his immune system. However, the need to boost his oxygen intake, increase his medications, and the continual monitoring of his oxygen saturation level did not dampen his spirits or limit his activities. Each week we received twenty to twenty-four containers of oxygen to keep him on the go.

He was always connected to a fresh tank daily and never left home without a second tank attached to the back of his electric wheelchair. It wasn't long before David's bedroom was filled with various new types of equipment, supplies, and materials that were a *must* for us to have at home to keep his health stabilized. Each piece of equipment had its own set of flashing lights, bells, warning signals, and the like to notify us of any mechanical or physical malfunctions. Sara Belle laughingly told David one evening his room looked like an airport runway with all the flashing lights and crazy sounds. In all seriousness it was estimated the combined inventory of medical equipment, machines, materials, and supplies located in all areas of his bedroom cost approximately thirty-five thousand dollars. These items were rented, but you can believe we made sure they were covered by insurance.

As time progressed David needed more help during the night. For years he could not turn over in bed by himself. Now it was even more difficult for him to sleep comfortably with so many attachments to his body. For several months we would take turns sleeping while the other stayed awake near by in case he needed help or one of the machines failed.

Prior to David's last three months stay in the hospital our dear friends Don and Joan Davis took time from their busy schedule to investigate ways to make our life a little easier. We had a real need to renovate our bathroom into one more functional for David's and our use. Sara Belle's continuing health problems, her inability to lift David and her lack of strength in making the necessary adjustments in his positions made it difficult to provide for him without assistance.

We were eventually given state funds that helped us construct a handicapped bathroom connected to David's bedroom. We will always be grateful to Don and Joan for their intense efforts in guiding us to the appropriate sources for assistance. With the help of Paul Mysak from the disabilities division of our health department, Ernie Cornbrooks' legal assistance and Andy Booth's architecture advice and guidance, David lived to enjoy his handicapped facilities. Eventually, we had to arrange for help to sit with David during the night so we could get some much needed rest.

David's health began to deteriorate rapidly in the winter of 2002. He began to reach out to his friends, especially Kathy Montelone, Donna Thompson, and Jane Graves as he searched for ways to share his anxieties and fears for the future. Many of David's friends have told us of the positive and uplifting conversations they had with David during this period in his life. Several sources told us he started his conversation by saying, "I don't want my mom or dad to have to worry too much but…" Then he would begin to talk about how he had enjoyed life and wondered when the time was coming for him to meet Jesus.

We are indebted to one of David's closest confidants at PRMC, Donna Thompson. We are blessed she kept running notes of her conversations and encounters with David. These she shared with us after his passing. It is important we share them with others to give an unbiased insight into his thoughts at the time. The statements presented below are typed directly from the handwritten notes Donna gave us:

> March 11, 2002: "I get very emotional when I think about things anymore. About life in general. I think about my death—where I am going to go. Sometimes it's hard to express what I'm feeling. I want to protect my mom and dad. I think about what heaven is going to be like. I have no doubt in my heart and mind that I will be in heaven. I've been told so. It seems every time I make plans they fall through because of my health. It makes me feel depressed. This has been going on since the beginning of the year."

> March 12, 2002: David wants to share his feelings with JoEllen, Holly, Kathy, Jane, and me. He said, "I want to bring out more of the feelings in my heart. I am afraid of dying—not of death itself but of the process. How much am I going to have to suffer before I go to heaven? What's going to happen from point A, now, to point B?" When I

asked David about sharing his feelings with his mom and dad he stated, "I can't. I don't want them to worry. I need to do this on my own—this is my own struggle. I'm going through it with my faith, with Jesus beside me."

March 17, 2002: "It seems the devil has been trying to get me down since January. I had a bad night last night. My nose was stopped up without the mask, and I was having a hard time breathing. I kept praying, 'Lord, get me through this night.' Mom took my temperature. It was 102, and I had the chills. I was fine this morning. When these attacks come I get very tense. It makes me very emotional inside. I wonder each time if this is the end."

March 23, 2002: David was thrilled about the response from Trinity and St. Peters churches in helping him raise monies for the March of Dimes Walk-A-Thon. The concert Peter's Voice held to help raise funds for David's walk raised $623.20 which added to his total monies of $3,603 to date. With a big smile David's response was, "Great! I may go over the $4,000 mark." He added, "I go see Dr. Silvia today for a follow-up, and I have an appointment with Dr. Nagel next Tuesday with my parents. They are two nice doctors." At David's request, I scheduled some time with Dr. Nagel for next week so we could discuss end of life issues with him.

March 25, 2002: David and I have an appointment with Dr. Nagel next Friday to talk about questions he has about end of life. Comments from David during this time together were, "I know everybody goes through changes at one time or another. I get really emotional when death comes up. When I have spells my parents ask me if I'm scared, and I tell them yes. I feel better with one on one than having a whole group around. I feel comfortable with Dr. Nagel because I think he knows where I'm coming from, at least I hope. When Dr. Nagel sees us hopefully he'll know what I should do to help me feel better about myself and what will happen to me. It's not an easy thing for me to deal with, but I have the faith things will be okay. I am ready to hear what Dr. Nagel has to say."

On Saturday, April 13, we were busy around the house doing laundry, working in the yard and beginning to get our spring and summer clothes in order. As the morning continued I noticed Sara Belle was not herself. She stopped frequently and sat in her lounge chair. This was so unlike her. Fortunately, I was with her when she stood up, stated she was dizzy, and immediately fell to the floor. She lay in a dead faint. I shook her awake and slowly moved her to the couch. She seemed to be coming around; however, I called my sister in Laurel and Sara Belle's sister, Ellie. By the time Ellie arrived, my sister, Faye, had already traveled from Laurel and was at Sara Belle's side. The best way to describe Sara Belle's condition was dopey. We called the ambulance. However, before it arrived Sara Belle began to go in and out of consciousness. This scared us to death! By the time she arrived at the hospital her condition had improved somewhat. After several tests, numerous examinations and monitoring over the weekend she was released. The diagnosis: Simply fatigue. The plan for recovery: Rest.

> April 15, 2002: David and I visited today. He told me about his mom and her spell over the weekend. He said, "She felt weak and fainted in the floor. The ambulance took her to PRMC. They couldn't find anything wrong. She is coming home today. She has an appointment with Dr. Bird tomorrow." David told me he has to stay focused on his work so he won't worry as much. David had a follow-up appointment with Dr. Nagel this morning. His oxygen level is constantly fluctuating. He told me Dr. Nagel said he needs a respirator at home that will cost over $10,000. David is hoarse today because he just had a coughalator treatment. It gives him a sore throat and makes him hoarse for most of the day.

April 18, 2002: David and I met with Dr. Nagel to talk about what will happen at the end of his life. David wanted the truth. He said he didn't want anything held from him. He said, "It may be scary. I don't want any heroics." Dr. Nagel was open with David and showed great compassion. I know it had to be hard for him to talk with David. They had developed such a close relationship. Dr Nagel shared, "David, when your oxygen and carbon dioxide elevate we will increase your oxygen input until we reach the maximum. There may still be an increase in shortness of breath. Sometimes morphine is given so it will decrease your anxiousness and difficulty in breathing. It may help you in being more peaceful. Eventually, respiration failure will occur, and you will probably go into a coma. Sometimes patients fall asleep and don't wake up. There is no pain. It will be hard for your parents to watch, but you will not know. You could get a urinary tract infection causing you to go into septic shock or you could suffer a fatal heart attack. David, you know we will do all in our power to make your passing as easy as possible. Try not to worry. You know I'm here for you anytime." David left Dr. Nagel's office satisfied with their talk and ready to face the rest of the day.

Sunday 14, April, 2002, was a big day for the Harris Family. Dan and Michele's oldest son, Aaron, was to be confirmed into the Catholic Church. Our family was invited to the 3:00 p.m. service and to the reception following the ceremony. We readied ourselves for the day preparing to attend morning services at our church. David was very sluggish as we began to get him dressed. Rather than to push him to get ready we suggested we stay home from church. We told him we thought he needed to rest before we went to Aaron's confirmation. He said, "I'll be okay. After all, the reason I got up this morning was because I thought we were going to church. So we are going to church." During church

SHELDON LARMORE

David was having trouble breathing. His portable oxygen supply was turned up as high as it would go.

"David, are you all right?" I asked.

"Dad, don't worry. I'm okay," he said.

As the service rambled on and on I looked about the congregation and noticed many were becoming as restless and distracted as I was. However, when I turned to look at David he was totally focused on the sermon unaware of happenings around him.

After church as we made our way to the van we had to stop. David had a severe coughing spell. Our first concern was to make sure he was not choking and was able to breathe. After a time David regained his composure and his breathing became normal. As soon as we entered the house he had another attack. This time frightened us more than any other time. He totally lost control of his body and began to turn blue.

Following this episode, his words to us were, "Please don't worry. I'm just tired. Next time just let me go. I'm ready."

We were shaken by this response. There was no way we expected this. He looked at us and said, "Mom, Dad, I'm okay. I'm just tired. I'll be okay." Our son was strong! Strong spiritually, strong in his faith, and strong in his love for us. He was determined to live life to its fullest and carry on any tasks that he felt were for the glory of God.

Later that day he insisted Sara Belle go to Aaron's confirmation. Shortly after Sara Belle left David had another coughing, choking spell. I increased his oxygen level on his portable tank. I used every device in reach and every piece of equipment in the room I could possibly manipulate to help him breathe. The windows were down. The phone was out of reach. It was useless to pick up something heavy to throw through the window to draw attention for help. No one in the neighborhood was around. His oxygen level continued to fall. Once I managed to get it up some and attempted to move him near a machine that would help, his level would take another nosedive. This continued for well over an hour. I was exhausted. After he stabilized enough to talk he looked at me and said once again in a quiet, labored voice, "Dad, just let me go. I'm tired. I'm tired of fighting. Please, just let me go."

I was distraught with hidden emotion, drowning in quiet tears, and physically drained. I hugged him tightly and held him close. I couldn't speak at first fearing I would not be able to hold back my outburst of emotions. Eventually David recovered enough to busy himself by watching the Orioles game. I guardedly sat near by trying to comprehend what had taken place in the last hour or so.

April 24, 2002: David brought good news today. Dr. Bird had called his mom to tell her the spot on the MRI was a cyst—nothing more to be done. Praise God!

April 25, 2002: David tells me he has seizures now at night and they are getting more involved and violent. He will be going to see Dr. Bird, his neurologist, soon at Dr. Nagel's request. His alarm to the machine regulating his oxygen intake and another alarm indicating heart irregularities are going off 10 to 12 times each night. He falls asleep, stops breathing and his alarm sounds. When he wakes up he has these seizures, his body gets really stiff and he gets really scared.

May 2, 2002: Dr. Silvia wants David to have an EEG, but they are waiting for a consultation with Dr. Bird. David had a severe seizure yesterday while waiting for lunch in the hospital's cafeteria. This was the first time he had a seizure during the day. His other seizures have always occurred at night. This one lasted an unusual length of time. He couldn't move. His eyes rolled back into his head. He stated, "Here lately I've been able to tell Jane, JoEllen, and Kathy my feelings, and we've gotten really close. I trust them with our talks. I can't talk to my parents. I don't want them to worry. They have enough on them."

May 3, 2002: David tells me he feels like he has fluid around his heart. He is supposed to see his cardiologist, Dr. Etherton, very soon. His feet and legs are swollen and have been for a good month. That's the reason Dr. Silvia has referred him to Jeff Etherton. He shared, "Dr. Silvia told Mom to get a pair of support stockings to put on my legs. My mom puts these support stockings on every day because my legs and feet are so swollen I can't wear my shoes. After a bit David began to talk about dying. I can't believe how mature he is when he talks about the end of his life. He said, "I worry. I'm not sure if my mom and dad are going to be okay after I die." We talked about his faith in God and his belief in the words of the Bible. He said, "I know in my heart God will be with them. He will comfort them." With that we prayed together and told each other we were so thankful to God for our friendship.

Sara Belle, bless her heart, constantly monitored David's appearance, moods, and physical behavior. She knew almost before he sneezed he was going to sneeze and just how loud. In early April she discussed with me her growing concern about David's increased quietness and periods of withdrawal from activities he normally enjoyed. A friend, Carole DiPietro, encouraged her to contact Hospice and ask for a counselor to meet with David periodically. This would provide David with a trained individual to share his thoughts with and receive professional feedback during their times together. She did and were we and David ever blessed. A lady by the name of Vera Patterson showed up at our door one day. She and David hit it off just great. He couldn't wait to meet with her during their scheduled times. She became another angel in our lives. Most times Vera and David would meet for lunch in the Junior Board Shop of the hospital or in the chapel. It was evident he felt secure in discussing his concerns, his dreams and his fears with her. She was another answer to our many prayers.

May 6 was David's thirty-second birthday. Even though he had a rough, sleepless night he would not stay home to rest. He felt it was his responsibility to volunteer since the week before his department had been really busy. Reluctantly as usual we consented to take him to the hospital with the understanding if he felt he needed to come home he should call us. We knew before telling him we were wasting our energy. Wouldn't it be wonderful if some of the healthy, able-bodied, young people in today's world had the same dedication, energy, drive and enthusiasm David had for life and for his responsibilities?

That evening David wanted to go to Tokyo Steak House to celebrate his birthday. He invited his two best girl friends, Kathy and Holly, and his Aunt Ellie and Uncle Bob to join us. Throughout the night David was David. He, as always, enjoyed being with friends and family, laughing hardily and enjoying every taste of food. His oxygen tank was at its maximum level with a full tank of oxygen at his side. We all enjoyed the on-site preparation of our food as the chef gave us an entertaining display of his culinary skills. We gave no thought initially when he lit the fluid causing the flame to rise some ten stories high in front of us. Then it hit us! David was attached to a potentially explosive gas. Thanks be to God! Nothing happened. And where are those of you who question the existence of angels and their whereabouts when we need them? Does this little near fiasco help you to understand why we believe?

Going Home to God

When the heart weeps for what it has lost, the soul laughs for what it has found.

Death is but the next great adventure.

—Unknown

The week following David's birthday was spent in doctors' offices. We had many concerns we felt needed to be addressed. He had an appointment with Dr. Etherton who explained to us David's heart was enlarged and becoming weaker. Dr. Nagel informed us what we already knew, David's condition was irreversible and would continue to deteriorate. Dr Silvia couldn't give us any encouragement. Since David continued to develop pneumonia even after being on the feeding tube he made the decision to drink and eat on special occasions knowing his next pneumonia attack may be fatal. In Dr. Genvert's office David had another coughing and choking spell. On our way out of the office he told David, "You're my man. Take care of yourself."

In a matter of seconds, he came out into the waiting room as we were leaving. He touched Sara Belle on the arm saying, "I want both of you to take care of yourselves. Call me if you need me."

Both Dr. Zant and Dr. Bird passed us in the halls of the hospital that week. They stopped to ask how we were and how David was progressing. David's doctors were genuine and caring individuals. Each of them knew ten cents worth of human understanding far out equaled ten dollars worth of medical science. We will forever be indebted to them for their kindness and compassion. We know them as doctors who know how to pray and obey God in their professional as well as their personal lives. We've thanked God often for sharing them with us.

That week David told us he had four things he wanted to do. Four things he *must* do. He had to finish the week volunteering at the hospital, he wanted to go with the Holly Center team to visit the third grade class in one of the city schools, he wanted to attend the May meeting of the City Council where the mayor was presenting him with an award, and he wanted to talk to the Rotary Club thanking them for presenting him with the distinguished honor as a recipient of their "Four Way Award."

Day by day David put a couple extra to-do items on his ever-growing list. He was able to participate in all of the events and complete all the things on his list except one. He never gave up teaching us to learn from yesterday, love to be part of today, and hope for tomorrow. He tried not to think of the future because he said he had too much to do each day.

Early on Friday afternoon we received a phone call from Vera Patterson, David's hospice counselor. She asked if she could come over for a visit. When she arrived she stated she knew she shouldn't allow herself to become emotionally involved with her clients. However, she said David was an exception. She wanted us to know she had met with David that morning and was so moved by their discussion she just had to see us today. She continued with dampness in her eyes, "David has taught me so much. He is one special young man. I'm not at liberty to share with you what we talked about, but you must be proud of him."

Our visit was an enjoyable one with conversations moving from one topic to another. I was so glad Sara Belle took Carole's advice and made contact with hospice. Sitting in front of us was a gift, a true gift from heaven, who had given a greater peace and meaning to our son's life.

Between the two of them they had built a bond of mutual respect and trust. She soon learned one of David's obstacles in life was his inability to cope with fear. Not a spiritual fear but a human, physical fear of the unknown. Through many sessions Vera was able to break through that barrier. She gave David permission to fear. As Vera prepared to leave she asked us not to share with David she had visited. We never did.

As we took care of household chores on Saturday we encouraged David to rest. We reminded him he had a very busy week ahead and kiddingly insisted he needed his beauty rest. He loved hearing that. Later in the afternoon, since Sunday was Mother's Day, David and I planned to go to the Country House to get Sara Belle a gift. It wouldn't be David or his dad if we didn't wait until the last minute to buy a gift and card. When the time arrived, I walked to David's room. He was hugging Sara Belle saying, "I want to wish you Happy Mother's Day." "David, you are a day early," she said.

"Yes, I know. But I'm not sure if I will be here on Mother's Day."

"Don't talk like that, David. Sure you are going to be here."

Hearing the conversation I waited before I entered. "Are you ready to go shopping, David?"

"Dad, do you mind going by yourself? I don't feel well," he said in a quiet voice.

When I returned, I walked into another conversation between Sara Belle and David. The mood, however, was much lighter. Knowing the topic of the conversation it was hard to think it would be less than tear jerking. However, they'd had this talk so many times in the past year both of them could now joke as they talked.

Sara Belle was saying, "Now David, when you get to heaven you are going to have to let mom and dad know you are okay."

David replied with one of his cute little mischievous grins, "Right, Mom. Just how am I going to do that?"

"You'll find a way. If I get to heaven before you and Dad, I will find a way. I might have to ask St. Peter, but I will, somehow, let you know I got there and am okay," Sara Belle assured him.

Sunday morning we went to church. On our way home we stopped at Dunkin' Donuts for a carry out of coffee and donuts. The afternoon was spent watching an Oriole's baseball game. Even though it was Mother's Day, Sara Belle prepared a delicious baked chicken dinner and a fresh chocolate pie for her boys. David began to slowly sink into a deep slumber after dinner. We called it an early evening, and all of us were in bed by nine.

Early on Monday morning I got up, dressed, and went to Salisbury University. I promised to fill in for one of my colleagues during his early morning class. He was only going to be gone a short while but needed someone to cover his class. Teaching at the university was a definite highlight in my career. I've never worked with such caring, generous, and wholesome individuals as I experienced the ten years I taught on staff.

David rested in the morning. His friend and ours, Barbara Webster, came in the afternoon to talk to him about his presentation to the Rotary Club on Thursday evening. David was planning to speak, but he asked Barb to be his backup if his congestion prevented him from finishing his talk. Together they rehearsed until they felt comfortable with how they were going to interact.

Soon it was time to begin getting ready for his appearance at the city council meeting. We received word to be in the chambers promptly at seven. The council had a full agenda for the evening. David was going to be the first order of business. Just before we left for the meeting David had one of his coughing and choking spells. After he regained his composure we tried to convince him to stay home. He was determined. He said they expected him to be there, and he needed to go. He kept repeating, "I'm okay. I'm okay."

We arrived in the council chambers with David's entourage of friends including his Aunt Faye, Uncle Lee, Aunt Ellie, Uncle Bob, Julia Ann Ball, Kathleen Johrden, Bob Caldwell, John Sharpe, and five or six others from the hospital staff. Seven o'clock arrived. No mayor in sight. After fifteen minutes the president of the council began the meeting. By seven thirty David was beginning to experience shortness of breath and started coughing. I carried him out into the hall to help him calm down.

"Let's go home, David. They will reschedule you for the next meeting," I pleaded.

"I'll be okay Dad I have to do this."

We re-entered the chambers. No sign of the mayor. I had to take David out of the meeting again about eight thirty. Again I pleaded with no avail. David was determined to get through the night. We re-entered the chamber about 8:50 p.m. The mayor was still nowhere in sight. The mayor arrived shortly after nine explaining there was a conflict in scheduling and an overbooking of meetings. At 9:15 p.m. David received his recognition. We left for home shortly afterward. By the time we reached the parking lot he was extremely warm and was coughing deeply. On our way home David's condition improved.

He stated half jokingly with his famous grin, "Don't you guys think I deserve a treat for what *I* have put you through? I need a donut, and while you are at it, I will take a cup of coffee."

Knowing better, our hearts melted. David's Aunt Faye and Uncle Lee followed us home where we all joined in laughter as David and his Uncle Lee joked with each other and got great joy out of making fun of the rest of us. Just before Faye and Lee left, David got quiet and sat back in his chair. Sara Belle asked,

"David, honey, are you all right?" Sara Belle asked.

"I'm okay." He just kind of stared about the room.

As we got him ready for bed, his Aunt Faye said, "David, how about I stay with your mom and dad tonight? They can get some rest, and I will be with you."

"No, Aunt Faye. We will need you more tomorrow," he said.

With that we all hugged and kissed David, tucked him in bed, and moved to the family room. Shortly, Faye and Lee left after we promised to call them during the night if we needed them.

Later Sara Belle and I went to David's room and stood in the doorway watching him sleep. He seemed to be at peace and resting well. We started for the family room when we both heard an odd noise coming from David's room. When we entered his room, Sara Belle noticed David had raised his electric hospital bed up as far as it would go. He had never done that before. I'm not sure if he ever investigated how his bed could be raised, especially since he could not move in his bed once we placed him there.

"David, I can't reach you. Your bed is too high," Sara Belle said. Jokingly she added, "Are you trying to get to heaven?"

His simple response was, "Yes."

"Well kid, we're not ready to let you go yet so come back down here," I said.

David just looked at me with a half smile.

Sara Belle and I planned to take shifts sitting with David through the night. Since I was taking the first shift, I left the room to prepare for the night.

As I stepped out of the shower Sara Belle entered the bathroom and said, almost as if in shock, "I think he's gone."

I grabbed a towel, and we both raced to David's bedside. I gently moved him about while we both kept calling his name. Sara Belle tried to feel his pulse while I felt his neck and placed a hand on his chest. Absolutely no pulse. Absolutely no heart beat. Absolutely no breath. We called 911 and within minutes they responded. They worked over David for at least twenty minutes as we stood in the corner of the room in total shock. We had no emotion. No tears. No feeling. Why? Neither of us could believe we were living this nightmare.

"Lord, take care of David," Sara Belle prayed.

SHELDON LARMORE

"Lord, take care of David," I prayed.

Without any exchange of words David was lifted from his bed, placed on a gurney, and carried to the ambulance. We followed behind, got in our car and waited. Once in the ambulance the paramedics took another fifteen minutes or so to work on him. We knew David was no longer with us. We could not talk. All either of us could do was stare ahead at the flashing lights of the ambulance. It was as if we were suspended in time. Someone else had control. We knew he was gone from us in body but not in spirit.

The ambulance slowly entered Gunby Road, turned on Mt. Hermon Road, and unhurriedly, without flashing lights, made its journey to the hospital. This confirmed to us that David would not be returning home. As we entered the emergency room one of the nurses on duty knew us. She approached with tears rolling down her face. "You're going to have to excuse me. I'm not supposed to do this."

Feeling her emotions we both took turns hugging her saying, "It's all right."

"How is he?" Sara Belle asked.

"They can't get any response, there's no pulse."

As we walked toward the area where they were trying to revive David, we both responded with a statement worse than a thousand deaths, "Tell them to stop. We know he is gone."

To See David lying so still, swollen, so quiet without any sign of life was unbearable. Sara Belle knelt by his side quietly praying between sober tears. I stood beside her in total shock, total disbelief. My prayer was, "God, take care of him. He is loved."

Driving home from the hospital at one o'clock the silence between us was deafening. We no longer were three on earth. A huge part of us had journeyed to a new home. Once home, we remained in shock. Without hardly a word spoken we stripped David's bed sheets, remade his bed, washed clothes, cleaned the house, ironed, and moved about the house aimlessly searching,

searching for what we were not sure. Just before dawn we sat at the computer, wrote a draft for his obituary and tentatively planned his funeral. A little after seven the phone rang. I picked it up expecting it to be my sister.

The voice on the other end said, "Hello, Sheldon. This is Kel. Just wanted to let you know Debbie and I are thinking about you both. If you need us you know where we are."

It was a most touching and appreciated call from Dr. Nagel. His call was the first we received expressing sympathy. By eight we began to have family, neighbors, and friends streaming in throughout the day. We never felt so loved and cared for, yet so very lonely and lost in the midst of friends.

A CELEBRATION
OF LIFE

If we have been pleased with life, we should not be displeased with death since it comes from the hands of the same master.

—Michelangelo

isitation for David was set for May 16 at the funeral home from 3:00 p.m. until 6:00 p.m. We arrived as a family by two thirty in the afternoon. There already was a line of friends waiting inside and stretching around the building outside to express their love and support. We were surrounded with kindness and love. We were so overwhelmingly surprised we changed from grieving parents to parents overcome by the tremendous tributes this community of people was showering on David. We never guessed. We never suspected such homage and unselfish expression of respect and admiration for our son. We were touched that our local television station, WBOC, was there to interview us and random mourners in the funeral home and was also present to film a segment of his funeral the next day. David was such a caring and humble person he wouldn't quite understand what all the fuss was about, but he would have loved it! He would have been hugging and kissing on everyone so much that by the end of the day he would have looked like one big red fire ball from lipstick smears.

The line of mourners stretching into the parking lot of Holloway Funeral Home continued well into the evening. Since the viewing was to end by six, Sara Belle and I were expected to attend the Rotary Club dinner meeting at seven. This was the last appointment on David's list of things to do that he was not able to fulfill. He was to speak to the members about his experiences over the last year and give thanks for all their support in the past. In preparing to leave the viewing we asked family members to stand in for us since there was an awesome line of friends still waiting to express their condolences.

As soon as we arrived at the dinner meeting we were met by Barbara Webster. As stated earlier she and David had met to discuss his presentation just hours before his passing. He wanted Barbara to be able to deliver his speech in case his health made it impossible for him to speak. Could it be David was listening and received a message from God telling him he would be with Him in heaven before this evening? Could it be God led him to meet with Barbara to prepare an alternative plan for the presentation? Barbara did a superb job, tears and all. David had to be smiling down on her from heaven. The members of the Rotary Club may never fully grasp what they did for our family and David. We are forever grateful.

When we returned to the funeral home a little after nine, there still were people waiting to share their love. By nine thirty we kissed David good night and returned home. Arriving home Sara Belle excitedly said, "Sheldon, you've got to go back to the funeral home."

"Why?" I asked in utter exhaustion hoping whatever it was could be put off until morning.

"David's not wearing his new watch."

"So?"

"I want him to have his new watch. He got it for his birthday, and he wanted to wear it to the Rotary Club." A little after ten, I arrived in the lobby of the funeral home. I asked the young man who greeted me if he would change David's watch. He did and without showing any outward signs that may have indicated he was thinking, *That old gentleman has lost his mind.* The next morning Sara Belle realized she had not set the time on the watch. So she called St. Peters Church where David's service was to be held and talked to Mary Scarborough, the church secretary. She asked if David had arrived and if she could speak with Keith Downey from Holloway's. When Keith (fortunately a friend of ours) got on the phone Sara Belle said, "Keith, David is wearing a new watch, but I don't think I set the time. Can you open the casket and make sure the watch is set and running?"

He did, and it was running. Later in the morning Clarice, the lady who gave David the watch, stopped by the house just as we were leaving for church. Sara Belle told her the story of the watch.

"Oh Lordy! Honey, I have that watch set to alarm at two to let David know each day that it's time to take his medicines," Clarice said. "Do you suppose it will go off during the service? You know it keeps alarming until somebody turns the thing off. Oh…Lordy!"

David's last afternoon at St. Peters Episcopal Church was a very blessed and uplifting celebration of his life. The church was filled with the Holy Spirit. The four individuals who reflected joyfully on his life were his friends, Rocky Burnett, John Sharpe, Dean DeFino, and Father David Tontonoz. David's very close friend and sister in Christ Kathy Montelone read the Scripture message. Following communion, the choir sang "Lift High the Cross" as the procession exited the church. This is a favorite of ours as well as one of David's. I still can't sing the words without getting emotional. After his committal services Sara Belle secretly arranged, as a gift to David, me, and others in attendance, the ceremony of doves flying above the burial site. Three doves were released to represent the Father, the Son, and the Holy Spirit. Then a single dove was released to represent the loved one going with the Holy Trinity into heaven.

Late that evening we were finally alone at home. We simply sat in the dark quietness of our family room with an unbearable emptiness void of all emotions. It was as if life had come to an end. Without David we could see no future. Our grief was the most intense feeling of sorrow and devastation we've experienced. Jay Neugeboren writes,

> A wife who loses a husband in called a widow. A husband who loses a wife is called a widower. A child who loses parents is called an orphan. But...there is no word for a parent who loses a child. That's how awful the loss is!

SHELDON LARMORE

A TIME TO MOURN, A TIME TO REFLECT

Death leaves a heartache no one can heal. Love leaves memories no one can steal.

—From a headstone in Ireland

The finality of the funeral, the stillness of the house, the absence of noise and frequent laughter shared by friends and family remembering times with David created a deafening silence. Life seemed void of any kind of existence. Nothing could compare to the enormity or devastation we felt in our grief. Grieving had taken over our lives. Everything came to a halt. The world around us moved on while our world had ended.

From the day after the funeral we knew we were becoming deeply absorbed in sorrow. We were moving, thinking, and processing in slow motion. Over time, we were so blinded and so shut down we had no desire to face the world. We gained some sense of peace praying and meditating some part of each day. We thanked God daily for giving us David. We asked Him, through prayer, to take care of him and let him know we were okay and missed him. Eventually we realized for our own sake we had to recapture life. David was far too great of a young man with tremendous spirit to have his parents ruin his memories in their grieving.

We soon learned one joy shatters a hundred griefs. We received a call from Vera Patterson saying she would like to stop by for a while. She wanted to see us and had something she would like to share. Her visit was the shot in the arm we needed. Vera's presence in our midst seemed to bring a calm, a peace to our otherwise somber existence.

After a time of reflecting on David's life and sharing hopes for the future, Vera surprised us with the greatest gift any grieving parents would cherish above all. She related to us the conversation David and she had during their last time together. His major concern was for us. He wasn't sure we would be able to cope with his death. She shared he was composed and mature throughout their talk. As Vera made notes, David talked about the things he wanted us to know and do after he was gone. The plan was for her to come to our house on Tuesday morning. At that time she and David were to type a letter from the notes Vera had jotted down during their discussion. David's plan was for Vera to give us the letter after his death. David passed away the night before, leaving this task incomplete. At our request, Vera compiled his notes into letter form. Reflecting on the events leading up to his last day, is it possible David had a divine communication with his Father? Is it possible David learned the importance to be quiet so he could hear the words and receive the blessings of his heavenly Father? Listen, listen to hear God say to him, "David, son, you have finished your work on earth. It is time to come home."

The following is the letter.

Dear Mom and Dad,

I am writing this letter to tell you how much I have appreciated all the sacrifices you have made for me over the years. I know there were many times when you put your own plans on hold to be able to take care of me. You have been wonderful parents, and I could not have had better ones. If I could have changed things, I would. But I must believe that God's ways are not our ways and that what He brought into our lives was for a reason. I believe that He is in control.

SHELDON LARMORE

I was afraid of dying—not of death, but the process. After many talks with Vera we worked on this, and I was able to realize that God will be with me and will not take me through anything without giving me the tools to do it with. Vera gave me permission to express my innermost human feelings without me experiencing any guilt. She helped me to understand that these are natural human feelings, and I received peace.

Please do not wonder, after I am gone, if there was anything you could have done differently. I have had a full life with your help. When I am gone I would want you to take some time to do things together that you were not able to do. Enjoy some time away from home and know this is what I would wish for you.

Always remember our good times together—"can we get a cup of coffee?" When you do have coffee remember me, and I hope you smile at the pleasure it brought me! We had many good times and I hope they are what help to keep you strong when I am gone. I will always be with you in your heart. I will always love you both.

Love,

David

Memories are the precious gifts of the heart. We need memories and soft whispers from our departed loved ones to help create a sense of inner peace, a closeness.

Time alone will not heal. The only thing time guarantees is change. We've learned in times of doubt, in times of sadness we must stop and be quiet until we feel the presence of the Spirit surrounding us in peaceful comfort. Listen for ways to make sense out of the senseless.

We don't know if we will ever or fully want to conquer the loss of David. To help us travel back into the human race we found great solace in walking on the beach early, early in the morning, looking into the pastel-touched sunrise of the morning and saying, "Hello, David. We love you. We miss you." At times, it seemed the clouds would do a quick, little dance as the currents above moved across the sky.

DAVID LIVES

We know you are not far away. We feel your presence around us. Our love binds us together always. We three are one, eternally.

—Unknown

We will not let death separate us from David. We can't consider David has gone to the "other side" because we don't have a concept of what the "other side" means. We describe his absence from us saying he has gone home. He is back with his Father who originally sent him on a mission when He put David in our care on Earth. We are presently on Earth working in faith waiting for our trip back home. It's our primary goal to keep David's memories happy and alive. He finished his part of the race. It's now time for us to pick up his torch—the light of hope, the light of life—and move forward until our race is done. David would want us to continue nurturing our faith. Believing life beyond death does exist we take great comfort in knowing David is still with us and will remain with us through eternity. When we are asked, "Do you have children?" we respond by saying, "Yes, one. We have a son." He is not in our past. He will always be in our present and future. When we lose a loved one we have to realize they have just moved home. They have just changed addresses but are still very much with us if we take time to receive their love and messages.

We have had times since David went home when life seems to be falling off the edge. If you recall Sara Belle had experienced health problems earlier that were thought to be coming from stress or a minor cyst. Six months after the loss of David it was discovered Sara Belle's problems were the result of a cavernmona on the pons of the brain. It had grown to the size of an orange and if it ruptured it would have been fatal. After three weeks of daily radiation at Johns Hopkins Hospital it is still present in reduced size but controlled. Since our loss of David she has also been diagnosed with lymphoma as well as Parkinson's disease, has had three hernia repairs, a major splenectomy with the removal of a thirty pound spleen, cancer of the nose resulting in reconstruction, and has Meniere's disease. Undoubtedly, we have learned to stop life periodically. We find a place where we can sit, relax and be quiet. This gives our souls a chance to listen and our hearts and minds an opportunity to accept thoughts of peace. We listen for messages of love received by our hearts and hear the unexpected and sometimes extremely vivid inspirations and dreams communicated to us by David or other loved ones. We always know David is with us from the title of my favorite song, "You'll Never Walk Alone." Believe, have faith and reach out. Communicating in spirit, in mind, with departed loved ones is not a complicated process. We shouldn't make it one.

We know of and believe in the many stories shared by individuals and families of messages and visits they have had from departed loved ones. We talk to David constantly. We thank him for watching over his elderly, forgetful parents. We thank him for the many times he has protected us from danger or guided us in making a decision. I will never let up on my relentless teasing of him. When things are not going right I teasingly blame him. Times when he doesn't seem to be around, when I need to talk with him I will say, "David, wake up! It's your parents. We need help," or "David, your lunch break is over. It's time to get back to work."

Frequently we take a cup of coffee and a donut to the cemetery and visit with him. He loved his coffee so much we'll share our coffee with him by pouring a little on his grave as we talk to him.

We remember the conversations David and Sara Belle had many times while he was living. She frequently reminded him he had to find a way to let us know he was okay once he arrived in heaven. She insisted we needed to hear from him. His statement was always something like, "Mom, be real. Now how am I going to do that? I can't let you know if I'm okay. Just know I will be okay." Well, David did find ways to let his parents know he is okay and he is with us always. Messages from David have been endless. Let me summarize some of the major ones we have received. They are known and have been witnessed by many friends and family members as well.

One example is finding dimes. David was active with the local March of Dimes. Therefore, he obviously decided to use a dime as one means of communicating with us.

1. Six months after David went home I was scheduled for rotator cuff surgery. While I waited in a room before the operation I got chilly. A nurse brought me one of those folded warm blankets and gave it to Sara Belle to put over me. When she unfolded it there was a shiny new dime in the very center of the blanket. Imagine our thoughts, our excitement. Immediately we knew it was a message from David. He had decided to use a dime to communicate with us. This was the very first indication David was near.

2. A month or two later we went to Johns Hopkins hospital for Sara Belle's checkup with her neurosurgeon. We found a lone shiny dime in the hallway just outside of the doctor's office.

3. We took a cruise a couple of years later. When the attendant unlocked our stateroom we entered and found in the center of the freshly cleaned and vacuumed floor a single dime.

4. In the middle of our dining room table on the first night of our cruise we found a dime.

5. Two or three times a week, without fail, we find a dime either in one of the rooms of the house or in the car.

6. One summer evening we visited David in the cemetery. Afterward we went to Ruby Tuesday's for dinner. As soon as we sat down we both spotted a dime in the middle of a freshly changed tablecloth.

7. We were having trouble with a drain in our kitchen. We called a plumber who in his investigation found a dime. It was the culprit stopping up the drain and costing us money. I just looked up at the ceiling and said, "Now David, why would you do something like that, Buddy? Now you had better work some magic and find a way to pay this bill you created."

8. We took a trip to Branson, Missouri, with Faye and Lee. At the time we had not been talking or thinking about David as we stopped to shop. When we returned to the locked car, Lee unlocked the door, opened it, and found a dime in the center of the driver's seat.

9. There was a period whenever we found a dime we *always* found a penny next to it. This became such a pattern we would say, "Well David, we see you have a new recruit 'in training' as you show him how to send messages to loved ones using a dime."

10. Placing a dime on David's headstone in the cemetery has become a type of ritual. Over the years many of David's friends have visited him in the cemetery. Most have left a dime at the base of his headstone symbolizing their love and remembrance of him. At one point the collection of dimes totaled $8.60. These dimes remained in place for a number of years until one visit we found them missing. For a moment we were saddened. But it was as if David

was speaking to us saying, "Mom and Dad, it's okay. The person who took them probably needed them more than we did." Dimes have continued to mount. In a recent visit the new total was $4.40 and counting.

These are only a very few examples of us finding dimes. Each time we find one we know David listened to his mom. He found a way to let us know he is okay. Below are a few other incidences where he has left dimes with friends.

1. Kathy Monteleno, David's friend, was swimming in the Atlantic Ocean and felt something hit the side of her leg. She reached for it and found a dime. A single dime in the Atlantic Ocean!

2. Michele Harris bought a new car. As she drove it home, her father was with her and casually began to investigate around the dashboard. He pulled open the ashtray and in the middle was a shiny new dime.

3. Jane Graves, a close friend of ours, had an automobile accident late one evening. Her car was totaled, but she and her family miraculously escaped without injury. When Jane exited the car the first thing she saw was a brightly shining dime in the middle of the road among all the broken glass.

PARKING SPACES

We hesitate to put this to a test for fear David or the good Lord will accuse us of not believing. However, many times when we go shopping we will tell David where we are going and ask him to save us a convenient parking space. Most times he will have us a vacant space closest to the store. We have experienced times when we have entered a parking lot with no spaces available. We say to David jokingly, "Okay, Buddy, you are falling down on the job. Where do you suppose we park?" Immediately in front of us we witness a car pulling out of a choice parking space near the entrance of the store. We pull in thanking David for a job well done and reminding him to stay awake for the next time. If we didn't tease him he would miss it.

FEELINGS OF TOUCH OR CLOSENESS

Several nights four or five years after David went home, I felt as if someone was getting in bed with us. On numerous occasions I would raise up in bed to look. Seeing nothing I did not say anything to Sara Belle. This went on over a number of months. Two or three times weekly I felt the mattress sink slightly as if some one was lying down. One night while awake, I saw Sara Belle sit up in bed. I asked her if she was okay. She said yes and then slowly lay down. The next night the same thing occurred. This time she asked, "Did you feel something move on the bed?" I told her about my experiences over the last months. Surprisingly, she had experienced the same things. We simply laughed and together said, "Hello, David. If you are going to sleep between Mom and Dad you are going to have to be still. You're keeping us awake. Good night."

Most everyone has faced a time of a grief. The loss of a loved one is traumatic and many times devastating to those left behind. Hopefully, it helps to realize that the loss loved one has just shed his or her earthly body and still exist in a spiritual body. We believe David and others who have departed from this Earth are absolutely capable of communicating with those they have left behind. Because of the bond of love they cherish they have a vested interest in continuing the relationships they have treasured over the years. To comprehend this requires a simple faith. However, faith is not a passive action, and it needs nurturing. It is not necessary to consciously seek communication from a loved one. Their messages many times are subtle and quiet. Just stay tuned in. Be quiet so you can hear. Listen so you can recognize messages from your loved ones. These messages may be in the form of an idea, a thought, or an answer placed in your mind by a departed family member, friend or loved one. It may be a whisper or a gentle, calming breeze assuring you everything will be okay. Just believe! For those who believe no proof is required.

To our readers we want you to know how much we appreciate your allowing us to take you along on our journey of love and faith. We are grateful David's life was filled with good friends, great times, many blessings, and true miracles.

David, we can still feel the afterglow of your love and smiles. God be with you, son.

We love you!
Until we meet again,
Mom and Dad

Appendix: Selected Tributes to David

*T*hree of the many eulogies shared during the Celebration of Life ceremonies for David were given by three close friends of his: Dean DeFino, John Sharpe, and Rocky Burnett

✝

The Quiet Man in the Chair (Eulogy #1)

The Scene: A Christian singles gathering, or perhaps a civic meeting or religious service where many are gathered for fun, such as a communal service or worship. It is noticed that everyone's heart seems to be a little lighter with the pressures of life momentarily removed from their minds. A slight smile across their face reflects an inner peace they are enjoying. This is because of the presence of a quiet man in a chair that inspires faith and hope in human kind. In that man's silence he speaks far more elegantly than the greatest orators of the world, not by words but through the love that he has for life and for everyone he meets.

The man who has seen some of the worst that life can offer, and yet has the ability with a spiritual fortitude that so few could ever reach, changed those conditions into a positive, rewarding experience for both him and all that he encounters. With eyes blurred with tears, I reflected on the impact that David had on my life. We could all describe him as a dear friend that loved and lived life to the fullest. He was a man who saw the best in people, and always had a positive outlook. David possessed all that we recognize as good when describing human nature. And in reflecting the uniqueness, the rarity of such an individual I realized that David was much more than just a friend.

Ministry occurs whenever the lives of people are touched by the presence of God. David was a unique and privileged individual who was viewed by an all-knowing God to be chosen as one of our heavenly Father's few special ministers to show a skeptical world that God loves and cares about each and every one of us. More powerful than the greatest sermon preached from the loftiest pulpit is the message that David spoke everyday through the way he lived and loved. He was a true emissary of God who ministered to me every moment that I was in his presence. Whether it was in a bowling alley, restaurant, theology class, or copying the Scriptures by hand, David always ministered.

David knew that the true meaning of *joy* is not the absence of sorrow but rather in entering the presence of God. And that is where David took each and every one of us, and that is why despite our tears we have joy in our hearts just by knowing him—just by being touched my him.

The shortest verse in the Bible is found in John 11:35, where it simply says, "Jesus wept." He did this upon learning of the death of his friend Lazarus. And so it is no shame for us to cry at our great loss, for no less than our Lord and Savior Jesus Christ wept at the loss of his friend. But Jesus did more than weep: He raised Lazarus to life again. He wants us to know, as He wanted Lazarus's sister to know, that David is now free of all the pain of a sin-cursed world and he is enjoying the blessing of heaven. David, now in the purest form, is in the presence of God hearing him say, "Well done, my good and faithful servant."

We give thanks not only to God, but to David's parents who shared this special gift they received from the Lord, with all of us. Thank you so much, Sheldon and Sara Belle, for giving us this gift for we are better Christians and better people because David touched our lives. Rejoice in the fact that we will see David again if we follow in the path that he set by his love for the Lord and the true Christian Character that he lived every second of his life. The message and ministry of the quiet man in the chair continues to live and enrich our lives.

— Rev. Dean DeFino, MDiv.
Foremost a friend, also Associate Pastor
of Trinity United Methodist Church

✝

A TRIBUTE TO DAVID LARMORE (EULOGY #2)

Our friend, David Larmore, had a motto. It went something like this: "But, seek first his kingdom and his righteousness, and all these things will be given to you as well." (Matthew 6:33). One of David's other mottos was, "Do your best and don't give up."

Our David, our unique and irreplaceable friend, lived by this verse of scripture and this motto, and by living a Christ-like life he encouraged others to live a godly and righteous life full of joy and love for one's fellow human beings.

David Larmore was a member of the Gunby Road Home Church, a ministry of St. Peter's Episcopal Church. One week in Home Church, our discussion turned to the disabled and handicapped, and a quick look around the room revealed that all of the members had some disability or another. And David, of course, had the most of all. But he also accomplished the most with what he was given.

In his adult life:

- David couldn't walk, but for twenty-two years he participated in the March of Dimes Walk America raising well over $70,000 in pledges.

- He couldn't talk very well, but he was a lay reader in church and a public speaker.

- His handwriting was painfully slow, yet he would hand copy entire chapters of scripture.

- He struggled when he read and had some trouble with comprehension, but he read his Bible every day.

- He had a great need for prayer for himself, but instead, he prayed for others daily.

- He could not run, swing a bat, catch or throw a ball, yet he coached a baseball team.

- He detested being in the hospital, but he looked forward to every day he could be at the hospital helping others and visiting with patients.

- He studied hard and struggled to graduate from high school, yet he went on to become a teacher, a coach, a Sunday School teacher, an evangelist, an advocate for the handicapped and disabled, a fund raiser, an encourager, an energizer, a spiritual advisor, a leader and guide, and an overall inspiration for all of us.

- He was small in stature, but a giant in his influence on this community.

- He did not have physical mobility, manual dexterity, speech clarity, or a high IQ, but he went to work every day and shared his special talents of love, consideration, compassion, faith, and inspiration with everyone he met.

When we examine what made David Larmore tick, we will understand that his mottos were not just things for him to claim or say. They were a blueprint for his life.

"Do your best and don't give up. Seek first his kingdom and his righteousness, and all these things will be given to you as well."

Because of his multiple physical handicaps, our David suffered and was in some form of pain each and every day of his thirty-two years, yet he maintained a positive outlook and refused to complain about his situation. Although an enormous amount of energy was expended by others to enable David to live a life of some normalcy, David's own focus was on others. He overcame his own handicaps and disabilities to be a servant for others, always seeking the kingdom first and always doing his best. Through his life, everyone around him could catch a glimpse of the Kingdom of God.

Because of the way he lived his life, the legacy of David Larmore will certainly be that he inspired us to excel in our lives as he did. He did his best, he didn't give up, he sought the Kingdom of God, he lived for others, and he knew and shared the love of Jesus Christ.

Our brother and friend, our David, lived a Christ-like life.

—John Sharpe
A much loved and caring friend and former member of St. Peter's Church Vestry

†

TO MY FRIEND DAVID (EULOGY #3)

Too often, we miss the loyal qualities in each other. It seems in the end we all wish we were better understood and appreciated. Sadly, we overlook or ignore some valued friendships because we just didn't strive hard enough. Sometimes we neglect the genuineness and intention in each other.

David Larmore was genuine and directed, even to the point of being a special messenger and example from God. There was a simple but intricate message from God through David. The Bible says, "above all things, persevere." Could it have been a life of handicap, disappointment, or just a different human condition that caused his resolution and his insistence to give the very best behavior and venture with his own efforts? Perhaps his relief and belief came from his determination to serve others, yet to leave himself and his own care to God. Possibly David sought to relieve his own condition by abetting others. It was his way. It was his best therapy.

This was my friend and brother, David. He was resolved to seek out others and be a part of their needs and life. He was not selfish and honestly believed God used him to serve his neighbor. That was his message. In the process, David was adamant about facing his own trials and errors and consequently we, his friends, saw through his bodily state and witnessed a spiritual courier.

To those of us who knew David well, he was steadfast in his faith, because he trusted God to be his protector and overseer. David was convicted in his faith, persistent with his spiritual disposition, and his practice was clear: "Never ever, give in or give up."

David carried the mark of God's spirit throughout his life. Though he rarely shared his deepest thoughts or moments with his closest friends, even his parents, Sheldon and Sara Belle, admit he seldom complained or questioned his life until there were only a couple of options to his health condition. His example illustrated time and time again David was a stable friend and steady volunteer. David was dependable, even during some of his most difficult times. Actually, it could have been his style and manner that presented such an ideal. This is how I see Christ.

When I looked at David, I saw Christ. When he touched me, I felt the touch of God.

Born and handicapped as David was, he would not have matured in spirit and tone without the love and attention of Sheldon and Sara Belle. With all our sadness with David's passing, we are not alone. Through David's father and mother, we see and feel the very spirit of our God. Sheldon and Sara Belle loved and supported David to the point of personal sacrifice that only God knows and expected. They have done what few of us could do—instilled the love of God in a challenged child and gave him a hunger and thirst for the company and concern of his fellow man.

I thank God for the life and memories of David Larmore. His father and I teased him incessantly, but it was all welcomed and anticipated. Most of all, I thank God for his persistent smile and his enduring friendship. I am a better person and a more attentive Christian for the truth of David's message and the spirit of his example. Thank you, God, for loaning David to us for this short time.

—George "Rocky" Burnett
A true and devoted friend and former Vestry member and senior warren of St. Peter's Church

TRIBUTES IN THE LOCAL NEWSPAPER

Weeks after David's death, there were tributes printed in our local newspaper, *The Daily Times*, in his memory. A very special one was written by a very amazing individual and a dear friend of David's and ours, Paul Rendine. Paul is chairman of the Lower Shore Governor's Committee on Employment of People with Disabilities. Due to a motorcycle accident while on a vacation in

Bermuda, Paul is permanently paralyzed from the waist down. He was an inspiration to David and us over the years. Below is the article found in the newspaper a couple weeks after David went home.

"DAVID LARMORE, A SPECIAL PERSON, WILL BE MISSED"

I first met David Larmore about 17 years ago. I had just taken on the chairmanship of the Lower Shore Governor's Committee on Employment of People with Disabilities and had begun a major effort to revamp the committee to make it a much more active and representative committee for and about those people with disabilities who were residents of the Lower Shore three county area.

I really met David through his father, Sheldon. Sheldon, who is now retired, at that time worked in the central office of the Wicomico County School System. I had asked Sheldon to talk with me and the Lower Shore Committee to educate us about the various ways in which all of us, working together, could develop a number of positive methods in which the educational experience could become as independence-developing and socially mean-ingful as possible for our county's children with disabilities.

Although I can't precisely remember when I first met David, I recall it was at a weekend activity in our county where Sheldon was working as a volunteer, a caring and sharing effort that was to become a major part of David's life. My conversation with David was the type that stays with a person because of its special impact.

While my disability was caused by an accident just over 20 years ago, David's disability was present from birth. What struck me the most, though, about this young man in the motorized wheelchair was how much he seemed to enjoy life and how large his smile was. As a matter of fact, I can't ever remember a time when David didn't have a smile.

As many of you may know by now, David is deceased, having passed away suddenly and unexpectedly just a few short weeks ago. While he was only 32 years old at his death, he left behind an incredible legacy of care and service to others from one of the most unselfish, selfless and compassionate individuals I have ever met, whether able-bodied or disabled. His example is one that anyone and everyone should also strive to replicate, whether able-bodied or disabled.

Thanks to his parents for the values that they instilled in him, David embarked on his almost single-minded job of making life better for others by involving himself in thousands of hours of volunteer service to our hospital, Peninsula Regional Medical Center, to our center for individuals with various developmental disabilities, the Holly Center, and to various elementary schools in five counties and two states on the Delmarva Peninsula.

As a matter of fact, according to PRMC, David donated more than 12,000 hours as a volunteer at the hospital, making life better in any number of ways for patients, medical professionals and staffers. And these are nowhere near all of the various volunteer activities David was involved in.

David had also just recently been recognized with awards from an incredible number of entities—from local civic organizations to the state of Maryland—for his giving and caring personality as evidenced by the countless hours he gave of himself to make life better for someone else. In a manner somehow fitting of his life, on the evening of his death, David had been honored by the city of Salisbury for the many different awards he had just recently received for his volunteer efforts—just hours before passing away in his sleep.

David was a special person—not just because of his volunteer efforts for others, but also because of his volunteer efforts in spite of his own disability. As PRMC said in its special edition issue of *Life Works*, the employee information publication, "All David ever asked for was the chance to make life better for someone else. Not a bad example for each of us to follow."

They are correct—he will be sorely missed!

Submitted by: Paul Rendine

This editorial appeared on Sunday in the Daily Times two days after David's funeral.

"LARMORE'S SHORT LIFE OF SUCCESS"

Success is defined in different ways by different people, in our own society usually by some form of professional achievement and monetary gain. But a more profound form of success can be seen in the relatively short life of David Jefferson Larmore, who died Tuesday at the age of 32 years. Larmore exemplified success as a human being. Disabled from birth and confined to a wheelchair, he never seemed to let his physical condition get in the way of living life to the fullest.

He was well known to elementary school students in the area, for whom he served as an ambassador representing the humanity of disabled individuals. He also volunteered many hours at Peninsula Regional Medical Center and the Holly Center. In fact, he received so many awards for volunteerism and community service, it would be impossible to list them all here.

Through it all, Larmore smiled and kept on giving. If ever there was an inspiration to which we can look when things are not going the way we would like, Larmore is it. He never complained about the hardships he must have endured as a result of his disabilities, but focused always on helping others. His presence and his example will be sorely missed in this community.

Peninsula Regional Medical Center Publication:

LIFE WORKS is Peninsula Regional Medical Center's weekly employee information publication. As stated previously David passed away a few minutes after midnight on May 14, 2002. As the employees at PRMC started their morning shift at 8:00 a.m. they were greeted and saddened with a special edition of LIFE WORKS announcing the passing of David. Roger Follebout, a very true and devoted friend and Christian felt it necessary to inform the hospital's employees and medical staff of David's death. Below is the article found in the special edition prepared in the early morning some 6 or 7 hours after David died in the emergency room.

Remembering David Larmore

"We lost David last night." I'm guessing those were the first words many of us heard here at the Medical Center this morning. A terribly sad start to the day, but exactly the way it was meant to be.

David was one of the kindest, gentlest men you'll ever meet who lived twice as long as medical science said he would only to give ten times more of himself to this organization than any of us ever will in our lifetime. Respect, admiration, and love: David Jefferson Larmore earned them all. He didn't have to, but he did. Just being our friend was good enough for all of us, but never quite to the standards set by David. His spirit and his will were nothing short of remarkable!

So isn't it fitting that this wonderful gentleman, with everything going on inside this "city within a city" we call Peninsula Regional, was front and center on the minds of everyone on this health care team this morning? And isn't it remarkable that we all had the privilege of knowing David and sharing in his life for as long as we did? It was exactly as it was meant to be. Monday night's storms passed, the sun shined brightly, a new Tuesday dawned on Delmarva during National Hospital Week and David left us for his next volunteering assignment. There are bigger plans for our friend, be assured of that.

Also, be happy you had the opportunity to be a part of David's incredible time here on earth, his incredible contribution to Peninsula Regional Medical Center and his unbridled enthusiasm for life—all limitations aside. There is no question he was proud to share that with you, our patients, visitors, physicians, and everyone whose life was made better by simply spending time with David. All he ever asked for was the chance to make life better for someone else. Not a bad example for each of us to follow.

It's impossible, when speaking about David, to measure what he meant to all of us by mere facts and figures. However, we felt it important that you know David had just celebrated his 32nd birthday on May 6th. He joined our team in PLUS Volunteers on October 21, 1991, and donated an astounding 12,002 hours to the program. That ranks him second in the history of PLUS Volunteers in hours donated. David was a mentor for the "Developmental Disabilities Awareness Program" through the Holly Center…an outreach teaching program to elementary schools in Wicomico, Worcester, Somerset, Dorchester and Sussex Counties. He was a recipient of Maryland's "Most Beautiful Award," the Governor's "Innovation Award for Independence" for Wicomico County and just last month received the state of Maryland's top award by the Governor's Commission on Employment of People with Disabilities. Ironically, but somehow fitting for David, he was honored by the City of Salisbury-and even feeling ill-showed up last night to be recognized for receiving that honor just hours before passing away in his sleep.

We would encourage any of you who would like to share your thoughts about David to please forward them, via email or campus mail, to Roger Follebout, Jr. in Community Relations and Marketing by Noon on Monday, May 20, 2002. It's our plan to share as many of those as we can in the May23rd edition of LIFE WORKS. Also in that edition, we'll tell you more about David's many contributions to us, the community he loved and lived in and we'll share the thoughts of his friends in PLUS Volunteers.

David will be missed tremendously. He was a friend and an inspiration to all. As Barb Sturgis of PLUS Volunteers said earlier today, "*God Bless You David! Thank you for a well-lived life that you shared with so many. And thank you Sara Belle and Sheldon (David's parents) for making it possible for him to do so.*"

✝

From the pages of "Holly Center's Volunteer Newsletter":

DAVID LARMORE
"A BRIGHT SHINING STAR"
A Tribute to a Special Friend and Volunteer

The day we lost David was a day of eminence, memories, and love. He has left us with a remembrance of goodness, sweetness and beauty that will forever glow from the face, heart, and mind. David Larmore, indeed, was "a bright shining star."

Everything that David did, he did for the love of God and to better serve mankind. As we know, life has its demands, and being mature involves discipline and responsibility. David Larmore wrote the book! He always found a way to do more, more than what was required. David had a vision. He had a Christian message that was as clear as looking at your very own reflection in the mirror. His vision was to "be all that he could be."

Without question, David was a "yes" man—yes to everything or anything that would help others or give someone encouragement or a new lease on life. If ever there was a person who put others first on their "to do list," it was definitely our David! That's called serving others in love. No matter what the challenge, David continued to rise to the occasion with steadfast principles and unassuming dedication to his commitment. Many lives have been touched in some way by the caring effect created by David's service. Those who had the opportunity to know him have been improved immeasurably by his uninterrupted perseverance. His parents, Sheldon and Sara Belle, were the catalysts in helping David live his life to the fullest.

The commitment David exemplified serves as a shining example of his love for all. The lesson I have learned from David is to take the time to reflect. Take time to stand in front of the mirror and study the scene silently, thoughtfully, alone, and at length. I am left with the feeling of being grateful to God for all of his wonderful blessings, especially David, that he has so generously bestowed upon us.

—Marlina Belote
Director of "Developmental Disabilities
Awareness School Program"

✝

In Memory of David

In memory of David, the Medical Center with funds from David's friends, the hospital employees, and medical staff and people throughout the region has constructed a Remembrance and Tribute garden area in David's honor. It is along the path leading from the parking garage to the Volunteer Services entrance he so often rode through, grinning from ear to ear. The hospital encourages employees and visitors to stop as they pass through the area, read the tribute to David, reflect and take a moment to remember and thank David for sharing his genuine, kind, and compassionate manner. As quoted in one of the LIFE WORKS, "There will never be anyone who can replace what David meant to this organization or gave, under extremely challenging conditions, to each of us. As you pause, be happy when reflecting on David's bright smile, cheerful disposition and upbeat attitude on life that we should all be so fortunate to exhibit. It's exactly what

David would have enjoyed from us and without question, exactly what he deserves."

At the Memorial Service held by the Medical Center, The Board of Trustees presented us with a resolution honoring David for his service. In this resolution, the Board noted that David, "was an active, gifted, and cheerful young man who shared his enthusiasm for life with countless patients, visitors, volunteers, employees, and physicians..." The resolution also notes that David was "a kind and gentle man who earned respect, admiration and love for his smile, his faith, and his unmatched generosity..." An exact duplicate of this resolution is framed with David's picture and is hanging in the hallway outside the volunteer office of PRMC.

In David's memory, the Peninsula Regional Medical Center placed a sculpture of an angel in the garden with a commemorative plaque that reads:

DAVID JEFFERSON LARMORE
1970 – 2002
PLUS Volunteer
1991 – 2002
12,002 Hours of Service
He was a celebration of life. He led by example.
His smile was infectious.
Angels dance and David again leads,
As his spirit is alive in us all.

During the holiday season following David's passing, the star atop the hospital was illuminated and dedicated to David.

DAVID'S AWARDS AND RECOGNITIONS

From reading David's story it is hoped the reader envisioned him as a very caring, compassionate young man with great humility. He journeyed through life looking on the brighter side of opportunities and enjoying the friendships and victories of those he met on the way. He truly was a cheerleader of life, the benefactor of many good deeds that found their way into his world, and certainly the giver of hope, promise, and love toward others. His faith and his devotion to his Lord served him well as he lived his life for others. His rewards came from the feelings he received in working with and helping others feel better about themselves. He loved to share compliments and talk about his faith and his love for Jesus. In his personal passage through life David received numerous tributes, awards, and various types of recognition. He was always surprised, most appreciative, and felt quite honored to be selected. His humbleness and unassuming nature always allowed him to accept honors with great gratitude, but he never saw the need to flaunt or display these accomplishments unnecessarily. This is the main reason they were not highlighted in his story. He treasured them but spent time dwelling more on the good deeds or loving tasks they represented.

Major awards David received are:

- From 1980 to 1984, he was the Lower Shore March of Dimes Poster Child.

- In his senior year of high school he was one of fourteen national finalists for his work on entrepreneurs with a disability.

- He was selected by his senior class as the "Most Spirited" and recognized as a Sensational Senior and outstanding young man in the community.

- He was the first graduating senior from Parkside High School to receive the Lana K. Reinhart Memorial Award given to the senior who exhibits outstanding citizenship and has triumphed over hardships.

- In 1988, he received a resolution from the Maryland House of Delegates for helping students understand the free enterprise system and for his outstanding achievements in distributive education programs throughout Maryland.

- In 1992, Governor William Schaefer presented him with a Governor's Citation in recognition of his impressive commitment to the people of Maryland and especially individuals with developmental disabilities.

- In 1994, he was selected Wicomico County's recipient of the "Maryland, You Are Most Beautiful" award given in recognition of outstanding volunteers throughout the State of Maryland.

- In 1996 he received a proclamation from the Wicomico County Council for his demonstrated genuine love of his fellowman and his commitment to the services of others through volunteering countless hours of his time, sharing his unique talents and providing an example of the generosity of the human spirit.

- In 1996 he was selected to be the Honorary Grand Marshal in the Salisbury Christmas Parade.

- In 1998 he received the "Volunteer of the Year" award from Holly Center.

- In 1998 he received recognition for his leadership in forming the Easter Seal Official Little League Team for children with disabilities.

- In April 2001 David received the Rotary Club's covenant Four-Way Test Award for exemplifying the ideals of the four-way test in his daily life.

- In March 2002 the State of Maryland Governor's Committee on Employment of People with Disabilities presented David with an award recognizing him as an Outstanding Marylander with a disability.

- On May 13, 2002 just three hours before his death Mayor Barrie Tilghman and members of the City Council of Salisbury presented David with a certificate of appreciation for the valuable and distinguished service he rendered the City of Salisbury and for serving as a model to other persons with disabilities.

Each award was meaningful to David because they each came from people or organizations he cared for and held in utmost respect. As we reflect on the many times David was fortunate to be recognized for his efforts or received an award for an accomplishment we remember a saying, "The best way to measure any man's character is how he takes praise." As parents, we are proud of how David was able to accept the love and admiration showered upon him without affecting his goals or focus.

REMEMBERING DAVID

David's impact on our community and those who knew him reflects on the kind of caring, loving, and unassuming person he was. He would be pleased, yet humbled, by the recognition he has received in his memory.

- Peninsula Regional Medical Center has established and dedicated a memorial garden on the grounds of the hospital in his memory.

SHELDON LARMORE

- A picture of him with a proclamation from the Board of Trustees of the hospital hangs on the wall outside of the Volunteer Office at PRMC.

- A scholarship in memory of David is being funded to provide financial assistance to handicapped students entering college.

- A song, "David's Song," composed by Rick Fahey and sung by Peter's Voice of St. Peter's church is available locally.

- During the March of Dimes Walk-A-Thon in 2003 and 2004 over 125 walkers from PRMC wore tee shirts with the logo and statement, "Walking in the Memory of David Larmore." The combined total raised by the team in those two years was well over $40,000.

- Parkside High School's French Club designed a Christmas tree with a lighthouse theme and donated it to the Festival of Trees annual fund raising event in memory of David. David's tree went for $1800. It was the second highest bid of the evening. Monies received were donated to the local March of Dimes.

- In memory of David, the March of Dimes presented us with a framed certificate from the International Star Registry showing a star in the universe that has been named, "David" in his memory. It is now listed in the *Hubble Guide Star Catalog* which is recognized in the astronomical community as the most accurate source of the location of stars.

- Surprisingly, one month after David went home Benedict's, a local florist, notified us that the National Perennial Plant Association selected a flowering phlox as its 2002 Plant of the Year. They named it David! We like to think of this as a God-incident. Needless to say we have numerous David's in our garden.

- Several friends and especially David's Aunt Faye and Uncle Lee have donated time and funds to help make a garden area in the backyard of our home representative of David's life. The garden contains cement statues of a baseball and football player, a dog symbolic of those David loved so much and a beautiful pond with fish representing life which David so much valued and enjoyed.

✝

DAVID'S SONG

Composed by Rick Fahey
Sung by Peter's Voice from St. Peter's Episcopal Church
in Salisbury, Maryland

Peter's Voice is a music group dedicated to bringing smiles to people's faces. Is there any wonder then, why they were one of David's very favorite musical groups? They do a mix of Christian and popular music as well as fun comedy pieces. Each member of the group is employed full time but several times a month still find time to sing gospel songs and songs that lighten the hearts of others. This is their way to relax. They truly find joy as they use their God-given talents to serve the Lord. Their reputation as an inspiring Christian musical group is well known throughout the Eastern Shore of Maryland.

A year or so after David went home to be with his Father Sara Belle asked Rick if he would be willing to compose a song in memory of David. The song is titled, "David's Song." The words and a short explanation of each verse follow:

DAVID'S SONG

I carried you within my womb
I rolled the stone upon your tomb
I watched the light within you grow
The fire of faith begin to glow
At times it seemed my cross to bear
And then the joy was everywhere

(This verse is intended to provide an image of his mother, Sara Belle, watching him grow and the mix of joy and hardship that came with it.)

I carried you up steps of stone
I prayed with you upon His throne
I helped you where you could not go
You shed a light that warmed my soul
At times it seemed my cross to bear
And then the joy was everywhere

(The above verse paints an image of me as David's father carrying him up the stone steps in the church to the alter to receive communion and to pray to the God he loved so much.)

There is a star in skies above
That lit our world with selfless love
And though the light left long ago
It traveled far and keeps the fire still aglow

(This verse creates the image of a star. The March of Dimes named a star in honor of David. It was an appropriate gift because the light from a star travels until it is absorbed and becomes the energy for new warmth and new growth. David touched so many people with his genuine love for them and by the radiant warmth of his smiles.)

We watched you tread where others feared
Your actions spoke with a voice so clear
We saw you grasp what we could not
We saw you touch the face of God
And when we thought we carried you
Your legacy revealed the truth

(This speaks so much of David's faith as he approached the unknown without fear. He seemed to understand the meaning of God's love and communicated with Him as if they were sitting in the same room. We thought we carried him through rough spots, but in reality he was the one with great faith and spiritual knowledge who actually carried us through many crises.)

There is a star in the skies above
That lit our world with selfless love
And though the light left long ago
It traveled far and keeps the fire

And when we thought we carried you
Your legacy revealed the truth
There is a star in the skies above
That lit our world with selfless love
And though the light left long ago
It traveled far and keeps the fire still aglow

SHELDON LARMORE

This is David's song. But it is every bit as much about those who knew him and learned from his life, how much we can do with whatever gifts we are given.

 e|LIVE

listen|imagine|view|experience

To download your free copy of
David's Song sung by Peter's Voice:

1. Visit www.tatepublishing.com and click on the e|LIVE logo on the home page.
2. Enter the following coupon code:
   d9ea-5495-0da0-d098-e4c5-c3d1-9833-b7ba
3. Download the song from your e|LIVE digital locker and enjoy!